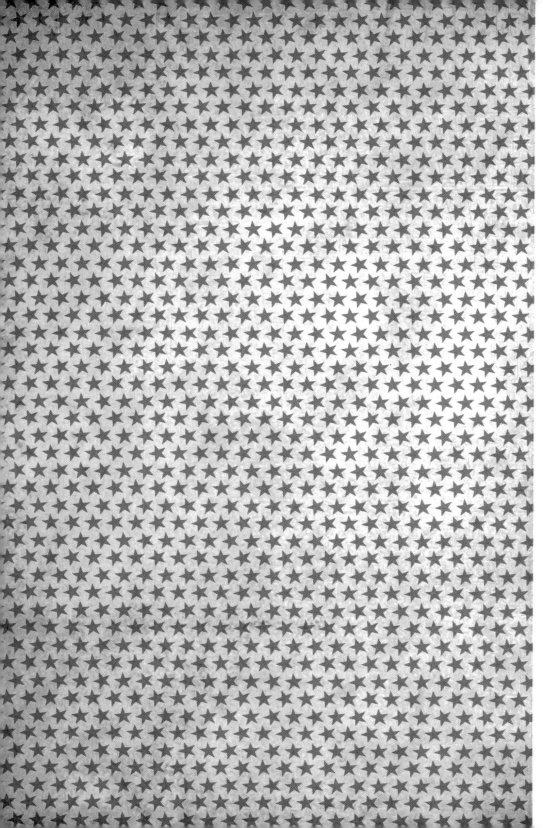

LOVE & WHISKEY

The Remarkable True Story of Jack Daniel,

His Master Distiller Nearest Green,

and the Improbable Rise of Uncle Nearest

FAWN WEAVER

MELCHER
MEDIA

NEW YORK

MELCHER MEDIA

Melcher Media, Inc.
124 West 13th Street
New York, NY 10011
www.melcher.com
greatbooks@melcher.com

Distributed to the trade by Two Rivers Distribution, an Ingram brand.
For ordering information please send inquiries to: ips@ingramcontent.com

Love & Whiskey

10 9 8 7 6 5 4 3 2 1
Printed in the United States of America

978-1-59591-134-6 (Hardcover)
978-1-59591-135-3 (Ebook)
978-1-59591-139-1 (Audiobook)

Cover art direction by Launi King and Creative Play
Cover design by Launi King and Blue Kangaroo

Uncle Nearest and Uncle Jack,
thank you for choosing me as the keeper
of this legacy for this leg of the race.

I will hold on to this baton for dear life
until it is time for me to pass it to the person
assigned to the next leg of the race.

I trust they'll be born on September 5, too.

—◄✦►—

"THE WAY TO RIGHT WRONGS IS TO TURN THE LIGHT OF TRUTH UPON THEM."

—IDA B. WELLS

★

THE
BEGINNING

⎯⎯⎯⎯⎯⎯⎯⎯⎯⎯⎯

IN THE REALM of imagery, where a single frame can speak volumes, there exists a picture from circa 1904 that captures more than mere moments; it ensnares entire narratives. This particular image, steeped in history and shrouded in mystery, was my gateway into an extraordinary account. Central to this enigma was a Black man, seated with striking prominence to the right of the legendary whiskey maker Jack Daniel. When I first encountered this photo, his identity was a mystery to the world and me. But as I delved deeper and secured the original image, it became clear that this man was more than just a figure; he was a symbol of something profound and unspoken.

In this photograph, taken in Lynchburg, Tennessee, a place and time barely a generation removed from the shadows of slavery, this Black man's presence beside Jack Daniel was a statement in itself. If you peer closely, two remarkable details emerge. Firstly, while it appears that all the men are seated, Jack Daniel, standing at a mere five foot two, is actually upright. By the time of this photo, his right leg had been amputated, adding to his already diminutive stature. Secondly, and more significantly, this Black man is not merely positioned beside Jack Daniel; he has been granted the central spot, a place of honor, by the whiskey icon himself.

This man, George Green, son of Nearest Green, was more than a companion or an aide to Jack Daniel. He was a chosen confidant, tasked with a role that went beyond companionship; he was there to obscure Jack's physical limitations, a sort of guardian against the vulnerabilities of a man revered in history. This repositioning, this deliberate choice to cede the center stage to George Green, intrigued me deeply. In him, I saw not just a figure by Jack's side, but a man entrusted to shield another's frailty, a silent yet powerful testament to an unspoken bond and a hidden chapter in the annals of a famed whiskey legacy.

GEORGE GREEN, center, with arms crossed

★
AUTHOR'S NOTE

$\mathbf{S}$ INCE 2016, I've conducted hundreds of hours of interviews with residents of Lynchburg. I've worked with over thirty historians, archivists, archaeologists, conservators, and genealogists, compiling more than three thousand hours of collective research. The information in this book reflects the most accurate knowledge we have in 2024, but I hope and expect that additional information about Nearest Green and his family will continue to come to light as time goes by. At least, that is my hope.

Nearest's name has been spelled many ways over the last 170 years. I've seen it recorded phonetically in official documents as "Nuerst," "Nuress," "Nerus," "Norris," and even "Nerice." His birth name was Nathan, but his children and grandchildren referred to him exclusively as Nearest in legal documents. As I've come to learn, those who knew him best called him Uncle Nearest. For ease of reading, I have spelled his name "Nearest Green" wherever possible.

KEY
FIGURES

NEAREST'S FAMILY

Nearest and Harriet Green

THEIR CHILDREN: George, Jessie, Eli, and Minnie

GEORGE'S DESCENDANTS:

- ★ Charles and Maggie Green, George's son and daughter-in-law
- ★ Otis Green, George's son
- ★ Annie Lee Green, George's daughter
    - • Helen Butler, George's granddaughter
    - • Wilma Jean Tate, George's granddaughter
    - • Geraldine Tate, George's granddaughter
        - • Dr. Geri Lovelace, George's great-granddaughter
- ★ Townsend Green, George's son
- ★ Curtis (William), George's grandson
- ★ Theresa McGillberry (Aunt Tee), George's great-great-granddaughter

JESSIE'S DESCENDANTS:

- ★ Annie Bell Green Eady (Mammie), Jessie's daughter
    - • Debbie Staples, Jessie's great-granddaughter
    - • Jackie Hardin, Jessie's great-granddaughter
    - • Jerome Vance, Jessie's great-grandson
    - • Victoria Eady Butler, Jessie's great-granddaughter
    - • Jeff Vance, Jessie's great-grandson
- ★ Nellie Mae Green (Aunt Nell), Jessie's daughter
- ★ Geneva Eady (Sis), Jessie's granddaughter

ELI'S DESCENDANTS:

- ★ Henry Green, Eli's son
- ★ Hubert Green, Eli's son

NEAREST'S DESCENDANTS BY MARRIAGE:

- ★ Leola (Miss Dill) Dismukes, Jessie's step-granddaughter
  - • L. B. and J. B. McGowan, Jessie's step-great-grandsons
- ★ Mickey Murphy, Otis Green's step-grandson
- ★ Claude Eady, George Green's great-nephew by marriage, and his wife, Dorothy (Miss Dot)
- ★ Jo Anne Gaunt Henderson, related through her mother's aunt to one of Nearest's grandsons
- ★ Juanita Dunlap (Miss Neat), Nearest's great-great-granddaughter by marriage; Juanita's mother was the daughter of Jessie's widowed wife
- ★ Kevin Eady, Victoria's cousin

JACK'S FAMILY

Jack Daniel

Lem Motlow, Jack's nephew

"THE SHIRTSLEEVES BROTHERS": REAGOR, ROBERT, HAP, AND CONNOR MOTLOW, Lem's sons

MARY AVON MOTLOW BOYD, Lem's daughter
- ★ Judy Boyd Terjen, Lem's granddaughter

Tom Motlow, Lem's brother

Franklin "Spoon" Motlow, Lem's cousin

JOEL PITTS, Spoon's great-grandson

Margaret Tolley, Jack's great-niece by marriage

AT UNCLE NEAREST (contemporary)

Fawn Weaver

Keith Weaver

Katharine Jerkens

Victoria Eady Butler

Sherrie Moore

Steven Henderson

Michael Senzaki

Shannon Locke

Evette Martinez

AT JACK DANIEL'S (contemporary)

Mark McCallum

Nelson Eddy

Steve May

Melvin Keebler

Debbie Staples

Jerome Vance

Jackie Hardin

IN LYNCHBURG (historical)

Dan and Mary Jane Call

Felix Waggoner

Ned Waggoner

George Daniel

JAMES DANIEL, George's son

JESSE DANIEL, George's son

CLINTON "POSSUM" DANIEL, George's son

William and Mary Stone

IN LYNCHBURG (contemporary)

Chuck Baker

John T. Bobo

The McGees

Oscar McGee

Carol Roberts

Kathryn Hopkins

Christine Pyrdom

OTHERS

Clay Risen at the NEW YORK TIMES

Brittany Hampton, Fawn's niece

Ben A. Green, author of JACK DANIEL'S LEGACY

Stephani Ross, Fawn's research assistant

★

PROLOGUE

UNTIL ALL TOO RECENTLY, you could walk into any restaurant, any bar, and make one simple request: "Tell me one whiskey or bourbon on your back bar that represents someone who is not a white male." Then just wait while they look over bottles named for Jack, Johnnie, Pappy, and so on.

Before I started the Uncle Nearest Premium Whiskey company, white males represented 30 percent of this country's population and 100 percent of the available whiskeys—*100 percent.*

The world has only learned of Nearest Green, the first known African American master distiller in the world, in recent years. But to the people of Lynchburg, Tennessee, his contributions to American whiskey were no secret. His family passed down the story of his mentorship and friendship with famed Tennessee whiskey maker Jack Daniel for generations.

But outside Moore County, Tennessee, Nearest was largely unknown—not unusual for a formerly enslaved person. In fact, if there is anything unusual about Nearest's story, it's that anyone knows it *at all.* Nearest couldn't read or write and left behind no personal correspondence or journals; beyond a few county records and family anecdotes, there is very little to help us understand who he was as a person or how he saw his world. For decades, scholars have been trying to piece together African Americans' many unacknowledged contributions to US foodways—a difficult task considering that, for three centuries, records of Black people in America were erased, lost, or never collected in the first place.

So far, there have been five keepers of Nearest's story—five souls, connected across more than a century, who've kept his story known. The first was Jack Daniel himself, who learned his trade directly from Nearest and worked with his sons after that. The second was journalist and historian Ben A. Green (no relation to Nearest), who published a biography of Jack Daniel in 1967. The book detailed Jack's relationship with Nearest and would go on to be considered "the Bible" for the people of Lynchburg and required reading for executives at Jack Daniel's. The third was Nearest's granddaughter, Annie Bell Green Eady, who proudly told her many grandchildren all about how Nearest and his boys made whiskey for Jack Daniel. The fourth was Clay Risen, the *New York Times* journalist who wrote about Nearest in 2016 and ushered the story into the twenty-first century.

I'm the fifth. Clay's article is how Nearest's story found me. I may be in the spirits business today, but growing up in California, spirit had a totally different meaning. After my dad, Frank Wilson, moved away from his career as one of the original Motown hitmakers, writing and producing some of the greatest Motown songs of all time, to become a minister, my parents became teetotalers.

But it wasn't just luck. I've paid close attention to true stories my entire life.

As a kid, I refused to read fiction. I never made it through a single novel by Judy Blume. Instead, I devoured *Encyclopedia Britannica* entries about actual people. I grew up listening to Smokey Robinson and Stevie Wonder tell stories at my parents' kitchen table. When I left home at age fifteen and high school early into eleventh grade, other people's stories became my entire education. I read business books and memoirs and absorbed their wisdom. I listened while others spoke in the homeless shelters where I found refuge as a teen, trying to understand what we could do to change our circumstances. I read the Gospel, unfettered by my strict parents' interpretation. And at age twenty, when my first business venture faltered, I listened to my former employees' critiques, studying my mistakes so I would not repeat them.

Throughout my entire professional life, I've tried to practice what Motown taught my father and what my father taught me—the significance of listening, empathizing, and seeing people's hearts instead of their wounds. He taught me to see the world through the lens of grace rather than the prejudice of race.

So in 2016, when I first learned about Nearest, I knew I'd stumbled upon a damn good story.

I later learned that all five keepers of Nearest's tale share the same birthday: September 5. As I discovered each person's date of birth, one by one, it felt monumental. It gave me chills and still does to this day. Annie Bell Green Eady was born September 5, 1901, and Ben Green was born a year later on September 5, 1902. And Clay and I are exactly the same age, born on September 5, 1976. No one has been able to say conclusively when Jack Daniel's birthday is, but until the 2000s, when Jack Daniel Distillery began celebrating the entire month as his birthday, the world celebrated Jack Daniel on September 5, with the exact year unknown. My research conclusively proved his year of birth to be 1849.

My life looks a lot different than it did back in 2016, but I've never doubted the rightness of raising up Nearest's legacy and his amazing friendship with Jack. Both men were bigger than their time, and their actions reverberate on through today.

Telling stories like Nearest's is part of reclaiming Black American legacies that have been lost, hidden, and destroyed. Against the whitewashed backdrop of US history, Nearest's story stands out as the kind of example I longed to hear about and see, and I can already see the impact it's having on others.

For Black History Month at E. A. Cox Middle School in Columbia, Tennessee, in 2023, the fifth-grade students made figures of famous Black Americans with Styrofoam heads sitting atop soda-bottle torsos. Students built figures like Rosa Parks, Martin Luther King, and Harriet Tubman. One little girl, whose father had recently taken our distillery tour, built Nearest Green. Principal Kevin Eady, who grew up just down the street from Jack Daniel Distillery, went to look at the projects and was shocked to see Nearest.

"You may not believe this," Kevin told the girl, "but I have a family relationship with him." The next thing Kevin knew, he had twenty fifth graders crowded into his office, asking questions about his distant relation, about his dad—who had worked at the distillery—and about his cousin, Victoria Eady Butler, who is our master blender and Nearest's great-great-granddaughter.

To hear Kevin describe the look on that fifth grader's face, to discover just how much Nearest's story has rooted itself in the imagination of the next generation, reminds me of what this all means. It excites me every day that this generation of Black children will have so many more examples of Black success and excellence in work and leadership than I ever had. To be able to be a part of that brings me immense joy.

I've always said one of my superpowers is that, when I'm gripped by an idea, I find other people who are passionate about it and create a passionate community. Because of the Nearest Green Distillery—and the hundreds of people who have worked tirelessly to spread its message of love, honor, and respect—Nearest's story is no longer in danger of disappearing. Instead, he has become the stuff of Black History Month projects, immortalized in Coke-bottle likenesses alongside Rosa Parks and George Washington Carver.

After over a century, he is where he has always belonged. And nearly a decade after he became part of my life, I can rest easy knowing he will never be forgotten again.

PART

ONE

✦ ★ ✦

AUGUST 2016

THROUGH

NOVEMBER 2016

THIS STORY starts in Singapore, but to understand how I got there, you really have to start in LA. By the time I was born, my parents had become leaders in the evangelical Southern Baptist church, studying under the cofounder of the Southern Baptist Leadership Conference. My dad's past as a bigtime Motown writer and producer was behind him. Parties with the Temptations and the Supremes morphed into hundred-person Bible studies in the living room. Famous artists still came by, but now it was because my father was their minister. My mother was the bestselling author of relationship books for women with titles like *Liberated Through Submission* and *Your Knight in Shining Armor*. They were drawn into their church's strict interpretation of scripture. Their pastor was a proud male chauvinist who preached that women should only wear dresses and skirts, never pants. From a young age, that didn't sit right with me—I couldn't figure out why on earth God wanted me to wear a skirt in the middle of winter. I've been wired from day one to challenge everything.

When I was fifteen, my parents had another baby. My mother felt she'd made mistakes with me and my sisters. She wanted a fresh start with her youngest, but I was constantly pushing back on everything. And so my parents gave me an ultimatum: conform to the rules of the house or leave. I left. I was saying no—no to the rules I didn't understand, no to women being subservient to men, no to being someone else. Just no. My mother watched me walk down the driveway. I think we both understood that living in that environment would no longer work for me, but it was still heartbreaking.

This was in 1992, less than a year after Rodney King was brutally attacked by the police. I moved to Jordan Downs, one of the housing projects in Watts, dropped out of high school, and spent several years in homeless shelters.

The last shelter I stayed in was Covenant House. They helped you get a job, save your money, and get on your feet. My first morning there, the staff helped me put together a résumé and sent me out into LA to pound the pavement. I went to a bunch of different places, handed out my résumé, and did some interviews. One was for a job as a server at BB King's Blues Club. I walked in, interviewed, and was offered a job. You were supposed to be twenty-one to work there. I had just turned eighteen, but I only got a few questions about my age before management soon forgot about it. They saw someone who carried herself with the confidence of an adult, not a homeless teenager. I got three more job offers by the end of the day.

From then on, my confidence only grew. I knew I would be all right. I took a second job at Camacho's Cantina as a hostess, and I started saving up.

In addition to my restaurant jobs, I got an unpaid internship in PR. Back then, you'd send out a press release, see who picked it up, and watch someone run with the story. But I thought PR could be more experiential. It just seemed to make sense that if you took the products someplace where the press was already going to be—for example, filling the greenroom where a celebrity would be interviewed with an artist's paintings and sculptures—then a natural conversation with the press could follow. I reached out to celebrities I'd grown up calling "aunt" and "uncle" to introduce me to entertainers who might allow me to do this.

Today we call that *brand integration*, but at the time, it didn't really exist.

I pitched it to my boss, who didn't fully get it. "But if you can execute it, go for it," she said. So I took it to two clients. They were hesitant, but they knew what the PR firm had been trying wasn't working, so they were open to giving this idea a try. After successfully placing their products a few times, both clients came to me and said, "Listen, we're not going to stay with this PR firm. We're going to go somewhere else. But if you ever decide to start your own firm, we'll go with you."

I was still a teenager, but suddenly I had two clients. After an initial trial, each offered me $5,000 dollars a month to take on their accounts—the same amount they'd been paying the other firm. By age nineteen, I'd established FEW Entertainment and had ten employees. My dad even helped—he had a mostly unused office for his nonprofit, Black American Response to the African Crisis (BARAC), that he let me use to set up my headquarters.

FEW Entertainment's clients were happy, but within a year the business started to falter. I knew how to do PR, but I didn't yet know how to run a company. I made the hard decision to let go of every employee, although I didn't completely shutter the company just yet.

Those years were ones of turmoil, marked by a lack of hope. I tried to take my own life twice by the time I was twenty. I remember tubes down my nose and charcoal being pumped into me to pull out everything I'd taken. The second time I thought, *All right, God, so I tried to take myself out twice and you're not allowing it, so how about I figure out why I'm here?*

In one of my mom's books, she challenges women to make a six-month commitment to put an "Under Construction" sign on themselves and figure out who they are without being in a relationship. That idea resonated with me. *I'm going to be under construction*, I thought. For six months, I did nothing but go to work and read. I cut out all TV and radio. I read the Bible every day and read some sixty other books, anything that seemed like it could be helpful.

In that six months, and for years after, God worked his own charcoal in my spirit. I found this truth in the Gospel: "For where your treasure is, there your heart will be also." In other words, wherever your focus is, whatever you give attention to, that's what grows. I've lived by that and focused on my strengths ever since.

I stayed in California and worked earnestly to build a career and life that sustained and nurtured me. By twenty-five, I had become the co-owner of one of the top restaurants in Los Angeles. Chef Gerry Garvin (now G. Garvin) wanted to open his own restaurant and needed help on the business side. One of my former employees suggested me to him. Although my fledgling company was barely surviving, I had enough work that by the time Gerry contacted me, I had built strong credibility in the industry, and very few knew of my company's challenges. I advised him to focus on his catering business, which had attracted a lot of celebrity clients, while I put together a business plan for him. I became a minor shareholder and the business manager, and I oversaw the successful, celebrity-filled launch of G. Garvin's Restaurant. It quickly became *the* place to go in LA.

In 2003, I was getting my hair done once a week at a great salon. I tried to keep my head down and avoid taking in the celebrity and local gossip. I'd bring a book or spend the time on calls with staff or payroll in order to avoid chitchat. The only thing my hairdresser ever talked about was her only son, who sat just a little lower than the angels in her estimation. She never got involved with celebrity gossip. Hair and her son were her only topics. One day she had my head in the wash bowl and leaned over and said, "I've been watching you all these weeks." She liked that I ran a business at such a young age. "You have to meet my son."

It took her over a month, and four attempts, to finally convince me to give her my number. Then, she had to convince her son to call me, which took another month of relentless appeals. "I met your wife," she told him point-blank.

"This must be the Second Coming," I said, when I realized who was calling.

Keith burst out laughing. "You've been talking to my mother," he said.

Our first conversation lasted for hours. Before meeting up for a date, I asked God to let me know if Keith was the right person for me and to close the door if he was the wrong one. I knew, from our first conversation, that Keith was it for me. He was absolutely the right door.

We didn't even have that much in common. His parents were divorced. Mine were marriage counselors. He likes to think things over for a long time. I'm eager to make a choice and follow my gut. I often think and act in the same motion. But we respect each other, we work well together, and most importantly, we love each other.

I believe who you partner with in life is one of the determining factors between success and mediocrity. I wouldn't be where I am without Keith. I was a whole person by the time I met Keith—perfectly content with going to the movies alone, sitting by myself in restaurants, and loving my life. Keith was a whole person as well. Our relationship is not one of two halves making a whole. Our marriage is one multiplied by one to equal one. Folks often describe me as a strong, independent woman, but that's not exactly right. I am a strong *interdependent* woman.

I also started to see my parents in a more nuanced light through Keith's eyes. People had always talked about how important my dad was, but as a kid, I never got excited by his music; I couldn't relate to it. Growing up in his house was a little like growing up in Orlando and being utterly unimpressed with Disney World. When Keith and I got serious, though, I brought him home to meet my family.

He walked in the door and looked around at the gold and platinum records that bordered the walls of the entire living room.

"Did you forget to tell me something?" he asked.

I'd never mentioned it. I never thought to! He asked me what songs my dad had produced, and I couldn't remember any beyond "You've Made Me So Very Happy," "Love Child," and "Still Water (Love)."

When I got home, I got a text message from Keith with a link to my father's Wikipedia page. *You should know more*, he wrote.

We got married nine months after we met and considered moving to San Antonio, Texas. I always knew I was Southern at heart and wouldn't live in California forever. But Keith was an executive at Sony Pictures Entertainment. LA was home. So we compromised and found a community in Old Agoura, about thirty miles outside town. It's like time froze there. Our neighbors had cattle and dozens of horses, and chickens crossed the roads. We had a dream home with enough room and stables for four horses, a lifelong dream of mine. We called it Serenity Ranch.

For years, our life was wonderful. I built an investment company, and Keith and I became real estate investors. I wrote two bestselling books and traveled the world.

But nothing great ever comes with ease. My father passed away in 2012. Following a decade of fertility treatments, in vitro, and unsuccessful adoption and surrogacy attempts, Keith and I came to terms with the idea that the family we'd long dreamed of might not be our purpose in this life. I named my investment company Grant Sidney,

Inc., after Grant Edward and Sidney Elisabeth, the kids' names we'd chosen early into our marriage. The push I felt to mother and nurture found fulfillment in my niece, Brittany. We were her respite from a very tough world for a teenager. Whatever tools she needed in life to succeed, she knew she could come to us and we'd supply it without ever asking a question. We loved Brittany—an audio engineer and animal lover—as a daughter, but my work with Grant Sidney was often so all-encompassing that I didn't have the time to spend with her that I wanted.

One of the companies Grant Sidney invested in was struggling. I tried to help its founders turn it around, but it was a stressful experiment. In June 2016, after a year of nonstop frustrating moments, Keith invited me to join him last minute on a business trip to Singapore. I jumped at the chance for a break. For better and for worse, the trip turned out to be much more than I bargained for.

EACH MORNING during our time in Singapore, Keith and I would take the elevator to the twenty-first floor of the Grand Hyatt to enjoy breakfast in the club lounge and pick up a copy of the *New York Times* international edition, which runs about two days behind the version Americans see. Donald Trump was the presumptive Republican nominee for president, Hillary Clinton would soon clinch the Democratic presidential nomination, and both parties seemed to be intentionally creating a greater divide among the diverse population of America than I'd ever encountered in my lifetime. We wanted to stay connected with what was going on back home.

On our second day, the top-floor lounge was crowded with Keith's colleagues and their spouses, all bent over their morning papers or iPads. As Keith returned from the buffet with a hodgepodge of smoked salmon and miniature dumplings, I leafed through the paper, pausing to read a below-the-fold headline that grabbed me: "Jack Daniel's Embraces a Hidden Ingredient: Help From a Slave."

A photograph of Jack Daniel, the real-life whiskey maker behind the brand, and his leadership team accompanied the article. Jack wore a white hat and mustache and sat slightly right of center. He'd ceded the center of the photograph to a Black man with a steadfast gaze, a tilted hat, and a distinctive mustache of his own.

My eyes went wide.

"Babe, babe, what's wrong?" Keith asked. "Is everything okay?"

I flipped the paper over and showed him what I was reading.

The article, bylined Lynchburg, Tennessee, began: "Every year, about 275,000 people tour the Jack Daniel's distillery here, and as they stroll through its brick buildings nestled in a tree-shaded hollow, they hear a story like this: Sometime in the 1850s, when Daniel was a boy, he went to work for a preacher, grocer, and distiller named Dan Call. The preacher was a busy man, and when he saw promise in young Jack, he taught him how to run his whiskey still—and the rest is history.

"The distillery, home to one of the world's best-selling whiskeys," the article continued, was trying to "tell a different, more complicated tale. Daniel, the company now says, didn't learn distilling from Dan Call"—but from a man named Nearest Green, an enslaved person.

The photo caption suggested that the man in the picture could be one of Nearest's sons, but no one knew for sure.

Keith and I were genuinely stunned. I didn't know a lot about Jack Daniel's at the time; my drink of choice tended to be Colonel E. H. Taylor or Blanton's. But I knew from nearly twenty years in the hospitality industry that the Jack Daniel's brand was owned by a public company named Brown-Forman, valued at $22 billion. One of the most successful products and ubiquitous brands in history originated with an enslaved person. And now it was giving him credit on the world stage!

We rode the elevator back to our room, wondering aloud whether there could be more to this story still waiting to be discovered. After that, our morning quickly turned into the hustle and bustle of our normal life. I put on my daily gospel playlist, listened to some Kirk Franklin, CeCe Winans, and Fred Hammond, and began answering emails from business partners and employees back home as Keith dressed for a long day of meetings.

But that photograph stayed with me. I wanted to understand who that man was.

The only photographs I knew of from that era depicting white people surrounding a Black person were of lynchings and beatings—images with a very different meaning than this. Photography in general was not that common, either, especially in a little town like Lynchburg. To this day, there are only a few photographs of Jack Daniel. But photographs of Black people were even rarer. Even more unusual, the photograph was of such good quality! Critics as far back as W. E. B. Du Bois have noted that "the average white photographer does not know how to deal with colored skins." But in this image, the viewer got a real sense of personality and presence from the mystery man in the center.

I did some cursory digging online. There was almost nothing out there on Nearest Green beyond a thin, brand-new Wikipedia page with a reference to *Jack Daniel's Legacy*, a biography from 1967. The article had been out for a couple of days in the States, but so far only news aggregation sites had picked it up, regurgitating the same story.

I just knew there had to be more to this. I remember thinking, *This is going to be a story people remember.*

IN 2016—the same year I read that *New York Times* article that changed my life—Jack Daniel Distillery celebrated its 150th anniversary. Ownership had changed hands over the years, passing from Jack Daniel to his nephews Lem Motlow and Dick Daniel and then to Lem's sons, Reagor, Robert, Hap, and Connor. These four, nicknamed the "shirtsleeves brothers" for their hands-on approach to their work, sold the company to Brown-Forman, a wine and spirits company based in Louisville, Kentucky, in 1956. Reagor stayed on as president and then eventually moved to sitting on the executive board, but the family remained heavily influential until Reagor's passing in 1978.

Jack Daniel, with his top hat, tailcoats, and shoe lifts (he was only five foot two) was a walking PR campaign in his day. He'd enter a saloon and put down a silver dollar for every person there and dare them to give his namesake a try.

I make the best whiskey there is, and I'm going to prove it to you, he'd say. This drink's on me.

Channeling that spirit in the 1950s, Jack Daniel's embarked on a forty-year ad campaign of black-and-white photos and simple, heartfelt ad copy centering the people who made the whiskey. Nelson Eddy, a Nashville-based managing partner in the public relations firm that manages Jack Daniel's media relations, has been the brand's historian for close to forty years—and an expert on all things related to Jack. Ask him a question, and if he didn't know the answer, he'd consult the Jack Daniel's archives in Washington, DC, and comb through their wealth of material by hand.

One thing Nelson kept encountering was people who didn't realize Jack Daniel had been a real person. They thought he was a figment, a brand persona, like Betty Crocker. And they tended not to know—at least until they came to Lynchburg and took the distillery tour—that what really distinguishes Tennessee whiskey from other spirits is the process of charcoal mellowing, where the whiskey is slowly filtered through charcoal made from sugar maple trees to remove impurities prior to going into the barrels for the aging process.

In March 2016, Jack Daniel's media relations team had emailed Clay Risen at the *New York Times*. "With your expertise on both whiskey and civil rights," the email read, "I wanted to reach out with a story that has gone largely untold."

The message was written in the warm, homespun style that has been the signature of Jack Daniel's marketing copy for decades. It was pitched right after Black History Month in 2016. Clay could tell the story had potential. As someone acquainted with the spirits industry, it seemed familiar to him, but it was definitely not a story he or anyone else in the whiskey world knew well.

The last line of the email was key: Jack had learned his distilling skills from Nearest Green, "an African American slave who continued to work as a master of the still house after he was freed." That term, "master of the still house" and its modern incarnation, "master distiller," is a title that commands respect in the whiskey world. It doesn't have a standardized definition like "master sommelier" but rather a know-it-when-you-see-it quality within the industry. It conveys deep knowledge about distilling and a responsibility for making a brand's whiskey consistent and reliable.

While Nearest was master of the still house, he was responsible for making Jack Daniel's taste like Jack Daniel's in every barrel. Nearest's sons went to work with Jack after Nearest stopped working, the email continued, and several of Nearest's relatives still lived in the area. "The families have been closely connected ever since."

The pitch was the best idea for a Black History Month story Mark McCallum had ever heard. Mark was the executive vice president at Brown-Forman and responsible for stewarding the brand. "Jack Daniel's is one of the most iconic brands of all time," he later told me. His job was to "not screw it up." They thought they "were the cleverest white people in the world, pitching this Black History Month story," Mark said.

The article was supposed to be a historical human interest piece. Instead of running shortly after Black History Month and being a PR win for Brown-Forman, though, the article ran in July. Its eye-popping headline became a hand grenade in the culture war of the summer of

2016. "Oh my God," Mark McCallum said, after reading the piece. "Why did they choose that headline?"

In retrospect, he realized that he had been naive. An Australian, he'd been in the States since 1997. "I'm not claiming ignorance to the racial tensions in the US," he said, "but I don't think I was as alert as I would have been had I been more immersed in this country." Mark realized that the feel-good piece could become "an abject disaster" for Jack Daniel's as a brand and Brown-Forman as a company.

The "Hidden Ingredient" and "Help From a Slave" phrases took hold in readers' imaginations, and as people shared the story on social media and it was picked up by other sites, public perception of what it was about was amplified by the facts. People interpreted the story in so many different ways. The day the article was published, a commenter wrote, "The 'whole' story of America never seems to be in the history books because white affluent WASP males always seem to control the presses." The next day, another user commented about "the jaunty way [the Black man was] wearing his hat! Look at the expression on his face! That's a man who has DEEP thoughts."

Others immediately misinterpreted the article to say Jack Daniel was an enslaver who'd stolen the recipe, hidden Nearest's involvement, and never gave him credit—a story that persists online to this day. "Enslavers like Jack Daniels profiting from the bodies and minds of enslaved Africans in America is part of the larger white supremacy narrative of denial, forgetfulness, myths, and erasure," one user wrote. Another commented: "It is not clear to me why Daniel, who was hired by Call as a boy, would have owned slaves."

There was plenty of positivity in the comments, too, but it was hard to see among comments like, "Let's SMASH all the Jack Daniel's Bottles," "The Cynical Me says this is just PR for the brand," and "Nearest Green had no more to do with putting Jack Daniel's on the map than Jack Daniel did."

I couldn't blame people for jumping to conclusions. They were right, after all, that the contributions of African Americans have been systematically erased from the history books. They were right that companies often exploit stories like Nearest's for good press.

But this felt different to me.

CHAPTER

3

ON OUR way home from Singapore, on a short stopover on a nearby island, Keith and I got a call that stopped our world. Our niece Brittany had died in a motorcycle accident. A driver had been blinded by the sun and never saw Brittany on her bike—she never even slowed down. Brittany had just turned twenty-six.

Just a few weeks earlier, Brittany had come over to our house. While she and Keith sat in the kitchen chatting about life, her current struggles, and the lessons she'd recently learned, I sat one room away working on my computer. I overheard her tell Keith I'd always been like a second mom to her and how much she appreciated my love and how I was always there when she needed me.

That should have beckoned me to her, but instead, I continued answering emails and strategizing about next steps for my investment—in retrospect, things that could have waited until later. Now she was gone, taken from us all far too young.

I couldn't believe it. I'd never cried so hard in my life. Devastated, Keith and I prayed for Brittany's parents: my big sister Tracey and Brittany's father David. Then Keith held me tight. I'd never experienced such a senseless loss of a young person. I'd only been to three funerals in my entire life—my grandmother, my father, and a close friend. Keith was inconsolable, too. After a while, he walked onto our hotel balcony, stared out toward the sea, and doubled over, releasing the loudest cry I'd ever heard from my husband.

We flew back to California, where I threw myself into planning Brittany's celebration of life. I went over to Agoura Bible Fellowship, a gorgeous location with a small church and a lot of outdoor space.

"Is there any way that we could do a memorial here?" I asked.

Memorials are almost always kind of last-minute, but this was huge in scale. The folks at the church didn't even blink. They were incredibly kind and part of our beloved community. "Of course," they said.

That's how I met Stephani Ross. Born and raised in Elgin, Illinois, she worked full-time at Agoura Bible Fellowship. Stephani and I worked together to throw a great party, a real carnival—complete with a popcorn machine and snow cones, sports, and soul food. I wanted it to be about all the things Brittany loved. The church was packed, and several hundred people helped us lay Brittany to rest. I had no time to think, let alone cry.

A COUPLE DAYS LATER, I saw an unopened Amazon package on my desk with the copy of *Jack Daniel's Legacy* I'd ordered, its old-timey brown cover nestled in packing materials. With all the planning over, that was exactly what I needed. I'm the type of person who'll throw myself into work and let grief catch up with me later.

I settled onto my big round leather couch and started reading. It was the first time in nearly a month I'd allowed myself to think about anything other than Brittany. Being transported to nineteenth-century Lynchburg felt like a much-needed escape. Within a few pages, I found myself totally immersed in Jack's life and Nearest's world.

Uncle Nearest "is the best whiskey maker that I know of," the Reverend Dan Call told a young Jack Daniel when he introduced them. *Jack Daniel's Legacy* painted a picture of a relationship between colleagues and a mentor and mentee working hard, exhausting hours together. Distilling was truly skilled labor; the difference between whiskey that was good to drink and whiskey that was unpalatable and full of unwanted by-products was one of chemistry, timing, instinct, and know-how. After long hours at the still, Nearest played his fiddle on the porch and Jack danced.

When Jack established his own distillery later on, Nearest's sons George and Eli went to work for him as still hands. George and Eli Green were known for their strength. They challenged each other to lift barrels of whiskey, rest them on their knees, and drink from them. This was an epic feat, considering a whiskey barrel weighed more than four hundred pounds, and Eli earned the nickname Samson in the process.

When I learned that Jack's birthday was September 5, I thought that was a cool coincidence. That was my birthday, too, and it was coming up soon. Then I read toward the end of *Jack Daniel's Legacy* that September 5 was really Ben Green's birthday, and he had assigned it to Jack because no one knew when Jack was born. As I'd later learn, he got Jack's birth year wrong by two years, but his logic about the month and date were sound. Family lore said that Jack was born "in the fall of the year," so Ben decided to give him "the birth date of the only guy who ever set out to write a book about Uncle Jack"—himself.

I was a little bummed that Ben had assigned Jack his birthday, but as I continued to read and discover so many similarities between Jack and me, I was drawn to the connection.

"I really like this guy!" I called out to Keith as I read.

"Who?" he called back from the kitchen.

"Jack," I said.

"Jack who?"

I'd been so immersed that Keith didn't know what I was reading. I started reading excerpts aloud, sharing my discoveries about Jack Daniel.

I was drawn to Jack's story, personality, and seemingly innate gift for PR. He seemed sincerely warm, but I sensed a strength that he'd forged by leaving home so early. I connected with him as an entrepreneur who began very early in life, without parents to help guide him.

Jack's distillery had brought him great success in life, that was for sure. In his will, he had to carefully distinguish between his small diamond ring, his largest diamond ring, and his diamond stud when bequeathing them. He had a fine home with a large parlor where he frequently entertained. It was a sweepingly grandiose room with ceilings that were fourteen or sixteen feet tall and floor-to-ceiling windows hung with velvety red drapes. On the right side of the room was a grand piano; on the left was an enormous marble mantel above the fireplace with cupids and cherubs carved into it.

Jack famously held expansive barbecue dinners on the first Sunday in May each year, where guests would be served in several seatings of one hundred people at a time, and he frequently hosted balls and dances. "Never have I seen a man who had a more winning personality," his nephew Tom wrote in a December 27, 1962, letter. Jack worked the room, a consummate host, greeting everyone, complimenting the ladies, and giving everyone a smile and a pleasant word. "Never have I seen a man with a greater personality than Jack Daniel," Tom wrote. That was another similarity between us. When I walk into a room, you know I'm there. After I walk out, you'll definitely remember me!

That was Jack's innate sense of hospitality. I learned, too, about his widespread philanthropy. I believe his name will go down in history as one of the greatest philanthropists of the early twentieth century. Although he wasn't baptized until later in life, he's said to have donated money to nearly every church in Moore County. And most amazing of all, upon his death, there were thousands of loan notes between Jack and borrowers who would never have the money to pay him back. They were all forgiven when he died—he left strict orders that no one was to collect on those notes.

He also had a reputation for having "many great friends among the Negros of Lynchburg and Moore County." He employed formerly enslaved people, compensated them generously, and was said to take care of many Black people in their old age and help with their funeral expenses.

At one point he promised an elderly Black man, "I'll see that you get a good funeral." After the man's death, he honored his word. He furnished a gold watch and chain and a new broadcloth suit to bury the man in, and he purchased a casket and flowers. "He also paid the preacher an appreciated sum for holding the most ceremonial funeral in the Negro history of Moore County."

We don't know who all this finery was for. We don't know when Nearest died, but perhaps it was his mentor's funeral that Jack went to such lengths to arrange.

Ben Green's book had been written in a purposefully folksy manner in the South in the 1960s, so of course, I found some factual discrepancies in it. People's memories aren't always perfect, and they usually have reasons of their own for what they do and don't tell a reporter. Ben Green wrote that it was actually Nearest's son George who befriended Jack, which I later found out would have been impossible because George wouldn't have been alive yet (he was born sometime between 1863 and 1866). Ben Green was, by modern standards, an unreliable narrator, and he'd left no list of sources. Still, the factual discrepancies didn't change the crux of the story. They were just the buns of the burger—the meat was real and true.

My biggest takeaway was that the lives of Jack Daniel and the Greens had stayed intertwined far longer than necessity demanded. That was a fact that spoke for itself. Nearest worked with Jack long after Emancipation. George and Eli were the first of many Green descendants who would be an integral part of operations at Jack Daniel's. It was an extraordinary relationship in an unlikely time and place, and between the most unlikely people.

My father and I might've disagreed about religion and rules, but he had taught me to see the good in people, to see the world through the lens of grace, and from my first moment with *Jack Daniel's Legacy*, I knew this was a story of love. In 1967—when Green published the book—finding people who'd known Jack Daniel in life, who'd been close to him, would've been easy. After all, only about 450 people lived in Lynchburg at the time. It occurred to me just how many times those people must have mentioned Nearest and his sons for them to be included in the story more times than Jack Daniel's own family. I'd started the book skeptical of Jack, but by the end he struck me as a genuinely good guy in a time and place when any mention of his relationship with Nearest would have been unexpected—and would have undoubtedly been discouraged.

There was another reason I felt compelled to chase this story. Whenever I got up from the book to go to the bathroom or the kitchen, I noticed something—there were two white butterflies fluttering just outside the window. Even when I was reading in my office, where there were two big windows to the left and right of my desk, I'd look up and see them.

I'd seen those butterflies before. Shortly after we learned about Brittany's death, Keith and I had composed ourselves and gone out for a glass of Brittany's favorite tequila. We'd been walking hand in hand when we had to stop: hundreds of white butterflies surrounded us, circling our legs in a cloud so thick we couldn't move. They'd hovered around us, constantly moving, for a solid thirty seconds. Then they all took off together. That was Brittany ascending, we told each other.

Now, I told Keith, "these butterflies are following me." My heart was with Brittany and my dad. They were telling me things were going to be okay.

CHAPTER 4

IN **DECEMBER 1856**—the same year, I came to believe, that Nearest Green perfected his whiskey-making process—the Supreme Court heard the Dred Scott case. They later ruled that no Black person, enslaved or free, in a Southern or Northern state, could be considered a United States citizen. It was a pivotal time in American history. The Missouri Compromise—which banned slavery in new territories above the southern border of Missouri—was invalidated. Congress had no authority to ban slavery from a federal territory. The country took a leap toward civil war.

By 1857, there were sixteen free states and fifteen slave states. Tennessee, which borders eight states, occupied an important position between the North and the South. Much like you might find dots of blue in a red state today, there were people in Tennessee who were staunchly anti-slavery. Tennessee was the birthplace of America's first newspaper devoted solely to abolishing slavery: the *Emancipator*, published forty years prior to the Civil War.

The white man behind it was Elihu Embree, an iron manufacturer and former slave owner who had evolved, at age thirty, into an abolitionist. Elihu mailed his newspapers to Southern politicians, intent on persuading them to end the horrors of slavery. George Poindexter, the governor of Mississippi at the time, wrote back accusing Embree of trying to "sever the bond of social harmony." Elihu and others like him fought to make Tennessee—and the broader South—a place where freedom really was "the unalienable right of all men."

And they weren't the only ones. There were Methodist churches that officially opposed slavery, and a radical anti-slavery association organized as early as 1824—the Moral Religious Manumission Society of West Tennessee.

Just prior to the start of the Civil War, enslaved people accounted for 55 percent of the value of personal property in Middle Tennessee. The area held nearly 308,000 inhabitants, or 28 percent of the state's total population, and about four in ten residents were enslaved. When the state lifted its ban on the import of enslaved people in 1855, Nashville became a hub for the interstate slave trade.

In some of the farther reaches of the heartland, in poorer areas distant from towns and railroads, slavery was less common. Class was the primary indicator of who owned enslaved people and who didn't— it was a measure of success. One Bedford County resident wrote that "slave holders were the only men that could make enough money to do anything." Whether tacitly or overtly, even non-slaveholders in Tennessee acknowledged their stake in, and commitment to, the slaveholding society in which they lived.

This truth cut across race; even the wealthiest free Black man in Tennessee, Sherrod Bryant, owned enslaved people who worked his seven hundred acres. "I think at some point some of the members [of the family] might not have looked upon it very favorably, but the more we discuss it, the more we suddenly realize that to gain wealth during that time, if you had a lot of property, you had to have slaves to help you cultivate it," one of his descendants told the *Tennessean*.

Historically, Black people couldn't trademark a brand name, own a product (much less sell it to others), or own any type of patent. As someone who has gone from homeless shelters to being one of the largest Black landowners in Tennessee, I've spent a lot of my life thinking about upward mobility. Intellectual property law is a part of what allowed the wealthiest white American families to grow and secure their fortunes over generations, and it was the lack of those rights for enslaved people that ensured their families would never be able to compete.

In 1858, the attorney general's issued opinion, *Invention of a Slave*, stated that neither an enslaved person nor an enslaver could file patents for their enslaved person's invention "because neither the slave owner nor his slave could take the required patent oath. The slave owner could not swear to be the inventor, and the slave could not take the oath at all." Because it was so difficult to secure patents, some enslavers are believed to have surreptitiously patented the inventions of their enslaved people. Eli Whitney's cotton gin was said to have actually been invented by an enslaved man named Sam. Black people's mass exclusion from the right to own one's own ideas has had consequences that have reverberated for centuries.

I started to research whether website URLs and trademarks related to Nearest Green were available. I've learned the hard way to never work on something I can't trademark—I had a whole line of hats, shirts, and tote bags designed and mocked up for my book *Happy Wives Club* before I learned that someone else had trademarked a phrase similar enough that I couldn't use it. So now when I'm even remotely interested in a potential project, I look into copyrights and trademarks, and I buy all the URLs related to whatever it is I'm digging into.

Over the years, I've filed more LLCs than one can even imagine, and at last count I owned 838 domain names. If I think I might work on it, I file it. At one point, our accounting firm advised me to dissolve all the LLCs I wasn't using because they were too hard to keep track of. I wasn't excited about that. "I might still do something with all those later down the line," I told Keith. He likes to joke that most women collect diamonds, but I collect LLCs. I see it as being a hoarder of potential.

To my surprise, no one at Brown-Forman had ever secured the trademarks related to Nearest Green. I thought that was really odd, because Nearest's story seemed to have been publicly known for so long. Nobody at any time ever thought, *Hey, this might be an interesting story; we should do something with it.*

Then I realized Keith and I could be those people. I'd read enough business books throughout my formative years to know that sometimes being in the right place at the right time with the right imagination and resources is all it takes. *This is a story people are ready to hear,* I thought. *Maybe* WE *should do something with it.*

We trademarked "Uncle Nearest, Uncle Nearis, and Nearest Green" for spirits, "Nearis Green" for restaurant services, and "Nearis and Nearis 1854" for clothing and spirits between June 28 and the end of July.

I also applied for a federal tax ID number and a business bank account for a company. I didn't have any plans yet, just instinct and a tug on my heart. With liquor, food, and clothing trademarks secured, our bases were covered for the future. We could take all the time we needed to figure out Nearest's story and what it could lead to.

BY AUGUST, I understood that Nearest Green was more than a rabbit hole I'd briefly fallen into. I couldn't stop thinking about him.

It was clear that there was much more to Nearest's story than the article in the *Times* had captured. I learned that most local records were still kept in county archives in physical form; online research from LA could only get me so far. On top of that, many of the people I wanted to talk to most were getting up in years, and my California area code made phone calls suspicious. Of course, that was the biggest hurdle of all: I was an outsider with no local connections. I'd need to visit to keep digging.

I told Keith I wanted us to go to Lynchburg for my fortieth birthday, coming up in September.

"There's no way I'm going to go to a town with 'lynch' in its name," Keith said. "It's not going to happen."

For two weeks, we went back and forth.

Every single time I returned to my reading, I'd say, "Babe, I can't stop thinking about Lynchburg. I need to go. I need to do more research."

He'd smile at me and say, "What about Paris? Rome?"

I'd been to both cities twice. I wanted to go to Lynchburg.

Keith went down his list of locales. Each day, he'd Google a new place and try to get me excited about it. "Tahiti. This looks beautiful. There are rooms over the water."

But I only wanted Lynchburg.

Finally he said, "I know you have Prague on your bucket list. We'll go to Prague."

"That's perfect," I said. "We'll go by way of Lynchburg."

You can't tell your wife she can't go where she wants to for her fortieth birthday; it just doesn't work. He finally gave in. That's when I told him I wanted to go for a week.

"That's absolutely not going to happen," Keith said. He laid out his terms: "You've got four days. We get in, we get out. Whatever research you don't get in those four days, you're going to do the rest from LA. I'm not letting you go back without me."

I understood Keith's concern. Lynchburg sits right above the Alabama border. I knew as well as he did there'd been a strong resurgence of the KKK in Alabama, and there are pockets of the South that still don't exactly like that we're free. But the reality of two Black folks road-tripping through the American South didn't hit me until Keith admitted that he was so embarrassed to be taking me to Lynchburg for my birthday that he hadn't told our friends where we were really going—he let them assume we were traveling to Kentucky to explore the Bourbon Trail.

But everything I'd read about Nearest and Jack made me feel like Lynchburg was so much more than its awful name. And not every story about race was tragic. My dad's career in Motown had been all about bringing Black and white people together. Still, an even smaller voice reminded me that if something happened to us in Tennessee, nobody would know where to look.

But I was optimistic now that Keith was on board. I've always said he's my biggest supporter—and that's good, because I tend to find myself in situations that require a lot of support! With any ambitious goal, any business challenge, any cuckoo-for-Cocoa-Puffs idea, he is my Chief Encourager.

I got in touch with Claude Eady, who'd been identified as a Nearest Green descendant in the *New York Times* article, and asked if he'd be willing to talk when I got to Lynchburg.

"I'm ninety-one years old," Claude said, his voice gravelly through the phone. "I don't know that I'll still be here in two weeks' time. But if I'm still around, I'm happy to talk to you."

CHAPTER

5

WHENEVER I'M traveling, I say a prayer for traveling mercies. I always feel safe, and whenever I'm traveling with Keith, I'm doubly comfortable. I didn't know what we'd find in Lynchburg, but on the plane, I was glad we were going and happy to be with Keith. It was going to be a good birthday trip no matter what.

As Keith drove the seventy miles southwest from the Nashville airport to Lynchburg, I marveled at the scene out the window. I love to soak in the sights of a new place as I get my bearings. Neat little houses dotted the lush green surroundings, interspersed with cows and horses. By the time we saw a sign that read, "Jack Daniel Distillery Ahead. Exit 81A," I was vibrating with excitement.

Cruising along with Keith on the runup to my birthday and through all that gorgeous scenery should have given me a deep sense of peace and contentment, but as we drove closer to Lynchburg, I had a pressing problem—more pressing than the four or five Confederate flags I noticed along the route. I really needed to pee.

Just past a particularly large Trump flag, a billboard welcomed us to town. Keith and I headed for the white Greek revival building that housed Miss Mary Bobo's Restaurant. Listed on the National Register of Historic Places, everyone online said it was the best place in town to get biscuits. I'd later learn the Bobos were Lynchburg elites, with a long and storied connection to Jack Daniel's. I was excited to try their biscuits and walk into a part of local history.

But when we got there, we found out that the restaurant took reservations weeks in advance and only had a couple seatings a day. The first one wouldn't even begin for four more hours.

We went a couple blocks back to the town square, which was folksy and charming and had clearly been purposefully kept as it would have looked in the early twentieth century. There were signs for Jack Daniel's brownies, Jack Daniel's ice cream, and Jack Daniel's candy—anything and everything Jack Daniel's. But nothing was open yet.

Panicked, I noticed a café called "Lynchburg Fixins."

I bolted for the door, barely noticing the other patrons in my haste.

But when I returned from the bathroom, I realized all eyes were on me. I was like a speck of pepper in a saltshaker. Every face around me was white, and literally everyone was wearing camouflage.

Keith raised his eyebrows at me.

A waitress came by and said, "Welcome to Fixins," in the deepest Southern accent I'd ever heard.

"What's good here?" I asked.

"Everything."

I ordered the grits with butter and brown sugar, scrambled eggs, and a biscuit with gravy—one of my absolute favorite breakfasts growing up. I later learned it was the first day of a limited dove-hunting season—they don't all wear camo all the time.

Keith and I spotted another Black person in the restaurant as we were leaving. We smiled at each other, relieved, and discussed our game plan in the car. The Moore County Library, just across the street from the square, had popped up whenever I found photographs of

Green descendants, but it wasn't open yet. And we weren't ready to head to our rental on Main Street, two doors down from Miss Mary Bobo's.

"What now?" Keith asked.

"I've got another stop in mind."

"Of course you do," Keith said, grinning.

I'D BEEN DOING a fair amount of research into Ben A. Green since reading *Jack Daniel's Legacy*. A white man from the little town of Lonoke, Arkansas, Ben had attended the University of Alabama before getting his first newspaper job at the *Tuscaloosa News*, where he stayed for twenty-four years. I would later meet his son Duff, who told me: "He always tried to be as objective as possible, but also as personal as possible."

As the president of the Alabama Press Association and the Alabama Associated Press newspaper group, Ben was acutely aware of the inequities in the world around him and had a reputation for taking on the KKK in print and in person. "I inherited a certain amount of my concern about how we were treating Black folks in the South pretty early," Duff told me. "I knew that I lived a protected life. And we were not rich, not by a long shot, but I lived in a society that protected me" but not others.

After leaving the *Tuscaloosa News*, Ben went to the *Nashville Banner*, where he became interested in country music. As Duff told me, "Dad had a way of digging deep into where he lived." Ben wrote articles about the music industry that would run every Friday night.

By the time Duff graduated from college, his father had moved to Shelbyville, about twenty minutes from Lynchburg, to edit the *Times-Gazette*.

At that time, Jack Daniel's didn't have much of a publicly known history, although an 1895 advertisement bragged that the "distill" had "been in operation longer than any in the United States."

After World War II, advertising picked up steam as its own industry. Typical whiskey ads in the 1950s were aspirational—full page, four-color illustrations of men in smoking jackets being served drinks on a silver tray.

To extend Jack Daniel's reach, the Motlows hired the company's very first marketing person, Art Hancock. This was in the 1950s, shortly before the Brown-Forman acquisition. Art implemented a new strategy, running advertisements that were the color of newsprint, giving the ads a factual appearance. Under Art's guidance, the advertising emphasized the people of Lynchburg and the history of the brand.

According to Nelson Eddy, Art was "responsible for having a good deal of research done on Jack back in the day," and he even drafted an in-house history.

Then Art decided a biography of Jack would capture the spirit of the brand better than any ad campaign. It worked out perfectly. Ben Green was already interested in writing a book about the area. The book was written with Jack Daniel's collaboration, but it wasn't a work for hire—it was an independent work and more rigorously researched than it looked. A letter Green sent to Hancock on July 13, 1966, illustrates his process and exhaustion—his longing to complete the work, along with his detail-oriented approach. The researching and writing had, evidently, been a long endeavor: "This has been pending a real long time and it will relieve my mind if I can get it to the printer," Green wrote, after explaining the 1,500 miles he traveled to track down a source—a letter from a librarian confirming that Jack Daniel had in fact won a gold medal for his whiskey at the 1904 World's Fair in St. Louis. Triumphant, he wrote that it "really relieved my mind to get this proof." His reporting was extraordinarily ambitious, if a bit uneven.

I was hoping the *Times-Gazette* newspaper in Shelbyville, where Green was once the editor, would have more information. So Keith and I drove the twenty minutes over.

Shelbyville felt like a different world, with grocery stores, hotels, and bars that served alcohol (all amenities Lynchburg goes without). We also realized we were far more likely to spot Black people occasionally.

We parked outside the newspaper's small office, where I remarked that the red brick building with a white sign out front likely looked just as it had in the sixties. The roof was angled, the windows welcoming, but there was something slightly dilapidated about the place.

The *Times-Gazette* was still printing three paper editions a week with its on-site printing press. I was hoping to learn whether Ben Green had printed any information about Nearest Green in his newspaper articles that hadn't made it into the *Jack Daniel's Legacy* book. The paper was open and happy to pull out their books for us—but they were physical, old-school tomes of newspapers that needed to be flipped through individually. There was no index and no way to search by subject. And, concerningly, when Keith and I looked at the papers from the 1900s, the only Black people included were those who played on sports teams.

Exhausted and a little dispirited, we drove back to Lynchburg. The temperature was in the nineties, and I could feel the lingering summer air on my skin, even in the air-conditioned car.

But the library was open now, and blessedly cool.

CHAPTER

6

THE MOORE County Library is tiny and charming. That first morning, we sat at the one round table that stands near the big blue librarian's desk and beside the stacks of books. A little children's area was off to one side, and a beautiful quilt showing books of many colors hung behind the desk. It's the kind of library that looks minuscule to grownups but would feel immense to a little kid—and I kind of felt like a little kid again sitting at that wooden table. Reagor Motlow and his wife had gifted the building to the county in 1963, and Reagor maintained an office there for a long time as a state representative and senator.

Not many people lived in Lynchburg—only 6,742 as of July 2022—and only 1.7 percent of them were Black. It was an aging population, too; a solid 20 percent of Lynchburgers were sixty-five or older. Lynchburg has grown dramatically since Nearest and Jack's day, when there were only three hundred or so residents. So we began searching for any record that included Black people to use as a starting point.

The first settlers arrived in the area that would later be known as Lynchburg around 1800 from North Carolina and Georgia. These white pioneers brought enslaved people who worked hard to break the soil for farming. The area was a vast wilderness that had to be cleared and tamed in order to make it suitable for homes.

As families moved in, a country lane developed into the present-day Main Street. Though none of the original records survived, lots were reportedly laid out, numbered, and sold to the public. The settlers built homes west of Mulberry Creek and set up industry along its eastern bank near the present location of Jack Daniel Distillery. In 1809, there were just two log cabins in Lynchburg; by the 1830s, there was a cotton mill, cotton gin, grist mill, tannery, and general store. Main Street served as the primary thoroughfare with commercial and residential buildings lining the street.

Lynchburg's local Masonic lodge was established on the east side of town in 1866, and the Grand Central Hotel, which later became Miss Mary Bobo's Boarding house, was erected in 1867. Not long after, local residents asked the state legislature to create a new county. Moore County was established in 1871, just a few years after the Civil War ended, and Lynchburg—previously in Lincoln County—was made the county seat. Around the same time, a small Black neighborhood grew up around a school, cemetery, and church on the west end of town. In a time before cars, the road was more or less a worn-down walking path traveled by mules and buggies. This would later be renamed Elm Street, but at the time everyone called it Dog Row after the many stray dogs that congregated around the residents' backyards begging for leftovers.

Like most small towns, Lynchburg's growth was fairly slow, and like most rural counties, most industry was limited to agriculture. Other than a few mills, manufacturing never really developed.

But one industry did boom: whiskey.

The area in and around Lynchburg turned out to be one of the best in Tennessee for making whiskey. Smack in the middle of the state, the region is shaped like a bowl and has the perfect climate for distilling. There was plentiful water, good timber, and good land for corn. And distillers found the abundance of blue limestone made for good drainage and filtered iron and other minerals out of the water.

Around 1812, the county's first distillery was erected right near where Jack Daniel would later open his own facility more than half a century later.

As the county grew, so did the number of distilleries in operation. By the 1880s, there were fifteen registered distilleries in Moore County, including Jack Daniel's, which was producing 150 gallons a day. Collectively they could produce 33,680 gallons, or just over 842 forty-gallon barrels, every month. At two dollars per gallon, the county could draw in $67,360 *per month*—more than $2.1 million today.

After a solid hour and a half, Keith and I had learned a lot about Lynchburg, and I understood why someone would set up a distillery here, but we hadn't been able to find anything about Nearest or *any* information on Black families in the area. Not a single thing on any Black person. The exhaustion I'd kept at bay the last few months threatened to bowl me over. What if the story I was searching for wasn't there?

Eventually the young white assistant librarian came over.

"Can I help you?" she asked. "What are you looking for?"

I shared with her why we were there and my interest in Nearest Green.

"Oh my gosh! I know the story. I was so excited when I read it." She'd posted the *New York Times* story on her Facebook page. "I shared it with everybody I knew."

Her excitement buoyed me. I felt like maybe I was onto something. Clearly, she viewed the relationship between Nearest and Jack positively.

"Let me try to help you," she said. She started going to all the sections where she thought she might find records, but she couldn't locate any, either. I knew there had to be Black people still in Lynchburg, and yet there seemed to be no records of their ancestors anywhere in the library.

The assistant librarian called the library director, who pointed her toward a white binder from Hickory Hill Baptist Church. Inside it, we found a single piece of paper. "Dan Call, then only 17 years old had inherited a large farm, on Louse creek, near present day Lois, Tn," it stated. "Here Jack Daniel would learn to make Lincoln County Whiskey helping Dan Call's Slave, 'Uncle Nearest Green.'" It was the first mention of Nearest that I'd found since arriving in Lynchburg.

I shouldn't have been surprised that a church would be the repository of Black history I was looking for, but it was the wording that struck me the most. Jack was *helping* Nearest Green. He wasn't stealing Nearest's recipe from him. He wasn't even getting help from Nearest. It was a complete reversal of the power dynamic the *New York Times* headline had implied. I made a copy of it.

Years later, I'd read a *Salon* magazine article in which one of Nearest's descendants, Yvette J. Green—a Nashville writer, essayist, memoirist, and poet—zeroed in on the headline and its reference to Nearest as an "ingredient," diminishing his centrality in whiskey making. She also interrogated the phrase "help from," which falsely implied that Nearest was an assistant instead of *the* man who made Jack Daniel's whiskey possible.

I started pulling all the old deed books for Lincoln County. If I was right that this was a story about love, honor, and respect, perhaps I'd find that someone had deeded land to Nearest or his sons, and that would help me find the story.

I'll never forget sitting at that table in the middle of the library, reading entry after entry in the deed books. So-and-so deeds so-and-so a hundred acres, a record would say, and then go on to detail the property that went along with it: twenty cows, ten hogs, three Negros, twelve chickens. I was gutted. I knew, of course, that we'd been enslaved, and enslaved people were property. But I'd only known it in theory. Now, I was staring down at the cold numbers, the mundane legalese, that showed the reality. We'd been deeded on the same line, in the same thought, as farm animals. I was exhausted. We'd gone from a diner full of white people in camouflage to a library that seemed to have eliminated all mention of Black people, except those awful deed books. How was it possible that there were no Black people in all this history?

"I'm done," I told Keith.

We agreed we'd come back to it. For now, we'd call it a day.

AS KEITH AND I were packing up, we saw an elegant white woman in her sixties enter the library. Her black suit, silk scarf, and little black pumps immediately stood out. No camo for this lady. She instantly became the focus of the assistant librarian, who made a beeline across the room to her. Keith and I were both sitting still, watching this interaction out of the corners of our eyes, trying to pretend we weren't paying attention to their conversation. But the library was so small there was no way not to overhear.

"I'm going on a trip," the woman said. "And I want a few audio books."

As they headed back to the audiobook section, we heard her whisper something to the librarian.

"They're the people that are here doing research on Nearest Green and Jack," the librarian responded, at full volume.

The jig was up, and the older woman walked right up to us. Short, with sloped shoulders and almost translucent hands, she carried herself with a determination I recognized.

"My name is Judy Boyd Terjen," she announced. "I am the grand-daughter of Lem Motlow," Jack Daniel's nephew who'd inherited his distillery. Judy was the second eldest living descendant of Jack Daniel; her mother was the eldest. "I will be happy to help you with your research."

She sure didn't sound happy. She didn't smile, nor did she seem to find it particularly nice to meet us. I figured, "I will be happy to help you with your research" translated pretty directly to "I know what you're up to. Don't bother."

I later learned Judy was on the trustee board of the library, so it was hardly a coincidence she'd stopped in so soon after the library called the director. She clearly wanted to know how we might be spinning the story. I wasn't sure if I was writing a book yet, but I didn't want Judy or anyone else shutting me out. And I liked the way she carried herself. She was assertive and put-together.

"I know what you're thinking," I said. "But I'm not here to harm your family's legacy." It was a gamble to come out and say this, but had I been in Judy's shoes, I would have been worried about the same thing. "I think social media has this wrong. I think the *media* has it wrong." If Jack Daniel had been trying to steal Nearest's recipe, he would've done it. Most distilleries in Tennessee and Kentucky had Black distill-ers, including those brands still being sold in restaurants and bars around the world to this day, and yet, we only knew the name of the one who worked for her ancestor. And we only know that because Jack and his descendants ensured the names of Nearest and his boys were recorded and remembered. "I think that there was a relationship here that deserves to be celebrated and shared."

I told Judy about reading *Jack Daniel's Legacy* and my realization that someone—possibly Jack Daniel himself—had wanted to make sure Nearest's story endured.

"I only write books about love," I told her. I assured her I wasn't in Lynchburg as an investigative journalist or an overzealous blogger. I told her about the first two books I'd written, both on love and marriage. If I wrote this book, it would be a book about the mutual respect these two men had for each other.

"Well, in that case, I want to help you," she said. This time, her meaning matched her words. Many of Nearest's descendants remained in Lynchburg, and Judy knew them well.

This was a wonderful development. It was vital to work from the ground up. I needed to meet Nearest's and Jack's descendants before marching over to Jack Daniel's headquarters and asking questions.

"You need to talk to Juanita Dunlap," Judy said. "She's one of Nearest's descendants and was one of my best friends growing up. Her mom worked for my mom, and I looked forward to every day when her mom came over because that meant I could play with Neat."

I was amazed by this. I hadn't even met Miss Neat yet, but I could picture her and Judy as children. What an image: Jack's family and Nearest's family, playing jacks together.

Miss Neat, as she was known to all her friends, was Nearest Green's great-great-granddaughter by marriage. Apparently, she had come to the library every day to work on the genealogy of Lynchburg's Black population, including Nearest. The Moore County Library just didn't have the manpower to keep pulling records for her and, unbeknownst to the assistant librarian, had moved every record of every Black family in the county to a separate area for her at the Moore County archives on the town square. They hadn't whitewashed anything—quite the opposite.

Before she left the library, Judy added, "You know that farm that you read about where Nearest and Jack lived?" I certainly did—the Call Farm had played a central role in *Jack Daniel's Legacy*. Judy drew a little map on a Post-it note. "It's for sale. You should buy it."

I can't imagine she meant that as anything more than an offhand remark. But Keith and I have been real estate investors for a long time. We gave each other a look. I knew Nearest and Jack had met on Dan Call's farm.

"Day 1 in Lynchburg was a pretty big success," I emailed a friend that night. "Bring on Day 2!"

CHAPTER

7

C LAUDE EADY and his wife Dorothy, known as Miss Dot, lived on Main Street in a brick house with two white chairs on the concrete front porch. The garage door was open when I arrived. I later learned that if they didn't want company—that day or any other—they'd just leave the garage closed. It's a good system! Not sure what to expect, I knocked on the door.

The inside of their home was spotless—white rug, wallpaper, dark wood table and chairs. Miss Dot would get cold, so she'd sit in her sneakers on her chair with the cream-colored cushion directly in front of the radiator vent.

Claude was born in 1924 and began working at Jack Daniel's in 1946. He loved working there, and he loved talking about it. Claude was used to doing interviews—he'd been featured in any number of magazine stories, photo shoots, calendars, and even a TV commercial—and genuinely enjoyed them.

In 1952, he married Dorothy Hall. Born in Lynchburg, Miss Dot had attended an all-Black elementary school in the 1930s. When she was twelve, her father secured a position working at Jack Daniel

Distillery, where he helped tend the cattle. It was better work than the sharecropping he'd done previously. With Miss Dot's father working at Jack Daniel's, the family started living "halfway decent." They didn't have the finer things in life, but they were receiving a check every week. Because of segregation, she traveled to a different county to go to high school. Miss Dot studied at Tennessee State before returning to Lynchburg to teach at the segregated Highview School. After Moore County schools integrated in 1965, Highview was closed and Miss Dot transitioned to teaching Black and white children at Lynchburg Elementary School.

"What was integration like?" I asked her.

"I guess it was a nonissue," she said.

I was shocked. How was that possible?

She gestured in the direction of a nearby creek. The kids already played together there before and after school, she said. They already played together on the weekends. They were just excited to be able to play together during school hours as well.

And it wasn't just the kids. "I didn't have any problem whatsoever with the teachers or the students or the parents," she said. "Everybody just knew everybody. And the white people knew us. And when we'd have county meetings with the teachers, the Black teachers met with the white teachers. And we just didn't have any problem when we were integrated."

Claude and Miss Dot told me that Claude's mother had told him he was kin to Nearest Green, but he wasn't sure how exactly. Before Clay Risen came to town, they'd rarely discussed Nearest, and they hadn't known that Jack Daniel had learned his trade from him.

When I asked more about how he was related, they referred me to Juanita Dunlap—the same woman Judy had mentioned in the library. Miss Dot had been Miss Neat's elementary school teacher, and they both attended the same church. "Everyone would run from her when we saw her coming with papers. 'Here comes Neat with those roots,' we'd all say," said Miss Dot while letting out a laugh.

At the end of our conversation, Miss Dot looked me deep in the eyes and said, "I don't know why I feel like I need to say this to you, but I am just so proud of you."

I felt tears come to my eyes. This was a story that had to be told. I felt chosen to bring it to light, for reasons I didn't understand—but I knew I'd make sure it was told right.

LATER ON, Keith was on the couch in our rental on Main Street and I was changing clothes when the phone rang.

I answered and heard a Southern accent I couldn't quite parse. I was able to make out, "You met my cousin in the library."

I paused, one pant leg of my jeans on, one off, and shot a look at Keith.

"Jack's family," I mouthed.

We'd only been there two days, and I'd now met two people who were related to Jack Daniel. I wondered if it was fate.

I hobbled over to the couch, and the woman on the phone introduced herself. Her name was Sherrie Moore.

"Do you want to go see the Dan Call Farm? I'm a realtor; I can take you. Do you want to go tomorrow?"

I said yes, of course.

"What else are y'all doing tonight?" she asked. "Are you going to Celebration?"

Celebration turned out to be the finale of the eleven-day Tennessee Walking Horse National Celebration horse show.

"Would you like to go?" Sherrie asked.

"Sure," I said. If someone from Jack Daniel's family wanted me to join them at a walking horse show, who was I to say no?

Keith and I visited Sherrie that night at her house and talked about Nearest and my reasons for making the trip. We also met her cousin, John T. Bobo, a renowned local attorney whose family had deep ties to Jack Daniel's. I liked him immediately. John T. talked in stories, and when they got a little long, he said he'd "make it just as brief as a country lawyer can." He seemed to know nearly everyone in Lynchburg and Shelbyville, and he had been the attorney for a great many locals, including some of Nearest's descendants. Between him and his elderly mother, Marie, I would be able to connect with many of them. He couldn't remember the first time he'd heard the name Nearest Green. In Lynchburg, he said, "that name has been around."

At the horse show we met other descendants of Jack. We made friends and watched the show together. To my eye, walking horses pranced strangely—at half speed, they lifted their legs unnaturally high after every step as if they were unsticking them from quicksand. But the crowd loved it. There were probably twenty-five thousand people there, all crowded into the open-air grounds. It was a breathtaking introduction to Tennessee and to the deeply hospitable nature of Jack's family.

THE NEXT MORNING, we accompanied Miss Dot to a service at Berry Chapel AME. This was where Nearest's sons, grandchildren, and most of the rest of his descendants—except for a few who attended the Church of Christ across the street—had attended church across the generations. The fellowship hall had been named in Claude Eady's honor.

In the 1800s, the land the church was built on was owned by a Black man named George Daniel, who was a contemporary of Nearest Green. I'd go on to find lots of Black families in the area with the same last name as white families, and vice versa. There were Black Waggoners and Black Daniels, and white Greens. The shared surnames came from decades of slavery followed by decades more of sharecropping. This was a common source of housing and income for both white and Black families. In George Daniel's case, I don't know what connected him to the Daniel family. Jack Daniel never owned enslaved people, but his father did—perhaps that's where the name came from.

After the war, George Daniel became a boot- and shoemaker with a thriving business that was noted in the same line as many white "business houses" in an 1887 history of Moore County. A club-footed man, he routinely stayed at his shop in town during the week and on the weekends returned to his home on Elm Street. He had enough land to donate a parcel to the AME Church in 1904, two years before his death. George Daniel had a large family, and many of them remained in Lynchburg and were well-known to the townspeople.

George's son James Daniel married Nearest and Harriet's daughter Minnie Green, and another son became stepfather to three of Nearest and Harriet's granddaughters after their son Jessie died. All I could conclude from this was that Lynchburg, in addition to being a company town, was a *family* town. I learned pretty quickly that the families of the Black and white residents had lived near and among each other for two hundred years. Almost everyone's family tree overlapped. This meant I needed to look into Nearest and Jack, but also into everyone else—a scale I hadn't entirely understood.

At the church, we met Juanita Dunlap, who was George Daniel's great-granddaughter. Born and raised in town, Miss Neat got her start researching Black folks in the area after being laid off from her job as a contractor at the Air Force base. Miss Neat found work substitute teaching at the middle school her grandson attended and manning the front desk of a lawyer's office. When she wasn't working, she accompanied her ill mother to doctor's appointments in Nashville. And when she had free time, she drove the thirteen miles from Tullahoma to Lynchburg to visit the Moore County Library.

She'd always been interested in her family history, and she wanted to know where her people came from. So she went through census records, documents, photos, anything she could get her hands on. She learned that her grandmother Gertrude had married Nearest Green's son Jessie in 1899. After he died twelve years later, Gertrude married a different Jesse—Jesse Daniel, George Daniel's son, who was a carpenter and custodian at Farmers Bank—and they had several children. Their daughter Helen was Miss Neat's mother.

Then she kept going. Every name she'd heard, she looked them up and made copies of their information. When that got too expensive, she recorded by hand. She wrote down every single Black person in Lynchburg she found listed in the 1880 census. Then she tracked down their descendants.

Miss Neat's ultimate goal was to compile a book detailing the histories of local Black families and give it to the library to make things easier for future researchers. She was familiar with just how hard it was to find any information at all on Black people. She'd been active for a long time in the Moore County Historical Society, and she knew the Lynchburg newspapers—the *Sentinel*, the *Moore County Pioneer*—had, historically, rarely included Black people, unless they committed a crime. Occasionally a notice about a marriage license given to a Black couple would run. But coverage was generally sparse. And there was never a Black-owned newspaper there like there were in larger towns.

In more recent years, the avid historical community in Lynchburg and the surrounding towns has sought to rectify that, publishing a large, heavy bound book titled *The Heritage of Moore County, Tennessee 1871–2004* that graces many a coffee table in Lynchburg. This quickly became a handy resource. The book told the stories of those a much earlier history of the county had neglected—"the hard working middle class, factory and mill workers, former slaves, the less affluent farmers, and pioneer settlers of this county"—but left it up to the individual writers of each entry how they wanted to handle the subject. Some white families acknowledged slavery and some didn't; same with the Black families. Miss Neat had penned quite a few entries herself.

After starting her project, it was like a bug had bit Miss Neat. She couldn't let it go. She started talking to everybody in town. She would walk up to people and ask about their grandfather or great-uncle without knowing anything about them. She was just interested. "I guess old people would have said I was nosy," she said once, but I never thought so. She didn't want to offend anyone or expose family secrets. She just wanted to put something together that would make it easier for Black folks to find their roots.

After meeting Miss Neat at the church, Keith and I eventually visited her home in Tullahoma, where she laid out photos and documents on her kitchen table. We worked out Claude Eady's family tree and found that George Green was his great-uncle by marriage. There were direct descendants of Nearest in town for me to meet, though, and she and others were eager to help me find them.

This was more than enough to be inspired—and to convince me that Brown-Forman wasn't doing enough.

Miss Neat had heard stories about Nearest in her family while growing up but learned the most about him when she'd read *Jack Daniel's Legacy*. She was elated when the *New York Times* ran its story. Like me, she wanted to solve the mystery of the man beside Jack Daniel. And she felt credit for Nearest from Jack Daniel's was long overdue.

CHAPTER

8

AFTER CHURCH, we headed back to the town square. From those first days, I understood that everyone in town had a relationship with Jack Daniel's. The whole square—all eighty-two properties—was a registered historical landmark, and Jack Daniel's owned many of the buildings. Hell, even Miss Mary Bobo's was owned by Jack Daniel's! It was a company town.

And the distillery really was the center of all life. It went well beyond the Jack Daniel's knick-knacks, souvenirs, and themed desserts we saw for sale. Local farmers filled their trucks with "slop"—food for cows that was made of leftovers from the distilling process. "Distiller's mold" covered the trees and buildings in a nontoxic blanket of black residue caused by a fungus that thrived on the "angels' share," the portion of whiskey that evaporates as it ages.

During that first visit, I found that the story of Nearest was both well-known and frustratingly opaque. It was a story that everyone knew but no one really talked about or celebrated, like night following day.

As Keith and I walked around the town's small square, I started to think that the story I was chasing wasn't just Nearest's and Jack's, but Lynchburg's as a whole.

ONE THING ABOUT KEITH and me is that, no matter how excited we are, we don't forget to eat. Soul food and Southern food are my love language. (Keith says I'm the only person in the world who gets more excited about a really good piece of fried chicken than buying a million-dollar property.)

The manager of our rental, Fran, had told us to check out Barrel House BBQ, where the owner had been featured on *BBQ Pitmasters*. It was just a short stroll from where we were staying, and it looked like a good place to grab lunch before we went to see the Call Farm. Founded by Chuck Baker in 2012, the walls and shelves were plastered and loaded down with more Jack Daniel's paraphernalia than I'd ever seen. There were sealed bottles, posters on the wall from the Jack Daniel BBQ International, barrel heads, pictures of the master distillers going all the way to the early days. (No Nearest, though.) I was so focused on the decor that I barely noticed when a bald man in a sleeveless T-shirt grabbed a couple menus and led us toward our table.

"Where are you folks from?" he asked.

"Los Angeles," I said, tearing my eyes away from the posters.

"Wait." He turned to look at me. "I know who you are." He pointed at me. "Your name is—wait. Don't tell me." He closed his eyes. "Your name is Fawn." He snapped his fingers. "Your name is Fawn, and you're an author from Los Angeles. Someone called me about you. I can't remember who it was. But someone called and asked if you'd been into my restaurant." He sat us down. "It's nice to meet you, anyway. Someone will be by here soon to take your order."

"That's a problem," Keith said in a low voice as the man walked away. "Why does that guy know who we are?"

"I don't know."

"That man had your name, that you're a writer, where we're from—"

"I know," I said.

Our waitress stopped by, and I asked her to tell me about the most popular item on the menu. She directed me to the "grilled cheese on crack." She giggled when I asked what that was. "It's pulled pork on Texas toast with American cheese," she explained. I asked for her second most popular item. "Well, all our meat," she said. "The ribs, smoked sausage, pulled pork."

I ordered all three. Keith did, too.

As our waitress headed back to the kitchen, the man who'd seated us came by our table again. "Fran Bradford is the one. You all are renting Steve May's place, right? She told me you were in town and that you were a famous writer. She wanted to know if you'd been in yet." He pulled up a chair and said, "I'm Chuck Baker, by the way. This is my place."

Still uneasy, I told him exactly what I'd told Judy at the library. I understood that I needed clear messaging to gain people's trust. Chuck seemed to like what I had to say.

It didn't take long to realize Chuck was something like an unofficial mayor of Lynchburg. He'd been a brick mason before shifting to barbecue. "I fell in love with the whole meeting people thing," he told me. "You get to meet everybody in Lynchburg." We chatted a bit more before he left to check on some other tables. I noticed that he greeted everyone with, "Thank you for coming in. I'm grateful for you."

Lynchburg clearly relied on its tourist trade, and I could see from the very walls of the Barrel House that people traveled to visit the distillery from every part of the globe. I started to relax a little.

Lynchburg was definitely a small Southern town, but maybe it didn't have all the pitfalls that had made Keith so reluctant to come. Chuck was probably just a sweet guy with a steel-trap memory and a knack for picking up gossip.

We enjoyed our lunch—it really was spectacular—and Chuck returned to our table and said, "Let's have drinks together tonight."

Keith and I looked at each other. "Sure!" I said. "We're going to look at the Dan Call Farm and then we'll be back."

"Interesting," he said, cocking his head. "Are you guys looking at buying it?"

Maybe I had relaxed too much. *Why in the world did I mention where we were headed next?*

"We're definitely interested in seeing it," Keith hedged.

"Cool," Chuck said. "See y'all later. I close at eight, so come around then."

"You got it," I said.

We headed out to meet Sherrie Moore at the farm. As we were driving, she called to tell us that the sellers didn't want us to go into the house.

"Who sells a house but doesn't allow potential buyers to go inside?" I asked.

"Well, with such short notice, the owners said they didn't have time to prepare the home to be toured, so they said you should just come and see the farm." The property had been on the market for eighteen months, and they'd grown accustomed to looky-loos.

I shrugged at Keith but agreed. After all, we hadn't come here to buy a house. This was a great chance to see the setting of *Jack Daniel's Legacy*. We were going to see where Jack had grown up, where he had learned to make whiskey from Nearest, where all modern Lynchburg had really started.

It was easy to get to the farm from town. Straight on Highway 50 until it turned into 55, left on Louse Creek Road, and then another left on Ed McGee Road. At the library, Judy had told us that the last time she went by, there'd been a dead cow in the driveway. I was relieved to arrive at the property and find no dead cattle.

DAN CALL WAS BORN in 1836 in Lincoln County, Tennessee. The son of Joseph and Rebecca Call, who settled in the area in 1834, Dan spent his life in Tennessee, inheriting several hundred acres of land that included a country store. Call made whiskey and sold it at his store before deciding that he couldn't be a man of God and work in the spirits business.

Lynchburgers have long struggled to toe the line between their love of God and their love of liquor. Mount Moriah Primitive Baptist Church, where Jack Daniel was baptized toward the end of his life, was established in 1816 near a stream just large enough for the full-immersion baptisms they practiced. Members were known for participating in a foot washing rite, using tin pitchers and bowls to wash their pew neighbors' feet. The Primitive Baptists had no problem with whiskey and felt alienated by the growing temperance movement.

By contrast, Call's Union Lutheran Church, which sat at the other end of his property from his whiskey still, opposed alcohol and enthusiastically supported the idea of passing laws outlawing the sale of it. *Jack Daniel's Legacy* tells us the congregation hosted a revival staged by an enigmatic "Lady Love," a "woman evangelist" preaching Prohibition throughout Middle Tennessee. Hundreds filled the church pews. She said making and selling whiskey was just as sinful as drinking it. "Did you hear that, Dan?" Call's wife Mary Jane reportedly asked him. "She's talking about you."

Between Lady Love and his wife, Call was eventually convinced to give up distilling.

As Keith and I drove up the thousand-foot driveway, I wondered what my mom—a teetotaler herself, as was my late father—would think when she learned about my new interest in whiskey.

As WE parked, we were immediately greeted by two absolutely filthy farm dogs. I was wearing a bright orange summer dress and flip-flops, and within a few feet, I was covered in dust. I'm not usually a dog person, but these dogs were special. Something made me bend to pet them. One of them, a black-and-white beauty under all that dirt, immediately flipped onto her back and asked for a belly rub.

Keith watched this and was like, "Who *are* you?"

I was squatting to pet the dog when I heard someone yell, "Lucy and Chester! Get over here!"

Looking up, I saw Ophelia and Ed McGee, the landowners, and Sherrie Moore.

Sherrie began listing people she was related to and asking if the McGees knew them. Of course they did. Everyone knows everyone else in and around Lynchburg.

As they talked, the dogs returned to my feet. I reached down and rubbed Lucy's belly again, asking, "Do the dogs come with the farm?"

"Yes," Ophelia said.

"No," Ed chimed in after, and we all laughed.

I hadn't packed for a hike around a farm. My sundress and flip-flops were no match for the property's uneven terrain. It was clear I was slowing down Keith and Sherrie while they looked around at Ophelia's invitation, so I let them trek around the land's steep rises and dips while I hung back, played with the dogs, and took in the place Nearest and Jack had lived.

Ed McGee had been a dairy farmer. He was one of fifteen children; Ophelia, one of eleven. They'd known each other since their school days, and their families knew each other as well. "They grew up old school," their daughter Edwina said. They didn't have much, they worked hard, and they'd taken one vacation in their lives.

Ed and Ophelia had allowed Nelson Eddy to lead tours of the farm for the Tennessee Squires Association, a Jack Daniel's fan club. There were also lots of unofficial tours led by locals for tourists from all over the world. Jack Daniel's fans wanted to see the spring and the ruins of the enslaved people's living quarters. Ed was proud of the land and its history. "My dad loved to show it off," Edwina later recalled.

There were some modern aluminum cattle barns on the property, and over one hundred cattle head roaming around, but otherwise the land looked exactly as it would've in Nearest and Jack's day. It was incredible to see, and I was thrilled when Keith and Sherrie returned and Ophelia came up to us and said, "You all can go into the house if you want."

I stepped inside.

The home itself was beautiful, although it had clearly been seventies-ified. Ophelia and Ed had covered up original, hand-painted wallpaper and put shag carpet down over the wood floors. When Ed pointed to a stairwell and said, "We never used the second floor," I felt a chill. They'd closed off the part of the house where Jack had stayed while he worked as a chore boy. They had also pulled down the balcony over the porch when Edwina had been young, afraid it'd break and she'd fall. They probably needn't have worried; the house was sound and well-made, and the contractor who did it told Ed it was the sturdiest thing he'd ever taken apart.

We left Ed and Ophelia downstairs as Keith, Sherrie, and I went up the steep steps, careful not to slip. It was like we'd walked into a time capsule. The walls and floors were just as they'd been in the nineteenth century. A rectangle of newer wood planks showed where the stairs had originally entered one of the rooms. The walls of the bedroom on the right side of the hallway were adorned with a hand-painted floral wallpaper that had begun to peel off over time. Less than half the room was still covered. And behind every piece of wallpaper were remnants of newspapers from October 10 and October 11, 1898, that had been used as wall insulation. There were fragments of articles describing pension grants, Revolutionary War commemorations, and local happenings. The room was frozen in time.

In the room on the other side of the hallway, Keith pointed to barrel-head stenciling on the wall. It appeared someone had been practicing. "D. H. Call Sour Mash Corn Whisky," the stencil read. This helped us date that room. From the limited research I'd done, I knew Dan Call never registered a whiskey called "D. H. Call," and I also knew all the local distillers added an "e" to the word "whisky." Were these Jack's handiwork? They were in the room where his bed would have been.

We snapped a picture of the barrel stenciling on the wall and then went back down the rickety stairs, trying to find our poker faces. I couldn't believe that the barrel stencils were still clearly visible on the walls.

I was overcome by a sense of peace. It had been more than a century since Nearest and Jack had worked at the farm, but I expected them to walk through the back door together at any moment, sweaty from an afternoon of work.

The entire nature of our trip had suddenly changed. Keith and I didn't even have to talk about it. The farm was on the market for $1.4 million, and though we didn't really have the money because of the entanglements with the business I'd invested in, we knew we were meant to buy that farm. It was a piece of American history.

We walked over to Louse Creek, the original site of the still. Today it's easy to reach, if a bit of a hike for those used to city walking. Back in Nearest and Jack's day, the still had been strategically hidden under trees and underbrush. *Jack Daniel's Legacy* tells us that to reach it they had to climb "over rocks, through briars and under trees," looking out for snakes the whole time. The air smelled sweeter here, and the ground was covered in softer grass that was easier to walk on. There were more trees on this part of the land. It was a peaceful spot. It was easy to imagine things happening here 150 years before.

I could feel Nearest's and Jack's spirits with me, and I knew there was work to be done.

An unassuming spring gushed steadily out of a hillside. Hand-hewn foundation stones were scattered about, and daffodils waved beside the building that once stood there. Scattered throughout the overgrown foundation were pieces of broken pottery, medicine bottles, mason jars, tin shards, fragments of tools, and bricks crawling with ants. A rusted copper pipe with sections missing every few feet led from the stream, the missing parts proof of Jack Daniel's enthusiasts who had come to get their piece of history over the years.

Keith gave me a look. It said, *We have to have this.*

Real estate is one of his loves, and I'm usually the voice of practicality there. But I realized in that moment that I was certain I wanted to write a book about Nearest and Jack, and that I needed to do it from this farm.

The farm would be an expense, and finding the money would be stressful. The house was going to need a lot of work. Keith was already drawing up plans in his head—a new kitchen, a modern bathroom. I had no idea how Jack Daniel's would react to me writing a book in its backyard. And our families, our work, and our day-to-day lives were two-thirds of a continent away.

But we both felt in our hearts that we needed to buy the property. So much for staying in Lynchburg no more than four days.

WHILE KEITH and I were thinking through the logistics of buying a working farm in Tennessee, we went back over to Chuck Baker's place. It was close to eight, and he said he'd be right with us. While we waited, we enjoyed another sampler platter of meat. As we were having the leftovers packed up, his team busily worked around the restaurant, wiping down tables and refilling barbecue sauce containers.

When we finished, Chuck came over to us and said, "You guys are staying at Steve May's house, right?" I nodded, still a little disconcerted by his local intel. "I'm going to go pick up some beers and then I'll meet you there."

"At our place?"

"You'll want to follow me out to mine," he said.

Keith shot me a look as Chuck jumped into a black jacked-up Chevy. We drove our rental car back to our place, debating the merits of following someone we'd just met to their remote home. Chuck seemed trustworthy. But Keith and I were two Black people in Jack Daniel's country.

As we were discussing the danger of following Chuck out into the woods, he honked from outside our rental house. With no time to change our minds, we gathered our stuff and got back in the car.

By the time we arrived at Chuck's farm, it was dark, and his driveway was a long and winding dirt road with no light other than our high beams. This was a lot coming on the heels of our experience at the Call Farm. Perhaps we were rushing into things. Keith turned toward me in the front seat.

"The next time you want to do something on your birthday, it's not going to happen," he said.

"Babe, I'm with you. I won't do this again."

We parked a hundred feet or so from the front porch. Chuck got out of his truck and said he wanted to show us something. There was no sunlight remaining, but a small number of outdoor lights illuminated a tiny portion of his fourteen-acre property. As we walked away from the house, feeling quite afraid, I reached for Keith's hand. He looked just as terrified as I was.

"Check this out," Chuck said. It took a moment for my eyes to adjust. Then I saw a deep hole in the earth—the perfect size for a mass burial ditch. It was too dark or too deep for us to see the bottom.

"I dug it myself," Chuck said. "It's ten by ten and eight feet deep."

I kept one eye on the driveway and the other on the tree line. Chuck kept talking, and I tried to calculate how long it would take for me to run into the woods. What if someone came behind us and began firing shots? *Lord, I have lived a great life, and I am so grateful,* I began to say internally as my final prayer. But this wasn't how I wanted to go out.

Keith and I had traveled so far down a dirt road to Chuck's home that if he killed us, dumped our bodies in the pit, and refilled it with dirt, no one would ever be able to find us. And all our friends and family thought we were bourbon tasting in Kentucky!

I was half listening as Chuck talked about digging the pit by hand when I caught one critical word—"photographer."

Chuck proudly jumped down into the pit.

"This barbecue pit is going to be in a photoshoot for next year's official Jack Daniel's wall calendar," Chuck went on. That's when I realized what was going on. Chuck was helping Jack Daniel's with PR! That was a language I could understand.

I venture to say Chuck never had a clue that Keith and I were both scared out of our minds. Instead, he followed us to the porch, where his girlfriend offered us drinks. Sitting on the steps, we began to talk. As our conversation turned to business, I was in hog heaven. I love helping other entrepreneurs who want to grow their businesses. I wondered how involved Chuck was with Jack Daniel's—and if it was even possible to run a business in Lynchburg without having your interests totally intertwined with the biggest game in town.

"Hey," Chuck said, leaning forward. "Are you really interested in Ed McGee's place?"

"Maybe," Keith said.

"I'm going to tell y'all something. My first job almost forty years ago was for Ed McGee. I helped him feed the cattle and did other odd jobs around the farm."

Chuck and Edwina, the McGees' daughter, were about the same age and had played in the upstairs rooms. Chuck had first glimpsed the stencil drawings on the walls years before. He knew how special they were, but it was a good example of growing up so surrounded by history that you start tuning it out.

Someone had told Chuck that Jack Daniel's had tried to lowball Ed on the Call Farm, and that Ed wouldn't lower the price for them. But for us, perhaps he would.

I'd later learn Jack Daniel's just hadn't been that interested in buying the land. The McGees had offered the land to the distillery before it went on the market and met with their representatives multiple times. Jack Daniel's felt the price was too high. The distillery's priority was protecting the viewshed, the rolling hills that are such a formative part of everyone's experience when they drive into Lynchburg from Shelbyville or Tullahoma. Industry and development were the primary threats to that, not two Californians buying a farmhouse.

Of course, with Brown-Forman's leadership located a four-hour drive or a whole day's travel away by plane in Louisville, Kentucky, they might've just overlooked the value of owning the Dan Call place.

Keith and I decided to make it clear we were more than looky-loos, and we gave Sherrie a verbal offer of $900,000 in cash to take to the McGees. That made us serious buyers in their eyes, and we made plans to return to the property the next day.

Our headlights illuminated the dark backroads as we drove back to our rental house a few hours later, and I just hoped that parts of this story would become as clear as those stencil marks a young Jack Daniel likely left on the McGees' upstairs wall.

LYNCHBURG IS TINY, and it didn't take long for Keith and me to tour the rest of town. We walked the square, the sloped residential streets, and two cemeteries—a white one and a Black one. The first thing I noticed was that there was a stark difference between the two.

Jack's grave was at Lynchburg City Cemetery, which had two metal chairs installed alongside it for visitors. The dirt was worn from the frequency of tours. As we walked down the hill back to our car, though, Keith spotted something.

"I think that's a tombstone," he said. He was right. We'd found a second cemetery, a field with no discernable entrance but neatly tended stones. "Honey, I think we're in the colored cemetery."

It was a little bit of a shock to find ourselves there. It was called Highview, but there was nothing to indicate that. There wasn't even a driveway. Keith and I walked through the tombstones. Many names had worn away, and other stones had never been inscribed in the first place. I saw lots of familiar surnames, but I was searching for one in particular.

We split up, and after a little while of wandering the area, Keith spotted George Green's grave set back from the other stones. It was a tall monument with two columns; on one, George Green's name was clearly visible, the moss climbing the *G*s. On the other, I could clearly read, was his wife Missie's. It was extraordinary to find George Green's resting place. But where was Nearest's?

Many other Greens across the generations had been buried there, including the parents and grandparents of the people I was learning about and making plans to meet. *I want to give this place a sign*, I thought. *I want people to know that there are people who helped to build this town who lived here and are now buried here.*

I soon discovered that I was fifteen years too late to meet the person in Lynchburg I most wish I could have known. Her grave marker sat in Highview Cemetery, decorated with a laurel wreath, and showed she'd lived a remarkably long life, from 1901 to 2001. Her name was Annie Bell Green Eady, although she gave herself the nickname Mammie and went by it her whole life. She was Nearest's granddaughter.

CHAPTER

SHERRIE PUT me in touch with Debbie Staples, Mammie's granddaughter and the great-great-granddaughter of Nearest Green. As Debbie and her siblings Jackie, Jerome, and Victoria saw it, the whole story started on their grandmother's porch.

Mammie used to sit there in her rocking chair, less than two blocks from Jack Daniel Distillery, and tell her grandchildren about Nearest. As kids, her grandchildren could look up on the hills and see the warehouses full of whiskey.

"My granddaddy used to make the whiskey for Jack Daniel," Mammie told them. She was *the* reason why the story stayed alive when Brown-Forman stopped telling it. Mammie was the daughter of Nearest's son Jessie. She had nine children of her own, and the many aunts, uncles, and cousins on her branch of the tree were the only Green descendants they knew of.

Mammie was a loving person. She was a prolific cook who would throw everyone out of the kitchen as she made the men in the family who worked at Jack Daniel's the whole nine yards for supper, what those outside of the South refer to as lunch—chicken, pinto beans, cornbread, you name it. In the 1950s, she and her family ran a café on Elm Street. Her husband George had a secret-recipe barbecue sauce that rivaled any in the county.

I came across a newspaper clipping in a family member's photo album about Mammie celebrating her ninetieth birthday. "Things have changed a lot since Annie Bell came into the world on Sept. 5, 1901," it said.

My heart skipped a beat. *Wow! I share the same birthday as Ben Green and Mammie, and maybe even Jack.* I'm a believer that nothing in our lives happens by accident, so this certainly caught my attention.

When Mammie passed away in 2001, just shy of a hundred years old, she had twenty-seven grandchildren, thirty-five great-grandchildren, and six great-great grandchildren.

Some of the best family memories came from Christmas Eves at her house on the downtown corner of Lynchburg and summer nights on her porch. Mammie's grandkids remembered spending the whole night out there, cutting up and talking. They watched the sun rise and the slop trucks head to the distillery.

Nearest and his boys would stay back and make whiskey while Jack went off to sell it, Mammie told her grandchildren and many other visitors to her warm and hospitable home. "My granddaddy and his boys made the whiskey, then Jack would come with his wagon and pick some up and take it into town to sell."

Debbie, Jackie, Jerome, and Victoria grew up on those stories. "She was telling the story of Jack Daniel's, but really she just wanted us to know who her family was," Jerome said. "She was telling us about her daddy and her granddaddy."

"I wish I had listened to more," Debbie said recently. She was young, in elementary school, during those days on the porch. As a kid, Jack Daniel's wasn't a big deal to her. "I never really thought about it until I got older."

Like lots of other Lynchburg kids over the years, they'd walk up to the cave at the distillery and play on the rocks around it. There were security guards even back then, but the cave was essentially a playground.

"I guess we were good children, so no one ever said anything to us about being there," Victoria recalled.

The connection between the families remained strong. After Nearest and Jack, after George and Lem, the Daniel family and the Green family had stayed friendly across the generations. In 1918, Lem Motlow deeded a house to Mammie's grandparents for life, and in 1964 his widow and children sold the home and land to Mammie and George for one dollar.

As late as the 1970s, people were telling the story of Jack and his "head stiller" Nearest. But then, with no permanent memorial to Nearest—no building names in honor of him, no statues erected, not even a headstone—the story faded for people outside his family.

In 1978, the last of Jack Daniel's descendants to run the distillery, Reagor Motlow, passed away. The same year, Debbie started her Jack Daniel's career after going to school part-time at Motlow State College. By the time she arrived, it seemed like nobody was talking about Nearest. Her Aunt Sis was working at the distillery then and encouraged Debbie to come down and put in an application. Sis was fond of the product she helped make, often saying as a toast, "Up to my lips and down to my toes, where many quarts and gallons goes!"

Mammie was glad Debbie would be joining her uncles, Aunt Sis, and cousins at the distillery. Most of Mammie's kin had worked there at one point or another, even if just as a part-time stint, and now her granddaughter did, too.

When Debbie started in the bottling department, she did everything manually—empty bottles, cases, conveyor belts that kept getting faster, the whole deal. A lot of that's been automated since.

Some people today think her connection to Nearest is what got her a job there, but she laughs at that idea. "That's just what everybody did," Debbie recalled. "It's always been part of our family." Likewise, Jackie joined her in the bottling shop after a while, and the sisters worked side by side. Jerome became a foreman in the warehouse department. Victoria moved away from the world of whiskey, spending her three-decade career in law enforcement before finding her way back to it.

Most people I talked to felt Jack Daniel's had always been a part of the Lynchburg Black community. But by the time Debbie began working there, the demographics were starting to shift. Longtime Jack Daniel's employees J. B. and L. B. McGowan and Claude Eady all spoke to this changing culture, that when a Black person retired, resigned, or otherwise aged out, they would most often be replaced by a white person. Claude and Miss Dot's son Kevin noted it later on, too. He had his first job there, mowing lawns, moving furniture, and doing anything else needed through General Services during his high school years. "When you grew up, especially young boys, if your daddy worked at Jack Daniel's, you're going to work at Jack Daniel's," he recalled. But there were no new jobs there when he graduated.

It was bad timing for Debbie. When she would bring up Nearest, "People didn't want to hear it," she found. "They didn't want to believe it."

For decades, the siblings tried to tell others about their great-great-grandfather's role in Jack Daniel's history, but nobody listened. Most versions of the story told on tours or in promotional materials talked about Dan Call as Jack Daniel's teacher. Debbie tried to have patience with her co-workers, who she saw were in a similar sort of situation. "You've been told a story by your parents, and that's all you know," she told a co-worker. "Now you're a grown man and you're telling me what your mom and dad said."

At one point, one of her bosses tried to dissuade Debbie from talking about Nearest. Debbie resented it but said nothing. It was deeply hurtful, and she carried that anger for years.

When the distillery sent out an employee survey one year asking for interesting facts they could share for Black History Month, she wrote: "I am the great-great-granddaughter of Nearest Green, the man who made the whiskey for Jack Daniel." Her siblings filled out the survey the same way. "And do you know," she later told me, crying, "they came to us and said they couldn't do that because they didn't really know who he was or what he'd done?"

I later learned that executives at the top levels of Brown-Forman had always known about Nearest's story, but they effectively pushed it into the closet and closed the door because it never dawned on them that the story could be a positive one.

Then Clay Risen got involved. Debbie found her interview with Clay nerve-racking. Unlike Claude Eady, she wasn't accustomed to speaking to reporters, and here she was starting with the *New York Times* at the behest of her bosses at Jack Daniel's—a sudden turn-around from the years they'd dissuaded her from speaking about Nearest. What should she say? What *shouldn't* she say?

"For a long time, we kept it to ourselves," Debbie said. "You don't know who to trust and who you can't trust."

Debbie went next door to her mother's house so they could talk to Clay together. Debbie wanted her mom to tell Clay about Nearest, but she was at the beginning stages of Alzheimer's. She struggled to remember anything, even with prompting. It was hard on Debbie to know that if Jack Daniel's had shown an interest in the story earlier, her mother probably could've helped.

They got across that Nearest's story was part of their family and community, not news to any of them, but they didn't say anything that made for good quotes in the paper. Claude Eady wound up as the sole voice of Nearest's family tree in the *New York Times*—and that was a stretch, given he was George Green's great-nephew by marriage, not a direct descendant.

I love Clay, and he's an amazing journalist; without him, I wouldn't be running Nearest Green Distillery, my life's greatest work, today. But his piece was a story written from a distance. Clay did the best a daily news reporter could, visiting the scene and talking to the people in town he was able to. But as I came to learn, if you don't live in Lynchburg, if you don't spend significant time there, if the people do not trust you, you're not going to get the whole story.

CHAPTER

12

WE RETURNED to the Call Farm the next day. The McGees' realtor, who was also their cousin, took us out on an ATV to explore the various corners of the property. The land is beautiful, vast, and—importantly—hilly. She nearly flipped over the ATV.

It was September 5, my birthday, and we were flying home the next day, so that was enough of that. The jolt spooked us enough to tell her we didn't need to see any more of the land and could just go back to the house.

We decided to move ahead with the purchase. The McGees were enthusiastic and only asked us to put down a small amount as an earnest deposit. They also asked for a long, multi-month escrow to give them time to move out, which we were more than happy to go along with.

Good, because I don't know where all this money is going to come from, Keith thought.

It was a blessing, too, that we had met John T. Bobo our second night in Lynchburg. As he puts it, "My law firm has a pretty active real estate closing department." As I've learned to put it, he's involved in almost every legal transaction that happens in the area. Everybody I talked to, Black or white, told me, "John T's my attorney." Everyone loved him.

Things were falling into place. The story of Nearest and Jack would truly come alive because I would be working alongside Nearest's and Jack's spirits. Buying the farm was just like filing for the trademarks—it probably looked a little crazy from the outside, and it also felt crazy from the inside, but it was obviously and immediately the right thing to do.

IF I WAS GOING to temporarily relocate to Lynchburg to write about Nearest, I was going to wind up facing Brown-Forman eventually. I figured I might as well start by taking their official distillery tour at Jack Daniel's before packing up and heading back to LA.

Keith and I made our way over to the distillery, taking the small bridge over the creek where the famously iron-free water flowed. Inside, we bought tickets and waited in the visitor center. There were wooden cases protecting historical bottles, photos of Jack, and information panels about the town. I looked around for anything about Nearest, but he wasn't there.

The *New York Times* had somewhat prepared us for that. "The Green story is an optional part of the distillery tour, left to the tour guide's discretion, and the company is still considering whether it will flesh out the story in new displays," the article had read.

But I'd expected to find *something*.

As our tour started, we followed a pack of tourists and a guide with a deep accent and a hearty laugh who launched into a talk about how Lynchburg sat in a dry county. She told us about how her favorite day was the first Friday of the month, when every Jack Daniel's employee gets a free bottle of whiskey with their paycheck. She talked about what she called "our little town square," mentioning where to get ice cream or fudge with Old No. 7 on it if we wanted snacks after the tour, and encouraged us to visit Miss Mary Bobo's. After she pointed out the gift shop, we boarded a bus that drove us a short way up a steep hill. The first thing I noticed were the warehouses, which each held over twenty thousand barrels of whiskey. Black and gray, they towered over the trees. I found them imposing, especially when the guide explained that Jack Daniel's had its own fire department because whiskey burned so hot and fast. The eeriest part? Alcohol fire is invisible; you won't even see the flames. That said, the guide wanted us to know that they'd never lost a gallon of whiskey due to fire—they had more fire-retardant foam than the international airport. That got some laughs, as did the short lecture on taxes.

"Folks," the guide said. "These two warehouses will cost us over $13.5 million in federal tax. Sixty percent of a bottle of whiskey is taxed. You got your federal tax, your state tax, your local tax. Tax, tax, tax. We'll never have Prohibition again."

I knew that alcohol had not been regulated prior to the Civil War. During the war, the federal government started taxing distilleries with the passage of the Internal Revenue Act of 1862, which was implemented to help generate revenue for the war effort. It introduced, for the first time, an excise tax on beer and fermented liquor. Distilleries in Union states began paying those taxes right away, and when the North won the war, Southern distilleries had to start paying, too. (Part of the reason many people in the South still insist the Civil War was not about slavery but rather about taxes.) The law divided each state into districts with a local federal representative who assigned registered distillery numbers to each and collected their taxes.

The guide explained that every single drop of Jack Daniel's whiskey sold anywhere in the world, all 170 countries, was made right there in Lynchburg. She was careful to note that the process hadn't changed a bit; that although Jack Daniel's had expanded (from twenty-five acres to two thousand five hundred acres), they used the very same ingredients, the same charcoal filtration, and the same distillation process in the very same woods with the very same water that Jack did.

We watched a video that showed Jack Daniel's staff taking stacks of hard sugar maple, spraying them with four-hundred-proof whiskey, and lighting them on fire. The resulting charcoal was used to filter the whiskey in what was called the Lincoln County Process. Our guide said it took the liquor days to drip through, and in the process, the charcoal stripped away bad tastes and mellowed it.

I'd heard about the Lincoln County Process, but this was the first time its full importance resonated with me. The Lincoln County Process was why Tennessee whiskey *was* Tennessee whiskey. Since 2013, it's been part of state law: to be considered Tennessee whiskey, it must be made in Tennessee, be of at least 51 percent corn, aged in new charred oak barrels, and put through the Lincoln County Process. In other words, it has the exact same process as bourbon, and is legally categorized as bourbon, but it takes longer and costs more.

At Cave Spring Hollow, where the water used to create Jack Daniel's springs from the ground, there's a statue of Jack in his trademark broadcloth frock coat, vest, and bow tie, with his wide-brimmed planters hat at his side. There, looking at Jack, and in sight of a small, unassuming building with white siding and a porch that had been his historic office, our tour guide explained a bit more about Jack Daniel the man. I listened carefully to the story, eager to hear whether the guide would mention Nearest.

She started with Jack's childhood at the Daniels' home, where he was the youngest of ten siblings. He left home early to live with a family friend named Felix Waggoner, whose wife had wet-nursed Jack as an infant, when his mother died unexpectedly of Typhus Fever seven days after contracting it. Felix introduced Jack to Dan Call. Call taught Jack how to distill, and they later went into the whiskey business together as Daniel & Call. But then Call's wife gave him an ultimatum: his congregation or his distillery. The Reverend chose the Lord—but Jack continued to distill on his land for some time. What fascinated me about this version of the story was that it omitted not just Nearest Green but the entire Civil War, which I knew, from Ben Green's book, had been a major part of the narrative.

It also never mentioned slavery. I knew Jack never owned any enslaved people, but he was a boy during the Civil War and had grown up around the institution of slavery as a way of life. His father, Callaway, owned several enslaved people and had to sell them "and cut out the leisurely way of doing things" due to financial pressures, according to *Jack Daniel's Legacy*. The Waggoners owned many enslaved people who tended to the farm and horses, milked the cows, and worked the land. As Green tells it, Jack was affectionate toward his caretaker's enslaved people—they joined in Jack's birthday parties and taught him about their work. When he hastily left for Call's Farm, he asked Felix to "tell the workers on the place goodbye for me."

The tour didn't get into any of that. They skipped past the Civil War and Reconstruction to 1904, when Jack Daniel won a gold medal for his whiskey at the World's Fair in St. Louis.

I took the tour multiple times that day, and while each guide had a slightly different style, they all covered the same ground. There was not a word about Nearest on the Jack Daniel's tours, even as the tour guides each stood inches away from the framed image of Jack Daniel sitting next to George Green. It was all too easy to understand Debbie, Jackie, and Jerome's frustration with the distillery. Tentatively embracing Nearest's role would be one thing, but to say nothing was unacceptable.

People needed to know Nearest's name. Jack Daniel and his family had never been shy about acknowledging Nearest's contributions. Although no longer owned by Jack's family, Jack Daniel Distillery should've continued doing what Jack and his descendants had. They should've been telling the story of Nearest Green and the importance of his contributions.

I was getting impatient. It was time to get to work.

IT WAS surreal to go back to LA after that. Our lives had changed. The coincidences, the connections, everything we'd learned, the commitments we'd made—it was a lot to unpack. It all happened so quickly. *It's not like we were there for weeks*, we kept thinking. It had only been four days. But I'd left an important part of myself back in that farmhouse in Tennessee.

As Keith says, "She knew right away." And I really did.

It was good to take a breath and evaluate our decisions. Keith saw the purchase as an investment, and it was, albeit one we'd agreed to pay cash for and didn't even come close to having the money that would be required to close the transaction. That said, he's always ready to invest in real estate—I've said to him many times over the course of our marriage that life isn't a game of Monopoly, and he can't just pick up every property he lands on—so there was no second-guessing on that front.

But buying the farm remained a no-brainer even for me, which surprised him. He's a business-minded guy, and although he knew our time in Lynchburg had been transformative and it wasn't a one-and-done trip, he was still a couple steps behind me. He figured we'd do what we could to lift up Nearest's legacy and then settle back into our lives in LA.

"That was the plan," he recalled.

But in my heart, the plan had already changed. I was going to be spending a *lot* more time in Lynchburg and on the hunt for Nearest. I had realized that the story of Nearest and Jack *was* the story of Lynchburg. The town, with its interconnected networks of descendants and friends from Nearest and Jack's day onward, was practically its own character. That meant I absolutely had to be there.

I wanted to walk the grounds of the Call Farm daily and feel the spirits of Nearest and Jack. I wanted to travel, searching archives and assembling relatives, and dedicate a room in the farmhouse to serve as a central spot for everything I found. I knew I could write Nearest and Jack's story from there. It would make for richer storytelling and a better book—and as a PR pro at heart, I knew if we ever put out a commemorative bottle or otherwise found a way to act on the trademarks we'd taken out, the farm would be a perfect backdrop.

We were also in a moment of change, both personally—after losing Brittany—and as a country. Nearest and Jack's story was one of hope and love that everyone could use, and it was fading into history. That was a wrong that could be righted.

Deciding to buy the Call Farm was a combination of marketing savvy, business sense, and faith. We flew back ten days later to do a formal walkthrough of the farm and make everything official.

THERE WAS TOO much sleuthing, especially paired with the logistics of living in two places, to do alone. The first person I contacted was Stephani Ross, who'd helped me plan Brittany's memorial. Even—and maybe especially—in grief, I'm drawn to competence, and through my fog, I'd noticed the gift Stephani had for holding space for people and simultaneously cutting to the heart of a matter. She worked just around the corner from our house at Agoura Bible Fellowship, and so I asked her to drop by to read an article about Nearest. She was hooked immediately.

Stephani would become an invaluable research assistant and organizer for me, working from California much of the time and flying out to Lynchburg for weeklong stints. She has a great sense of humor and an even stronger sense of justice. And I thought Stephani, as a white woman, might also be able to connect with people who were less likely to talk with Keith and me.

The first step was to reconstruct as much of Nearest's family tree as we could. We started building it on Ancestry.com, then dove into census records. Those proved extremely tricky. I was, and still am, quite suspicious of the censuses taken of Black people prior to 1900. From 1790 to 1840, only the heads of free households appeared in the Federal Population Schedules. Everyone else, including enslaved people, were noted numerically under the head of household. Black people didn't "exist" yet; we were considered property. There was no name, age, sex, or place of origin recorded for enslaved people—only the number of people enslaved per household. In 1850 and 1860, Black people were enumerated on a record called the Slave Schedule, separate from the federal census. But they still weren't named. The 1870 census was the first postwar, post-Emancipation count, and while it recorded names, ages, and places of birth for four and a half million Black people for the first time in American history, it was plagued with inaccuracies and bias. Most could not read or write and did not know when they were born. Many of the white census takers were also extremely uneducated, and they took guesses or asked neighbors for information; records, including the census itself, were recorded entirely by hand. It was common to get a formerly enslaved person's age completely wrong. Ten years later, the 1880 census finally added each household member's relationship to one another.

The 1890 census, conducted a quarter-century after the Civil War ended, should have been a good resource. But it no longer exists. Fire and water damage destroyed or severely damaged three-quarters of the records in the early 1900s. The remaining documents were left to deteriorate in a warehouse until Congress authorized their destruction in 1933. A decision was made to burn the rest on the grounds that, 'Well, if we don't have all of it, we won't have any of it.' It was a bizarre decision that erased what remained of a decade of US history and precipitated the creation of a National Archives.

I was able to determine that Nearest was married to a woman named Harriet, and they'd had eleven children. I also confirmed that after the Civil War, Nearest referred to himself in legal documents as "Nearest Green." I'm still not entirely sure why he went by Nearest and not his legal name, Nathan. It could just be that folks in the South like nicknames. But it could also be that Nathan was his enslaved name. Nearest was undoubtedly aware of Nathan Bedford Forrest, the most prolific slave trader and well-known Confederate Army general in the region. Most of the men from his company, known as Forrest's Escort, came from what is now Moore County. Records show Forrest traded over a thousand enslaved people a year, and after the Civil War he went on to be the first Grand Wizard of the Ku Klux Klan. No matter his reason, Nearest joined many other formerly enslaved people who chose to give up their slave names and select a free name instead. I knew I was going to need better sources than the census to get a full picture of Nearest, Harriet, their children, and their world.

I decided to learn all I could about Tennessee distilleries and the history of distilling. From LA, I got in touch with the National Archives outside Atlanta, where there are records for all the distilleries in the South. The archivists there were incredibly helpful with pulling research for me. We'd go back and forth by email, and they'd send me scans of pages.

I really appreciated all their help, but I needed to see some things for myself. So I traveled to Atlanta to visit the archives in person. They don't allow you to make copies, and all you can take in is a pencil, a piece of paper, and your cell phone—no computers. So I took whole books, some five hundred pages long, and photographed each page. I filled up hard drives with five hundred individual files for a single book, multiple times over. Then I brought them home and printed them out.

I also traveled to Mount Vernon, President George Washington's home and estate, along the Potomac River in Virginia. Two years into Washington's first term, in 1791, Congress passed an excise tax on spirits to pay off debts from the Revolutionary War, causing tax-hating farmers in Pennsylvania to revolt, tarring and feathering tax collectors and ransacking the stills of farmers who faithfully paid the tax. Washington sent a militia to quash the rebellion, and distillers had to pay the tax until it was repealed in 1802. In the middle of all this, in 1797, Washington built his own distillery on his property. It was the largest in the country at that time.

I wanted to see what a working distillery would have looked like during the time that Nearest would have been distilling, and visiting Mount Vernon is as close as we can get today. It was a sobering experience.

After he retired from the presidency, Washington ramped up production of whiskey from rye and corn, plus brandies and other spirits. His stillhouse was mammoth and productive. In 1799 alone, Washington sold 10,942 gallons of whiskey in more than eighty transactions, for a $7,500 profit. Six enslaved men who were skilled distillers—known to us today only as Hanson, Peter, Nat, Daniel,

James, and Timothy—made the whiskey that Washington considered "a thriving moneymaker." This is what it looked like when enslaved people made whiskey and there *wasn't* an honorable man like Jack Daniel there to make sure history remembered them.

Archaeological excavations that ran from 1999 to 2006 yielded enough information to faithfully reconstruct the distillery and start producing and selling whiskey again using historically accurate methods. They also turned up lots of items the distillers themselves left behind—lost buttons, broken teacups, fragments of plates, drinking glasses. That's all that remains of the memory of the stillhands at Mount Vernon.

It was there that I fully absorbed how dirty and dangerous distilling could be. It was the enslaved people who took on the risks of scalding accidents and still explosions, not the white men in shirt collars doing the job of "distiller." Jack Daniel was a distiller because he *owned* a distillery, not because he made the whiskey it produced. He was, first and foremost, a businessman.

Jack and I already had the same role in one sense—we were keepers of Nearest's story. But I thought about the liquor trademarks I'd applied for, and I realized that if I ever ended up making a bottle, Jack and I would have *two* jobs in common.

THINGS RAPIDLY picked up speed. We flew back and forth to Tennessee constantly over the next several months to deal with the property purchase, have inspections, and start working with the companies that would do the painstaking remodeling and restoration work the house needed. The town and its people continued to captivate me.

My favorite place to stay in town quickly became the Tolley House. It was an old-fashioned bed and breakfast in a gorgeous old house, built by Jack Daniel's sister and brother-in-law, partway up a rolling grass hill. It was stately and white with a stone staircase out front. The hostess was always kind, and they had a great Southern breakfast.

But my favorite thing about the Tolley House was that it exemplified the special relationship between Nearest's and Jack's descendants. Early on in my research, I'd learned about a pair of friends, Leola Dismukes and Margaret Tolley. Miss Margaret was white and related to both Jack Daniel and Lem Motlow by marriage. Leola, called Miss Dill, was Black and a descendant of Nearest Green.

Miss Dill and Miss Margaret were so close that people in town referred to them as Bonnie and Clyde. Miss Dill had worked for Miss Margaret, but people who knew them told me they probably hadn't gotten much work done—they'd stop every day and watch the soaps together. When Miss Dill died, Miss Margaret was so heartbroken she died a month and a half later. Miss Margaret's obituary specified that she was "preceded in heaven by her siblings . . . along with her dearest friend Leola Dismukes."

I loved staying in a house that literally represented the connection between Nearest and Jack. But Keith didn't enjoy the experience. The house had a lot of nooks and crannies and, we'd come to learn, *lots* of doors. The room we stayed in had an entrance door and then a little door beyond the bed that connected to a small stairway, which led to another room with a little door that stayed locked.

It really didn't help that the room was decorated with black-and-white historical photos of expressionless people staring at the camera, or that the bed was lined with creepy dolls.

"This has got to go," Keith said, staring at the dolls. Stephani hated the ones in her room, too. But no one was happy knowing they were in the closet, either.

The dolls didn't particularly bother me. While Keith and Stephani fed off each other about the creepiness, I unpacked my suitcase. I always do that, no matter where I stay, because it makes the place feel more like a home, albeit temporary.

Keith told me one morning he kept thinking about all the doors overnight, wondering, *If someone came in, which door would they use?* And *Who would I punch first?*

"That was not restful," he recalled.

STEPHANI AND I built ambitious spreadsheets to structure my schedule—interviewing Nearest's descendants, meeting with archivists, and visiting local cemeteries. My days were packed full of history and the folks I needed to get it from, interspersed with long, beautiful drives between interviews and appointments.

All the while, I sought a breakthrough—to find Nearest's name on a deed or a marriage license, to find where he was buried, or to find anything that would help fill in the gaps in his life.

I had the greatest hopes for learning where Nearest was buried. That one didn't depend on dusty records or tenuous oral history—if Nearest was in a marked grave, there'd be a physical stone to find. I soon learned, though, that was a big "if."

Miss Neat suspected that Nearest and Harriet were buried in the woods near a small community called County Line because we found records showing they'd settled there after leaving the Call Farm. I worried they were in one of the countless other small family plots that littered Lincoln and Moore Counties, some known and some forgotten. They could be anywhere.

At least one Green descendant believed Nearest was buried in Highview Cemetery. That made sense to me, and although we had searched for Nearest's stone without finding it, I wondered if he could still be there.

Stephani and I returned to Highview and went to every gravestone, running pencils over paper to try to reveal their faded etchings. We were determined to find Nearest's grave. Neither of us had ever embarked on a project like this before. It was exhilarating, even when our nets came up empty. We'd go on to try this in several other graveyards, but a local archivist later told us that it wasn't uncommon for graves to be marked with only a simple blank stone in those days. It wasn't until much later, when recordkeeping improved, that graves were more consistently marked and cataloged. Lying on top of the tombs trying to take pictures, tilting this way and that with Stephani standing guard, I thought about just how important it is to have someone preserve a place's history.

I dug into the history of Highview Cemetery. Its original stock-holders, as noted in an 1891 minute book, included Nearest's sons George and Jessie Green, Ned Waggoner, and several others, including a Tolley and a Motlow.

In the old days, I learned, all the men of the neighborhood would gather to dig a grave when it was needed—the hard labor offset by lots of laughter, joking, and swearing until the hearse appeared. After the burial, families would wait nearby and stamp down the dirt to settle it atop the grave.

Eli Green's sons Hubert and Henry Green were longtime caretakers of the cemetery and worked for the Harrison Funeral Home for decades, using a pick and shovel to dig graves in the rocky land. "That's my job I chose to earn my bread," one of the Green brothers—it's unclear which—told a *Moore County News* writer in 1973. "Truthfully, I have never really gotten use to it. When people die they have to be buried and we try to do a good job for them."

Lynchburg's cemeteries were segregated, but "we didn't have no colored funeral home," a descendant of Nearest's later told me. "The white man buried the Black." I found records for the Harrison Funeral Home that included details of many Green family burials, although they didn't include Nearest or Harriet.

I went back to the burial question over and over again, but like so many historical mysteries, I was left with more questions than answers. I began to sense I may not ever find Nearest's resting place. To this day, I'm still searching.

CHAPTER

15

I SPENT A lot of time asking people in town for help, but I didn't broadcast what I was doing. I'd regularly stop into the Jack Daniel's gift shop to buy Jack T-shirts, and I wore them around town. I wanted everyone who met me to know I had no intention of harming the legacy of Jack Daniel. I was just looking for the truth about Nearest.

I didn't know if Brown-Forman would care that I was telling this story. But I assumed they would: so much of their advertising was based on Jack as a person, and here I was, proving the story was woefully incomplete.

They'd taken a first step in contacting Clay Risen, but they'd clearly gotten spooked. I didn't plan to talk to them until I had all the facts about Nearest that I could find.

Lynchburg is a *very* small town. As the locals are fond of saying, the only reason they bother to read the weekly newspaper is to make sure they got it right.

I've since learned that when we bought the Dan Call Farm, everybody at Jack Daniel's and Brown-Forman looked to executive vice president Mark McCallum.

"Late in 2016, the drums were beating down in Lynchburg," Mark recalled. "Of course, we knew what was going on." He'd heard about Keith and me buying the Call Farm and the questions I was asking but decided to wait and see what we were up to. "I was very aware of the fact that a California power couple had moved into Moore County."

The farm's been for sale on and off for twenty years, went the refrain. *If it was such an important piece of the history of the brand, why the hell didn't we already own it?*

It was a fair question, Mark thought.

"I'm not sure what all my predecessors would have answered," he said, but to him, at the time, it just didn't seem important. "It really wasn't something we were interested in. We didn't need it."

For one thing, the Call Farm was a little remote. Jack Daniel's was aware of it, but it wasn't on the list of properties they wanted to spend their money on. It was, as Mark saw it, "not as important to protecting the look and feel of the brand and Moore County."

At one point, there was talk of putting in a second stoplight in town, and Mark remembers saying, "There's no way we're putting a second stoplight in Lynchburg, Tennessee, because we've been saying for decades: 'Lynchburg, Tennessee, population 427, town with one stoplight.'"

The idea of Lynchburg was—in some ways—more important to Brown-Forman than the actual town. Mark remembered Ted Simmons, one of the men who created the advertisements for Jack Daniel's in the 1960s, telling him, "This is Brigadoon. This is a fanciful place. Don't screw it up."

THE ARCHIVES HAD given me a great deal of things to sift through, and so far several dead ends. But my main reason for being in Lynchburg was to get to know the people who knew about Nearest.

I worked closely with the two Black churches in town, Berry Chapel AME and the Elm Street Church of Christ, which sit about a block apart on Elm Street. I talked with the Black elders to see what stories they'd heard handed down.

The photographs they'd kept also told me a lot. The warmth between Nearest and Jack seemed to go beyond just the two of them. People kept sharing old pictures of Black people and white people sitting together, and several with Black people front and center. I'd expected to find Black people standing off on the perimeter, if they were photographed at all.

The photo of Miss Dill and Miss Margaret brought me so much joy the first time I saw it, and the search for additional photographs of Miss Dill brought me to J. B. McGowan's home.

L. B. and J. B. McGowan—descendants of both Nearest Green and George Daniel—were Miss Dill's twin sons with her first husband. I was hoping they'd have some more great images of their mother. As I found customary in Lynchburg, J.B. welcomed me into his home immediately, even though I'd stopped by unannounced.

"I'm hoping to look through your mother's photo album, if she left one," I said. "And I'd like to talk to you about growing up in Lynchburg and working at Jack Daniel's."

J.B. immediately suggested we call L.B., who lived right next door.

The McGowan twins were born in 1934 and grew up in Lynchburg. Both twins worked in their Uncle Possum's blacksmith shop, until he died in 1949. The shop occupied the same location on the town square as Barrel House BBQ today. When they were growing up, Lynchburg— like most of rural Tennessee—did not have electricity yet, but they enjoyed listening to the Grand Ole Opry on Saturday nights over a neighbor's battery radio.

They were drafted into the Army together in 1957. The Army kept them together the whole time—through their training in Arkansas and Kentucky and then for fifteen months in Germany. They did almost everything together, building identical houses side by side and dressing alike. Before they had indoor plumbing, they would ask each other, "Are you ready to go feed the chickens?" and head to the outhouse. The twins worked together at a shoe manufacturer and then at Jack Daniel Distillery until they retired.

J.B., L.B., and L.B.'s wife Barbara came over, and we sat in a circle in the living room while they gave me a history lesson.

J.B. told me that, at Jack Daniel's, there was a surprising amount of equality and tolerance between its Black and white employees. "At that time, the Blacks needed the whites and the whites needed the Blacks," L.B. said.

That was part of a tradition that had existed since Jack's day. In a 1906 deposition that was part of a court case concerning mules, Jack testified that his distillery employed Black teamsters "as a rule" to drive the mule teams that hauled liquor barrels, grain, timber, and coal between the railroad, the distillery, and the surrounding towns six days a week.

In July 1965, the twins began working as truck drivers at Jack Daniel's, earning two dollars an hour (at a time when federal minimum wage was $1.25). "It was good money at that time," they told me. "If a white person came in to Jack Daniel's to work and a Black person held the same job, the Black person would be paid more." What J.B. and L.B. were describing was pay based on tenure, not race—something quite rare in the American South at that time.

About half the workforce at the distillery was Black at a time when nine out of every ten residents in Moore County were white. That seemed remarkable to me, how sought-after positions at the distillery were. Jack Daniel's was even employing Black men from outside Lynchburg. It suggested a very intentional diversity. I loved that. It wasn't just an attitude; it was an initiative—real, material, financial action. That's how you achieve equality.

J.B. also told me the distillery would give the workers a bag with one hundred silver dollars as a bonus every Christmas, and a five-pound box of chocolate.

My jaw dropped and my mouth watered when I heard this.

"What did you do with all the chocolate?" I asked.

"We ate it throughout the year."

Following the death of Reagor Motlow, the twins recalled, the workplace culture around Jack Daniel's began to change. Although Brown-Forman purchased Jack Daniel's in the mid-1950s, it wasn't until much later that they brought in their own person from Louisville to manage it. L.B. and J.B. both remembered a new manager coming to Jack Daniel's from the parent company and completely changing the fabric of what had always been. "He didn't grow up in Lynchburg," they shared with me. "He didn't view race the same way as us." Whenever a Black person retired, he replaced them with a white person.

J.B. was one of the people who made a big early impression on me. Here was a man who'd traveled throughout the South and been stationed in Europe. In his opinion, tiny, close-knit Lynchburg was different than other towns. He recalled an idyllic childhood in Lynchburg in the 1940s. He'd been "raised to respect everyone no matter the color."

Nearly everyone, Black and white, was poor enough that their spending money varied with the crop cycle. There was plenty of food but no extra funds, and the twins' Uncle Possum wouldn't turn anyone away. Growing up in Lynchburg had been "100 percent positive!" L.B. said. "We always played with the white boys. We often enjoyed creek fishing with Bill Dance, Johnny Majors, Tommy, Henry, and Gerald Price." Johnny Majors, they told me, was a big-time football coach for the University of Tennessee. "I wouldn't want to grow up anyplace else." The white boys said the same thing: One of the Bobos recalled that "Clinton 'Possum' Daniel worked as a blacksmith and was the granddad of J. B. and L. B. McGowan, twins I played with."

L.B. said there were "white only" bathrooms and water fountains at the courthouse, and that a café on the square called the Coffee Cup made him and other Black people enter through the back door. But, he recalled, once inside, Blacks and whites ate at the tables together.

It was fascinating to talk to folks in town. I'd done more traditional research for my previous books, but I adapted to Lynchburg's challenges. I relied on my phone to unobtrusively and quickly take notes and photos. I didn't go into interviews with long lists of questions but let everyone I spoke with unspool their stories and steer the conversation. I kept everything I learned in my head and heart, using my computer mainly as a backup to refresh my memory. I quickly came to see this approach was the only one that could have worked in Lynchburg to tell this story. The only way to bridge being an outsider with folks was to no longer be one—to get to know them, let them take the time to actually get to know me, and then spread the word through the community. It was all about relationship building. One person led me to the next person. They'd lived this history; I was just trying to piece it together.

WHILE STEPHANI, Miss Neat, and I were reverse-engineering Nearest's family tree based on known descendants, I kept looking for the root of the tree: Nearest himself. As I pored over tax records in the local archives, I discovered eight separate tax ledgers from 1873 to 1884, each more fragile than the next, that mentioned Nearest. It was thrilling to see his name in each one, written in pencil. Sometimes he was listed in District 10 of Moore County, sometimes in District 9. Sometimes his name was spelled correctly, sometimes it wasn't. But every single year, he paid.

For the very first time, I had actual proof of Nearest's existence. Until then, nothing other than the census, which couldn't be trusted, showed that he had lived.

I took a picture of Nearest's name in the tax ledger and texted Keith and Stephani: *I found him! I found him! Right here in black and white. Nearest Green did indeed live.*

Chills ran down my spine. This was huge!

With more reliable information to go on, and better able to navigate the many spellings of his name, I was able to build an understanding of Nearest from other records. He was in fact named for the first time in the 1870 census, listed in his twenties with a birthplace of Maryland; in 1880, he was listed as several decades older with a birthplace of Tennessee. It is impossible to uncover his origin story when the United States didn't even recognize Nearest as anything more than property for half his life.

After the war, Nearest, Harriet, and their kids relocated from Call's Farm, five miles south of town, to Lincoln County's First District—land that would soon be incorporated into Moore County. He managed thirty acres of farmland there, five dollars' worth of farming equipment, and three hundred dollars' worth of livestock, which included two horses and seven swine. In 1870, the farm produced one hundred fifty dollars, including twenty bushels of wheat, one hundred fifty bushels of Indian corn, and forty-five dollars' worth of livestock slaughtered or sold to slaughter. He also had four hundred fifty dollars in "personal property."

By 1879, he and Harriet had settled down in the County Line community closer to town—a busy neighborhood with a grocery store, sawmill, blacksmith shop, post office, two churches, and the Tolley & Eaton Distillery, one of the largest in Tennessee. But Nearest continued his work at the Call Farm. When Jack and Dan started Daniel & Call, Nearest stayed on as head distiller—this time as a paid employee—and, by all accounts, he continued to work for Jack until the distillery moved to its current location at Cave Spring Hollow in 1884. After that, Nearest's sons George and Eli took his place. Eli developed vision problems and lived in a house behind his brother Jessie's, with a clothesline tied between the two so he could get back and forth. He continued to work at Jack Daniel's even after he was fully blind.

It was thrilling to learn specifics about Nearest's life. I also wanted to learn as much as I could about the history and events in town that Nearest and Harriet would have lived through. I had to start with the Civil War, of course.

Dan Call left his farm to join the Confederate Army, serving with the 44th Consolidated Regiment, Tennessee Infantry, instructing Nearest and his sons to look after his wife. That was typical for the area. An 1887 history of the county said public meetings had been held in Lynchburg, and the people were "almost unanimously in favor of a Southern Confederacy." Lynchburg residents wasted no time raising several companies of young men for the Confederacy in March 1861.

While Dan was gone, Nearest saw to the still. Jack and Mary Jane hid the silver and tended the store. It had become a place for residents to talk and share news. The war was at their doorstep, and neighbors who'd enlisted were dying on the battlefield.

Guerilla fighting made life terrifying for those who'd stayed behind. Everywhere you looked, people were fighting, starving, or sick. Civilians in the area lived in fear of bushwhackers, and as a rich agricultural area, Lynchburg and its surrounding communities were a target for foragers from both armies. Drunk soldiers were even worse, so Nearest and Jack worked together to hide every trace of whiskey-making, dousing the fire, ceasing work at the still house, and stashing barrels in the underbrush in the woods.

Dan was wounded, and records indicate that he deserted in November 1863 at Knoxville. He soon returned home.

Three years of enemy occupation left its mark. The North held the region from 1862 until the war's end, with Nashville as the center of the Union's western war effort. The result was physical devastation of Tennessee's lush, fertile landscape. A Union officer wrote in late 1862, "This is a dreary, desolate, barren and deserted looking country. . . . The houses and stores are either closed or smashed to pieces. Everything is going to utter destruction." A Confederate soldier marching through Bedford and Rutherford Counties wrote that "the country wears the most desolate appearance that I have ever seen anywhere. There is not a stalk of corn or blade of wheat growing." The land was left sterile, herds and flocks slaughtered.

The war came at a devastating cost to the area's residents. Seven companies were mustered in the area that would become Moore County. Of the 460 residents who enlisted, ninety-six never came home, and at least sixty-three more returned with injuries.

To make matters worse, there was no functional central currency. Just before fighting broke out, the new Confederacy had created its own form of money. Where the United States dollar was backed by gold, the Confederate dollar, or grayback, was backed by no hard assets. Instead, it was basically just a sloppily printed promissory note issued by a "nation" that had begun without a treasury. Since the money wasn't printed by a central bank, but rather by businesses, private banks, and states, the Confederacy suffered from hyperinflation.

Along with economic hardship, the region around Lincoln and Moore counties faced a growing crime wave as Tennesseans began fighting over limited resources. As early as October 1862, Lincoln County residents met to discuss the riots, robberies, and murders being committed. Courthouses had been burned, records had been destroyed. With the war's end, Confederate currency would be entirely worthless. Tennessee's social fabric was fraying.

It's hard to say when, exactly, word of President Abraham Lincoln's 1863 Emancipation Proclamation reached Lynchburg. The news traveled by word of mouth at places like Dan Call's store and in the press—but as we know, many enslaved people had been denied the right to learn to read. Instead, reality must have set in gradually. Enslaved people did escape prior to the Civil War, but often only as a last resort in the most dire circumstances. Once the war began, they realized that the white community was no longer organized enough to ensure escapees were captured, punished, and brought back, and they began to leave—often exchanging rural farms for homes in cities and towns.

Most, though, remained deeply tied to the land, churches, and way of life they knew well, and relocated nearby. Many continued working for their former enslavers as paid laborers.

"In defiance of the most vicious symbol of white dominance under slavery, the freed people rushed to county courthouses to legalize slave marriages and adopt surnames of their own choosing," historian Allen C. Guelzo has written. "In July 1865 Tennessee's Bedford County courthouse issued marriage licenses to 422 couples, 406 of which were black; in nearby Rutherford County that September, 431 black couples had their marriages legalized in a single week. Never again would a white man with an auctioneer's bill in his hand come between black husband and black wife, and never again would an African American be known simply as so-and-so's Tom or Dick or Cuffee or Caesar." Black people also "withdrew from the white churches where their masters had ruled over faith and practice, and formed their own congregations."

Life after the war was better, but not easy. In March 1875, there was a terrible hailstorm. It caused nothing but trouble for the area farmers, almost certainly including Nearest. In a town near Lynchburg, the fields were so damaged that they couldn't be cultivated anymore, and the hail permanently changed the course of a spring by two hundred feet. Lant Wood, a taster at Jack Daniel's and historian in the early days of the distillery, recorded that while Lynchburg wasn't hit by as much hail as some of the surrounding towns, it still "came down the creek taking everything in its path—chickens, ducks, geese, fences, water gates, and a whiskey warehouse."

It's easy to imagine Nearest—and probably Harriet and the children, in an all-hands emergency—trying to save their horses, swine, and farming equipment from the hail.

Nearest and Harriet would've also lived through the Great Fire of 1883 that swept through Lynchburg's Main Street business district.

This was before the square and the brick courthouse were built, and nearly everything was made of wood. The town lost twenty-four buildings, including its newspaper office, a blacksmith, a grain house, a drugstore, a hotel, a saddle shop, a law office, and any number of storehouses. It was a devastating loss for the whole community.

As I continued to uncover the history of the town, even small events made me think of Nearest. What did he and Harriet make of the eight inches of snow that fell in 1876, the deepest March snow in over thirty years? Were their kids able to play in the snow?

Did Nearest's hogs suffer from the hog cholera "raging" around Moore County in 1876? How often were the "Negro balls" held that were briefly mentioned in the *Lynchburg Sentinel*, and might Nearest and Harriet have attended? Could Nearest have played his fiddle there?

Envisioning Nearest's day-to-day life, his happy times, the moments of rest and warm-heartedness he may have shared with his family, overtook me with joy and helped me envision the man beyond the still.

ONE SUNDAY in October, I asked the Black elders of Lynchburg to come together at the Berry Chapel AME Church Fellowship Hall after church. I wanted their help filling out the family tree—not just for the Greens but for every Black family that had lived in Lynchburg. But more than that, I wanted to share this joy of discovery with them. I even hired a film crew to help me document their answers and stories.

Keith had been back in California, working and drawing up plans to restore the Call Farm. I missed him, of course, but even across two thousand miles, I felt his love and the strength of our union. I've always treasured the sense of tethered stability he gives me as I travel through the world, no matter what audacious goal or plan I've embarked on. I would often listen to "Easy Silence" by the Dixie Chicks when I missed him most, and let its chorus soothe me. I was thrilled that he flew in for the event.

Miss Neat invited many of the Black elders in town, expecting about ten and hoping for twenty. Instead, thirty-odd people joined us and shared their experiences of growing up in Lynchburg and, in many cases, working at Jack Daniel Distillery.

She was particularly eager for me to meet Jo Anne Gaunt Henderson, a friend she'd known her whole life and the financial secretary of Berry Chapel AME. Like Miss Neat, she was active in the local historical scene and had contributed many articles to *The Heritage of Moore County* book I was coming to rely on. She had retired after a long career at State Farm and was enjoying traveling the world with her husband.

Jo Anne had grown up in a tiny community called Hurdlow, about ten miles from downtown Lynchburg. "Bat your eyes and you've missed it as you're going through," she said. There was one little grocery store there in Hurdlow, and another over in Lois, closer to the Call Farm.

Jo Anne looked back fondly at her childhood. "Everybody on the road knew everybody," she recalled. "You were safe." As kids, they could start out in Hurdlow walking toward their grandfather's house in Lynchburg, and someone would stop, pick them up, and take them the rest of the way. "The milkman, the mailman, everybody knew us," she said. "If any of them was coming to Lynchburg, they'd say, 'Hop in.'"

I was learning from Miss Neat, Jo Anne, and others that Lynchburg's Dog Row had been a tight-knit place where everyone looked out for one another. People made sure all the kids were safe, fed, and looked after. Neighbors pooled resources, and no one went hungry or homeless. People were willing to share all they had.

Jo Anne's grandfather, Will Peppers, was known as the "peacemaker of Dog Row." He was a religious man and commanded a lot of respect among his neighbors. Whenever inevitable disagreements arose, domestic arguments escalated, or people drank a little too much Jack Daniel's, people would send for Will to calm things down rather than go into town and get the sheriff.

Miss Neat lived nearby, and she and Jo Anne went to school and church together. They became close as adults, with Miss Neat serving as the young people's director at church and Jo Anne assisting her.

Jo Anne's family had done a lot of genealogy work and had its own rich history.

She protested that she didn't really care for genealogy—at least not as much as Miss Neat—but she had penned enough entries about her extended family in *The Heritage of Moore County* book to chronicle a great deal of the Black experience in the county. (Besides, *nobody* cares about genealogy as much as Miss Neat did.)

The book's organizing committee asked everyone in the county to contribute memories about the church they went to, the schools they attended, and their parents, grandparents, and other ancestors. Most people were glad to contribute to a remembrance that could be handed down to the next generation. Jo Anne loved her copy, keeping it within easy reach and in perfect condition. Her grandchildren were more interested in their computers than a heavy book, but she was pleased it would be there for them when they wanted it.

Miss Neat was excited for us to meet at Berry Chapel AME because one of Nearest's grandsons had married Jo Anne's mother's aunt. It was an indirect line—like Claude Eady and Miss Neat, she wasn't a direct descendant of Nearest's—but her family had documented and could share their extensive family tree.

AFTER THE CHURCH SERVICE, Stephani and I unfurled the giant printed family tree we'd been working on, nearly as tall as I was, in the fellowship hall. We had filled it out as best we could based on what Miss Neat could tell us.

Standing at the front of the hall, I told the group how I'd come to Jack Daniel and Nearest Green's story: the article I'd read in Singapore, the copy of *Jack Daniel's Legacy* I'd devoured in LA, and my encounter with Judy Boyd Terjen at the Moore County Library. Now that I'd spoken with Jack's descendants and found some of Nearest's, it was time to stop and check with the wider community. I wanted to make sure I was understanding their message correctly.

"One thing that I do with my books is look for accuracy," I explained. I planned to base myself out of Lynchburg and hold events like this—with them, with historians, collectors, genealogists, and anyone else who could tell me about Nearest and Jack.

"It seemed to me that whites and Blacks in Lynchburg have a slightly different relationship than they had historically in other towns nearby," I said, "especially big towns like Memphis and Nashville. Here, Blacks and whites seemed to treat each other like friends and family, with a kindness and an honoring of each other during an era when I hadn't expected that.

"Am I on the right track here?"

I saw nods and agreement.

"Would anyone say I'm not on the right track?"

A sea of aged faces looked back at me. No one seemed to want to speak up, or at least want to speak first.

I pressed ahead. I said that nothing I'd turned up indicated that Jack Daniel had ever treated Nearest less than a fellow human being and distiller.

"Unless you guys tell me otherwise, I'll be writing a story of love and honor between Jack and Nearest during a time in the South when that did not exist between Blacks and whites," I said.

Folks seemed hesitant to respond. I don't have the personality of the South—I move fast, I talk fast. Here I was, meeting most of them for the first time, asking awkward questions. Besides, people were getting ready to eat. We'd asked Chuck Baker at the Barrel House to cater, and he'd sent over the works. I decided to try again after lunch.

While the group enjoyed ribs, sausage, "grilled cheese on crack," potato salad, and baked beans, I pulled Miss Neat aside. She had been an absolute godsend, researching, organizing this event, answering all kinds of texts, and I wanted to thank her. I presented her with two handheld fireproof safes. She could store her documents in them and keep them protected.

"It's heavy," I said. "But you can carry it with you."

She gave me, Keith, and Stephani a big hug.

After lunch, the mood of the gathering changed. We'd broken bread together, and Keith laughed and joked with the group, setting everyone at ease. Keith has a gentle manner and a big laugh that's never far away; you can hear it in his voice and see it on his face before it arrives. His voice is kind and knowing. He had an easy way with all the elders. It's always been like that—people trust him easily, which tends to help them trust *us*.

I started out with easier questions this time. As we filled out the family tree, I asked folks to say their names; when they were born, if they knew; and the names of their siblings, aunts, uncles, and so on. I told them we'd be pulling census records to make sure we traced everyone, but the more they knew, the more it would help.

It was a big undertaking. I wanted to know how many grandchildren and great-grandchildren everyone had. I wanted to know who'd been taught by Miss Dot, whether folks were familiar with the Dan Call Farm, or if they had any stories they wanted to tell me. The whole room cracked up when we all realized I'd confused Lost Creek, Louse Creek, and Lois—three distinct places, all pronounced roughly the same. It wouldn't be the last time.

One woman mentioned her father had come from Pulaski, which I knew was where the KKK had originated. "I have found a really strong presence of the Ku Klux Klan next door in Fayetteville, next door in Shelbyville, and pretty much all the way around Lynchburg," I said, but my research hadn't turned up evidence of it in Lynchburg itself in recent memory. In fact, Lynchburg seemed like it had been a little pocket of hope.

"Have there ever been any sightings of the Ku Klux Klan in Lynchburg that anyone is aware of?" I asked. I heard a chorus of noes, but this time I noticed one exception.

"Oscar, you're nodding your head," I said.

Oscar McGee said he remembered some KKK members collecting change at the one stoplight in town, near the library, on a Saturday morning back in 1979 or 1980.

"They were asking for donations?" I had to laugh a little bit at that pathetic image.

As we went around the table doing the family trees, Rev. Dickey Sebastian and his wife spoke about their observations of race in town. The pastor's wife had grown up in a rough town called Flintville, about half an hour away from Lynchburg. When Black people went there, "they were rocked out," she recalled. "Here is different from where I was raised." She was astonished when she came to Lynchburg and saw Black people and white people getting along so well in comparison. She was particularly taken by the intermingling at funerals, where Blacks and whites would hug and comfort one another on their losses.

"I've never seen Black and white people get along like that," she said. "It's totally different up here."

Her husband, the pastor, agreed. He had grown up in nearby Mulberry, in Lincoln County, which is so close to Lynchburg I was having trouble telling the two towns apart at the time. He'd gone to school in Lynchburg through the eighth grade. "It was a lot different," he said. "I just noticed how white people and Black people got along so much better up here. And it wasn't like that in Mulberry." There weren't big problems in Mulberry, he added, but "they weren't close like that. They were not close like that at all."

Two people even told me about times when Black children went to live with white families. One woman's father was taken in by a pair of white brothers after his father died. "He kept that relationship until they died," she recalled. "They'd eat together and go places together. So he was real close."

And Oscar McGee, who was one of twelve siblings, mentioned being raised by William and Mary Stone, a white couple. They formed a lifelong bond, and Oscar saw William as a father figure and mentor. In the seventies, Oscar thought about joining the Army to see the world, but William was dying. Oscar promised he would stay and take care of Mary. He kept his promise, living in an apartment over the garage until she passed away in 1988. Oscar found out the Stones had left him and his brother five acres of land in their will. He later told me it wasn't uncommon in the Lynchburg area for white families to leave their land, or a part of it, to Black people who worked for them. A lot of the land that had been passed on this way had now significantly increased in value. I was bowled over. In other parts of the country, Black people are only just beginning to become landowners. But here in Lynchburg, a great many Black families had owned land for decades.

"In Lynchburg, there was no difference between races," Jo Anne shared when I asked about their collective upbringing among a community in which there were far more whites than Blacks. "But as Lynchburg became the county seat, they really began to see the difference. Those coming in from the outside of Lynchburg would treat Blacks as less than. They clearly thought they were superior."

But Lynchburg's equanimity toward race tended to rub off on new people eventually, she told me. "If they stayed in Lynchburg long enough, they'd become more like us and not treat each other differently," she said. Plenty of out-of-towners visited since Lynchburg was the county seat, but "white people in Lynchburg didn't change for the racist whites coming in, so those whites would end up changing."

The day stretched out before us, with the pleasure of old folks remembering. The crowd got raucous and giddy at times, and Keith teased and goaded them right along. We heard the pride in their voices as they told stories about Tuskegee Airmen and show horse trainers in the family and the vast numbers of family members who'd worked at Jack Daniel's.

Some people knew their whole family trees by heart. But other folks' eyes flitted up as they thought of their mother's names. One woman shared that she was the last of her nine siblings. One man couldn't remember his grandparents' names. I could tell that just about broke his heart. It definitely broke mine.

Sometimes, the crowd corrected people. Other times, everyone nodded. They were seated at folding tables, which had been pushed together and covered in white cloths and colorful flowers.

I asked if there was anything else I should know before I jumped further into my research.

Now I could tell people had been searching their memories and getting into the spirit of things. Jackie, a handsome seventy-something-year-old man who didn't look a day over fifty, spoke up: "Especially in the early 1900s, there seemed to be an extraordinary number of people here, Black men, that either were businessmen or actually owned their own property," he said.

"Do you have any idea why?" I asked him.

He didn't, beyond speculation that it could have had something to do with white people leaving agriculture to work at the distillery. But someone else mentioned a nearby town that wasn't there anymore.

"It was a whole Black community," she said. "Are y'all aware of that?"

Everyone talked back and forth about it for a few minutes, but it sounded like they weren't very familiar with it beyond the name: Portertown.

"My dad owned property right at the Lincoln County–Moore County line during that time," someone else spoke up. "It was full of Black folks at that time. They even had their own school outside there."

"P-O-R-T-E-R-T-O-W-N?" I spelled. A whole town of Black land-owners? It was another question to add to our growing list. *We'll be looking into that for sure*, I thought.

CHAPTER

18

ONE DAY, Moore County archivist Christine Pyrdom handed me several brittle ledgers from the mid-nineteenth century. Christine was the Moore County archivist and one of a trio of archivists across two counties who'd been helping me sift through papers and search for answers. Over at the Bedford County archives, Kat Hopkins was a stellar genealogist, and Carol Roberts had worked at the Tennessee State Library and Archives for nearly thirty years, helping counties across Tennessee set up official archives. "We have ninety-five counties" in Tennessee, Carol told me, which meant "ninety-five ways of keeping records." In Moore County, Christine was no stranger to that—back in 2000, she'd helped do the hard work of moving informally preserved records from all over town to a new permanent home.

The ledger she wanted me to look at now was a name index listing every member of the local Masonic lodge from 1866 to 1908. Fraternal secret societies like the Freemasons flourished during those days and often formed the backbone of informal power structures in many towns.

"We're not supposed to have this," she said. "These are the Lynchburg Masonic Lodge books. They're supposed to be kept secret, but two of the books were with the lodge grandmaster when he died, and somehow the books weren't ever sent to the grand lodge in Nashville to be put under lock and key."

I opened a ledger and began flipping through. The books were like peeking behind the curtain of that secret society. They revealed that all the prominent distillers in the area had been Freemasons—except Jack Daniel.

The books also gave an incomplete accounting of someone being blackballed from membership. The Freemasons used an anonymous and efficient voting system when deciding on admitting new members. Those in favor would drop a white ball into a box; those opposed would drop in a black ball. One black ball was enough to veto the new member. Without the full set of books, I wasn't able to tell who had been vetoed. Was it Jack Daniel? We have no way of knowing, but it certainly is interesting that every other major distiller in the area was a Mason. D. H. Call, Alfred Eaton, J. D. Tolley, William Tolley, B. H. Berry, J. M. Hughes—the book was a who's who of the local whiskey distillers at the time. All the stories I'd accumulated of the local distillers raced through my mind as I peered into their lives as contained in this old brittle ledger with faded yellow paper and smeared black ink.

Put a pin in that one, I thought.

ONE THING I'D KNOWN even before we left LA was that shortly after the Civil War ended, six Confederate veterans made it home alive only to continue nursing their grievances. Home, for them, was Pulaski, Tennessee, a war-scarred, defeated, embarrassed, and impoverished area some forty miles from Lynchburg.

It was here that the Ku Klux Klan was born, supposedly as a fraternal secret society like the Freemasons or Odd Fellows. The group spread to other towns—even Lynchburg—as a novelty, and I saw that the *Lynchburg Sentinel* published a list of the charter members of the local Klan group. I noticed a striking similarity between the names on its membership roster and the names in the Freemason books. That could explain why Jack Daniel was the only major distiller in the area who wasn't a Freemason.

That could mean Lynchburg had not always been immune to the Klan—although danger seemed to come from without, not within. The Klan was active in its familiar, violent form in Lincoln County by the spring of 1867. Following a large reorganization meeting at the prominent Maxwell House hotel in Nashville, the Klan spread in towns near Lynchburg, like Shelbyville and Columbia.

A popular tale in Lynchburg is that of Dr. Dance, who caught his nephew—who also aspired to be a doctor—packing away a long white robe. Dance told the nephew to cease his participation in the Klan or he'd make sure he didn't make it as a doctor. The nephew went on to practice medicine, so locals believe that must've been the end of that.

The Klan went out of its way to hurt white allies. A Lincoln County white man in his mid-sixties who'd been taught to see Blacks as neighbors—"If God give a man a black skin, I was taught from the cradle not to abuse him, nor tramp on him for what God gave him," he said—was attacked and pistol-whipped for his beliefs.

The KKK really kicked into action around the 1868 election, which would be the first time Southerners voted in a national election since the 1861 secession and the first time Southern Black voters would help elect a president.

Miss Neat told me a story about her ancestor George Daniel and his brothers having their house shot at around the time Black people were first allowed to register to vote. Their house had stood right next door to Berry Chapel AME, so the story stood out for its immediacy—and the bravery of George and his brothers, who shot right back. Miss Neat was proud of her ancestors. "That hole in the window over there, that I hope to keep forever, is from them trying to vote."

ON THE NIGHT OF November 3, 1894, a mob of two hundred men assembled in the west end of Moore County. At 11 p.m., they arrived at a small house near the edge of the property where Jack Daniel lived with his sister and brother-in-law. None of the newspaper accounts I found of what happened next explicitly labeled the group as the Ku Klux Klan, but they reported that some of the men "wore white cloths over their faces," and "one was clothed in a gown of red."

Jack was in poor health. While he would famously go on to kick a safe in 1905 and injure his foot, kick-starting a chain of events that culminated in his death several years later, he found himself bedridden at earlier times as well. Nelson Eddy and others have speculated that perhaps he had poor circulation or was diabetic, which seems to line up. When he was ill, he hired several people to nurse him. One of these people was a Black man named Ned Waggoner, who had been one of the original stockholders in the founding of Lynchburg's Black cemetery on Elm Street.

Ned and his family lived in a house on Jack's land, and on this night, the Waggoner family had already gone to bed. When the mob came to the house, Ned rose and opened the door, and they forced their way inside.

The family was stripped and marched half a mile, barefoot and naked, to a beech-tree that stood at the very edge of the property. Ned's wife Margaret was interrogated, flogged, then sent home and told to leave town within three days. Ned, who weighed around three hundred pounds, resisted and was shot between the eyes. His daughter Mary was strangled, leaving behind two small children—one eighteen months old, the other three months. His son, Will, and son-in-law, Sam Motlow, were killed, too.

The victims were discovered the next morning, their bodies arranged methodically—"in the shape of a square to the four cardinal points of the compass," according to the subsequent inquest. All the murderers left behind was some loose rope and a placard, leaning on the tree, that said, in printed red ink, "Plenty More Rope. The Rest Look Out."

Word spread throughout the entire country. Headlines appeared as far as Los Angeles and San Francisco, indicating that a lynching on this scale was significant. The *Boston Post* called the lynching a "terrible crime." The *Knoxville Journal* called it a "horrible discovery" and even printed an anti-lynching op-ed condemning the lynching as "a severe blow to society."

But not every newspaper was aggrieved. Some implied that the victims got what they deserved. The *Nashville Tennessean* called it a "wholesale hanging" whose victims were "said to have been a very bad lot, and many felonious acts are laid at their door." Each of them had at some point been charged and spent time in jail in Lynchburg.

As I kept digging, I learned that, in the lead-up to the hanging, there had been a string of barn burnings in the area. That week, three barns were destroyed, two of them in the same neighborhood. Members of the Waggoner family were suspected as the culprits. But only, in the words of the *Boston Post*, because the Waggoner family "bore an unsavory reputation as petty thieves."

Nearly seventeen years earlier, the *Lynchburg Sentinel* reported that Ned had broken into a smokehouse and stolen six pieces of meat. One year before the lynching, Mary was accused of robbing a man named Hobbs. On the night of the hanging, the mob allegedly found silverware and "other articles" in Mary's possession that Hobbs claimed was his own property. We'll never know whether he was lying.

When I came across records of the lynching, I was horrified—at the descriptions of what had happened and at the idea that Jack hadn't stopped it. The natural thought was to wonder if he'd been involved, but that was unfathomable to me. I kept digging and learned he'd been bedridden the night of the murders and for two straight weeks leading up to the lynchings. There was nothing he could have done to stop it. He was as powerless as the Waggoners.

It seemed to me the mob had been communicating with Jack through the violence. They came onto *his* land and lynched the people he'd hired to help him from *his* tree—a horrific message. Jack's influence and power in Lynchburg would have kept people from giving him hell over hiring Black workers at the distillery and at his home. It would've kept silent those who opposed paying a fair wage and showing kindness to Black families. This cowardly, nameless, faceless strike in the night at defenseless people was the way they had to rebuke Jack Daniel—and they waited until he was incapacitated and helpless to stop it.

Jack was distraught. The *Tennessean* reported that Jack was "very much troubled over the lynching," and he paid for Ned's burial. The pastor held the service without referencing how the four were killed. "The grief of the wives and relatives was intense," the paper said. The funeral was small and simple, and all four coffins were laid together, side by side, in one grave at Highview Cemetery.

Decades later, a 1946 book by radical white journalist Robert Minor called the lynching "one of the great, bloody nightmares of the Negroes' history of Tennessee."

Miss Neat had heard of the lynching from her mother before I found these articles. The story had been passed down about a nursing mother whose breast dripped with milk as she was hanged. Shaken by that detail, Miss Neat maintains the charges against Mary must have been false. This woman had just had a baby, and she was out setting fires? "I can't believe that," Miss Neat said.

NINE YEARS LATER, in August 1903, a Black man named Allen Small, accused of assaulting a white woman in Tullahoma, was quietly taken to Nashville on a midnight train to await trial even though the woman couldn't tell authorities whether the man who attacked her had been Black or white. Ordinarily he would have been held in the jail in Lynchburg—the county seat, where he would be tried in Moore County Court—but authorities were concerned for his safety. Parts of Moore County and those around it were known to be "mob-infested," at high risk of vigilantes like the Klan and other groups.

The *Nashville Banner* and the Moore County press criticized authorities for taking Small to Nashville, and Lynchburg officials persuaded a judge that "all danger of mob violence, if there had ever been any, had passed away." Small was relocated to the Lynchburg jail.

But in September, in the dead of the night, a mob of twenty men from Tullahoma surrounded the jail. They called for the sheriff to throw them the keys. When he refused, the mob attacked the building. The sheriff and his wife raised the alarm, and townspeople ran to his aid—but they thought they were coming to help put out a fire, so few showed up armed, and no one had extra ammunition.

The mob broke into the cell and dragged Small from the building. They intended to hang him, but the townspeople were fighting back too hard. I recognized the names of Harry Dance and other Lynchburgers among those who protected the jail and attempted to protect Small.

It was a real firefight. As the Lynchburgers emptied their revolvers, some tried to break into the hardware store to get more, but everything happened frighteningly fast. The mob shot Small, beat him with the butts of their guns, and then ran away. Only thirty minutes passed between the time the mob showed up and when it dispersed.

"During that short interval," the newspaper noted, town officers and citizens "put up one of the gamest fights ever made in defense of a prisoner, and continued to fight until their last cartridges were gone."

This was a horrific act of violence based on a racist, bloodthirsty herd mentality. Murders like Small's were chillingly common throughout the South. But here's why I find the story remarkable: The town of Lynchburg had stood up against vigilante justice and in defense of a Black man's right to a fair trial at every chance it got. Its officials had vouched for Small's safety. When that was in jeopardy, the townspeople showed up to help. They braved gunfire to protect him, and they stood their ground even after they were outgunned and outmanned.

By contrast, none of the mob was from Lynchburg. They'd all come from elsewhere, and the Lynchburgers fought them with all they had and chased them out. A town marshal arrested one ringleader after "a lively chase," and he was "thrown down and gagged by the officer until the mob dispersed." He gave up information that led to seven members of the mob being arrested the next day, and the newspaper anticipated the rest being identified and arrested the day after that.

The Lynchburg jail sits just off the town square, so I walked past the site of Allen Small's murder nearly every day. With some effort, though, I found the site where the Waggoners had been murdered on Jack's land and visited the spot. The house where the four victims lived was no longer there, and neither was the beech-tree where the stagecoach driver found their bodies. The large one-hundred-plus acres of land had years prior been subdivided, and one-story condos were scattered where the mob had stood.

Unlike the Call Farm, I didn't have any feeling at the site of the lynching. Visiting the site didn't help answer any of my questions. I kept thinking of Ned, who had nursed Jack and helped found the cemetery Jack buried him in. And my thoughts lingered with Jack, who had tried to shelter and protect Ned and his family.

Although the townspeople couldn't save Small, the level of accountability and commitment to justice they demonstrated—less than ten years after the perpetrators of the lynching on Jack Daniel's property went unidentified and unpunished—speaks volumes about Lynchburg.

"The people here are unanimous in condemnation of the work of the mob and are determined to remove the stain from the county by a vigorous prosecution of the members," wrote the newspaper. "The community has never been so aroused as at present, and the law-abiding people are jubilant over the arrests."

I've always marveled at Lynchburg. The community that provided most of Nathan Bedford Forrest's Escorts was the same one that led the McGowan twins to say they wouldn't have wanted to have grown up anywhere else, and where Miss Dot said integration had been a nonissue. It was the same community that had produced Nearest and Jack. How did that happen? Could it be that once Jack Daniel had become the big man in town, it was impossible to remain racist with him flanked by African Americans? Was it possible that Nearest and Jack's relationship had persuaded Lynchburg to move forward in a different way, and the Black elders I interviewed just happened to be the recipients of that changed viewpoint?

CHAPTER

19

IT WOULD BE IMPOSSIBLE to understand Lynchburg without knowing the Motlow family, and I like to think I had the best guide. Motlow descendant and storehouse of family knowledge Joel Pitts, in his overalls and button-down shirt, was warm and friendly, if a little hesitant with new people. From the first time I met him in October 2016, he was an incredible resource. We'd have three-hour phone conversations where he'd tell me about his family and the area. He knew whiskey well; it ran in his family's blood and he'd made moonshine. He'd been president of the Lincoln County Historical Society and a member of the Moore County Historical society. He was also an ardent collector of Jack Daniel's memorabilia, documents, and rare bottles.

Joel explained that the Motlows were one of the founding families of Lynchburg, settling in the area around 1809. After Jack Daniel transferred ownership of his distillery to his nephews Lem Motlow and Dick Daniel in 1907, Lem bought out his cousin and later became a fixture in Tennessee politics. Joel's great-grandfather was Lem's cousin Spoon Motlow.

One Lynchburger recalled: "There was rarely any crime, hardly any poverty, and very little wealth other than the owners of the distillery, the Motlow family, and they did not flaunt their money."

Lem's wife Ophelia raised sheep and had a dairy farm near their grand colonial farmhouse half a mile from downtown—in addition to its tennis court and stable of Tennessee walking horses. The house was destroyed in a fire in 1936.

The Motlows owned thousands of acres across Moore County and were its major employers. Many of the Black people I met had female relatives who had worked for them in a domestic way—cooking, cleaning, child-minding—and many of the Black and white families of Lynchburg had male family members who had worked on their land, tending their crops, orchards, and animals. I've heard a story about some wealthy women snidely turning up their noses at Lem's work as a farmer and commenting to Ophelia that they didn't know how she handled a man who smelled like cow manure. "Smells like money to me," Ophelia said.

Lem's son Reagor went into state politics, too, and changed the fabric of the region with his donations: land to establish Motlow State College and a new building for the county library. Several Black elders told me they'd heard a story about him funding a bus to transport Black students a county over so they could more reliably attend high school under segregation. "I have heard that, but I have no way of verifying it," John T. Bobo, who knew Reagor well, told me. He added, "I believe it to be true." Official records appear to show the bus was controlled and funded by the Moore County School Board as far back as 1948.

The Motlows were also the major force behind Farmers Bank, which was for many years the only bank in Lynchburg. A group of locals, including Jack Daniel, Lem Motlow, and Joel's great-grandfather Spoon Motlow started the bank in 1888.

Tom Motlow, Lem's younger brother, grew up farming in Lynchburg but was naturally bright and highly educated—able to "cuss the mules in Latin or Greek," as one writer put it. He was urged to go into law by a mentor who felt he would rise to the Supreme Court, but Tom felt honor-bound to take a job his cousin Spoon had waiting for him at Farmers Bank when he graduated from Vanderbilt. The bank was paying him a salary to finish school with the plan that he would take up a position there when he graduated. All Tom would find back in Lynchburg were "whiskey, mules, and mud," warned the mentor, but Tom went ahead with his plans. He began as a cashier, then served as bank president for decades.

The Motlow family, like the Greens, remains a significant presence in Lynchburg, and I knew that I'd need to get to know them better to fully grasp Nearest and Jack's story. I'd met Judy Boyd Terjen, Lem's granddaughter, in the library my first day in Lynchburg. But it felt different to spend so much time with Joel. At times, Stephani and I joked that it was pretty bold to be working with this particular Motlow descendant while we were still trying to fly under the radar.

It was through Joel and his fellow history buffs in the area who participated in Civil War reenactments that I also learned you can be a Yankee even if you're Black and from California. And I discovered that what Yankees learn versus what Southerners learn about the Civil War are two extraordinarily different histories. When I was in school, I was taught that the war was fought by a bunch of people who didn't want to free the enslaved people they owned. In the South, they were taught it was the War of Northern Aggression. The things we're indoctrinated into become our foundation. When three generations, all your schoolteachers, and all your history books tell you the same story, of course it becomes "the truth." As a Christian, what I know for sure is that judgment and unjust weights and measures are an abomination. I can't take away what folks in the South were taught in school, by teachers they loved and trusted, by their parents and grandparents. That doesn't mean that I'm on board. But I do understand that they were indoctrinated this way, and it's been a pleasure to see the way many people in town have changed their views and evolved.

With the film crew in tow to document things for posterity, Joel took us down to his basement. He had thousands of items; literally every inch was stuffed with all things Jack.

There were Jack Daniel's flags on the ceiling, bricks from Lem Motlow's old barrelhouse, and a bottle made especially for Joel. He had letters about his great-great-grandfather, three checks signed by Jack Daniel Motlow, dozens of bottles, and a hardcover first edition of *Jack Daniel's Legacy* with its green cloth cover and a goldleaf image of Jack on the front.

This wasn't my first run-in with the Jack Daniel's collectibles market since I'd come to Lynchburg. I knew old bottles and memorabilia could command a lot of money on the auction circuit. "You can buy the best pickup General Motors makes" with the combined value of a few select old bottles in their original packaging, as one Jack Daniel's employee measured it. But it was the first time I understood how much it mattered to people and basically functioned as its own economy. Joel Pitts's basement was proof of it.

That first day I set foot in Joel's basement, he explained the Tennessee Squires, a Jack Daniel's organization that kept coming up. It wasn't *just* a fan club. Even Jack Daniel's official podcast later referred to them as "that group of rabid and devoted friends of Mr. Jack."

Jack Daniel's founded the Squires in February 1956 as a shrewd attempt to kick-start the whiskey market post World War II. This was another brainchild of marketing director Art Hancock and sales manager Winton Smith. I learned later that Smith was traveling through Texas and saw a sign in the airport advertising "a square foot of Texas" you could buy from a dude ranch. Smith and Hancock decided to try the same idea with Jack Daniel's. When consumers asked bartenders and store owners for Jack Daniel's and they didn't have it, they were told to write to the distillery. As people wrote in, they received personalized letters through the newly formed Squires Association. "Keep the faith," they were told. "One day we'll have enough to go around." In the meantime, they also got an honorary and unrecorded "deed" to a square foot of land at the distillery. (These days, it's a square inch.) The deeds aren't legal documents, and no property ever really changes hands, but Jack Daniel's aficionados display their framed deeds and pass them down to their children along with their Squire memberships.

Mark McCallum at Brown-Forman saw Jack Daniel's as a pirate flag—and the bottle's label had the colors to match. It was about independence and American grit.

With thousands of Americans based in Europe and Japan after World War II, Jack Daniel had been the drink of choice for the American military and spread throughout the world. When Mark was a young man in Australia, he knew Jack Daniel through the Rolling Stones.

"Many countries loved that little piece of America," Mark recalled. Jack Daniel's went on a push to expand its international reach in the 2010s. Mark saw the Squires as "brand acolytes," and it was important to consider them "an evolving group." As the brand focused on the world beyond America's borders, it became "obvious that the primary vocal ambassadors for the brand were all American and 90 percent white men." So Brown-Forman worked to expand Squire membership around the world.

Some perks of membership, I'm told, are confidential to Squires, but two of the evident ones are priority parking at the distillery—saving the Squire the journey from the large spillover parking lot across Lynchburg Highway—and admittance to several Squires-only spaces at the distillery and around town.

People take membership seriously. Various Lynchburg businesses sport "Squires Welcome" signs, and bed and breakfasts are known to bill themselves as unofficial Squire houses. Squires periodically get wholesome letters in the mail from the distillery, along with gifts and special perks. There's an annual barbecue that draws some two thousand Squires to Lynchburg each year. A special calendar gets mailed out every year that features figures around the distillery and citizens of Lynchburg, like Chuck Baker and his BBQ pit. Joel called the Squires "a Jack lover's society." But I wondered if it was more than that.

JOEL KNEW the Call Farm property well. For twenty years, he'd been going over it with a metal detector, looking for Civil War relics. A long time back, he'd found a metal jug stencil that read "Jack Daniel" buried nine inches beneath the original distillery site.

"This is the only known Jack Daniel jug stencil in the world," he told me. "I've had it in my collection all this time, but if you're bringing this farm back to life and will be telling the story of Nearest Green, it belongs here with you."

Nothing so far had brought Nearest and Jack's story to life like holding that stencil in my hands. I could see grain and malt being prepared for the ten-ton limestone grist mill. I could see the furnace where the whiskey was cooked, the spring where the yeast was kept cool, and men rolling barrels for sale in Huntsville and Tullahoma. I thought about the blacksmith who'd made the stencil, probably around 1880, and the young man he'd made it for—and Nearest, hard at work at the center of the whole whiskey-making operation.

This was real, physical history—something Jack or Nearest may well have handled. Joel had pulled it from the earth, preserved and protected it, and waited until the time was right to hand-deliver it.

LEGEND—AND *JACK DANIEL'S LEGACY*—have it that Jack left Dan Call's farm when he started Jack Daniel Distillery. This was, perhaps, one of the reasons Mark McCallum had never seen the farm as all that important to the Jack Daniel's brand. He'd read Ben Green's book when he started working at Brown-Forman—all Jack Daniel's executives did—and saw the farm as not much more than Jack's childhood stomping grounds.

When the IRS consolidated Tennessee's revenue districts in 1876, Daniel & Call's distillery number changed from Distillery No. 7 to Distillery No. 16. Jack protested in the newspapers and distiller group meetings with the revenuers, but his protests fell on deaf ears. Jack, being the great marketer and PR man he was, never changed the distillery number on his product. Jack Daniel's whiskey remains known the world over as Old No. 7 to this day.

But we found some documents that changed the whole picture.

"You've got to get down here—you have to see this," Christine Pyrdom said over the phone.

I met Christine in her office in a bare brick building just off Lynchburg's main square. She'd discovered three documents. Each showed Jack Daniel had agreed to lease Dan Call's distillery, the two surrounding acres, and the nearby spring and rename it all the "Jack Daniel Distillery." The spidery handwriting in the record books shows the arrangement went into effect on October 1, 1877.

This is amazing, I thought.

Until that point, everyone always assumed Jack Daniel Distillery began where it is now at Cave Spring Hollow. I thought so, too. But the records Christine found specifically stated that Jack wanted to lease the distillery area of Call's property—two acres surrounding the spring on Call's Farm—and rename the Daniel & Call Distillery to Jack Daniel Distillery.

The IRS had changed the distillery numbers in 1876, and the leases Christine found were dated 1877. That made the Call Farm, not Cave Spring Hollow, the original site of Distillery No. 7—and Nearest Green had been its master distiller.

This discovery changed everything. Old No. 7 had started on our grounds, just behind the house where Jack had grown up. Unbeknownst to Mark McCallum, Ed McGee, or anyone else in town, Keith and I had purchased the site of the original Jack Daniel Distillery. That meant Nearest hadn't just been Jack's teacher or mentor. He was the first Black master distiller on record in the United States.

It was also a moment of personal realization: we could never renovate the Call Farm the way we'd planned. It was a historical monument; we couldn't change it and make it into a Southern home.

We learned that Jack Daniel's collectors from all over the world had traveled for years to the Call Farm. They seemed to instinctively understand the mystique of the Call Farm in a way Brown-Forman did not. We'd already seen how they'd sawed off several feet of the mid-1800s piping that carried the water from the original spring to the still. They'd walk off the property with stones from the still's foundation, and if it weren't for the pure size and weight of the millstones still there from the original grist mill, there's no doubt someone would have attempted to remove those from the property, too.

The McGees had let tour buses come onto their property, but we needed everyone to know that would no longer be allowed. Our work was preservation-based. We posted twenty-four-hour security guards at the farm until we could put up a gate around the entire perimeter. The days of looting the original Jack Daniel Distillery were over.

I was still concerned, even with security. Locals claimed that a lot of local records burned in fires that had swept the town, first in 1883 and again in 1913, but along with those fires, some of the more inconvenient records seem to have been misplaced, too.

As a local historian told me when handing over new documents, "Make sure to hold on to these. Documents with inconvenient truths have a way of going missing or into the Jack Daniel's archives never to be seen again." I took her advice to heart, making copies of every single page of the books I found, often more than once. My goal each day was to keep my research close enough that even if someone broke into the house and tried to destroy it all, I'd have copies of everything on my laptop. And my laptop never left my sight.

At the Call Farm, I put up photos of Nearest's descendants—young women in fine hats and jewelry and men in uniform. I was surrounded each day by artifacts and photos, my constant, tangible reminders to tell the truth and to get it right. People showed up almost every day, and the security would call me and let me know someone new wanted to meet me. I'd invite them into the house, because that's what you do in the South. But it did not take long for everyone in town to know the types of artifacts the home now contained. I drove up to the farm every day and prayed that the Greek Revival home where Jack Daniel once lived had made it through the night once again.

ONE OF THE RENTAL homes I stayed in frequently on my trips to Lynchburg turned out to be owned by Steve May, a Jack Daniel's executive, which didn't help. I wasn't comfortable speaking about this project in that house. I was concerned it could be bugged.

One morning, I was sitting in the kitchen, reading and sipping coffee, when I saw something peculiar: two men in a white pickup truck parked right across the street. The driver was staring intently at my license plate. His eyes never left my car. He was speaking with someone, presumably the man in the passenger seat, but he never turned his head to look at him. He just sat there staring.

I walked over to the window and watched him staring at my car. He glanced up at me and then back down to my license plate. One thing about being in a small town is everyone knows what everyone drives. And everyone knows where everyone lives. And it was known throughout town that the author researching Nearest Green was living at Steve May's house on Main Street. And really, my car stuck out like a sore thumb—a white BMW utility vehicle in a town filled with Ford F350s and Dodge trucks.

I went into the living room and partially closed that window shade so I could see them without them seeing me. *Maybe they are after me after all*. I felt like one of the *Boston Globe* reporters in the movie *Spotlight* as I thought about how some folks at Brown-Forman might respond when they learned about my research.

I was afraid, but not of what they'd do to me. I've always been convinced I'm going to heaven, and that heaven is better than here. But I was afraid they were going to burn the house down.

I knew if I called Keith and told him about the man sitting out front staring at my license plate, he'd insist I return to LA immediately. But I was uncovering so much. Each passing day I was in Lynchburg, the more friends I made, and the more documents I found, the more progress I made toward securing a lasting legacy for the Green family.

I don't keep secrets from Keith, but I knew if I called him, my research would be all but finished. So I watched the man as he watched my car, and then he took off. Just like that. After almost five minutes of simply staring at my car, he threw his cigarette butt into the street and drove off.

Lynchburg is a great town with beautiful people, but I had to keep the truth at the forefront of my mind that I wasn't there on vacation. I was investigating a story that many people saw as damaging to their hometown hero—and the town's biggest source of revenue.

That night, like every night before, I brought my laptop, wallet, and phone into the bedroom, locked the door behind me, and prayed until I fell asleep.

CHAPTER

21

THE FILM crew, Miss Neat, and I all trooped out to Nashville. We had an important appointment: we were going to interview Nearest Green's eldest living descendant, and she was 106 years old. Time was of the essence.

Like so many other leads, this one came from Miss Neat and her "roots."

"You know his granddaughter is still alive, right?" she'd asked me.

"Huh? Really? Is that even possible?"

I immediately searched her name in our records: Nellie Mae Green. Miss Neat was right. She was Mammie's sister, and had grown up in Lynchburg. Aunt Nell had worked as a house cleaner and a window dresser at one of the department stores downtown. She'd also worked for Miss Mary Bobo's son in West Virginia. She'd married a man named Joe for the first time at twelve years old, then married him again when she was "fully grown."

"Miss Neat, I have to interview her before she's gone." I said it with such a rush of excitement I think I startled her a bit. "I don't know how much longer she could possibly live. Can you set that up?"

When we reached Aunt Nell's brown-brick and slate-roofed home in Northwest Nashville, we found her sitting in an armchair with a blanket draped over her. Her hair was pulled back into braids. I had hundreds of questions for her, but Miss Neat's voice carried better than mine. We looked through Miss Neat's photo album together, showing Aunt Nell photos of all the different Greens that she'd grown up with. But her memory was deteriorating. She couldn't recognize most of them.

What I really wanted to know was what Aunt Nell remembered about growing up in Lynchburg. She recalled being raised by various aunts and uncles. Her father, Jessie, came to visit often, but she didn't see him much. Children were often raised by other relatives and neighbors while the parents worked for white families day and night. It was not uncommon to call every adult around you "Aunt" and "Uncle" So-and-So. I grew up this way, too. It must have been my father's Southern roots and his years of picking cotton in the fields of Texas.

At one point, I shared the photograph that had run in the *New York Times* with Aunt Nell and asked if she recognized the man with Jack Daniel.

"Yes," she said as a wide smile took over her entire face. "That's my uncle!"

She couldn't remember, however, which one of Nearest's sons he was. She thought it could be her uncle Eli, but I'd found some known pictures of Eli and was fairly sure it wasn't him.

She was absolutely certain, however, that the man in the photo was one of her uncles.

"Aunt Nell," I said. "Have you ever heard of a man named Nearest Green?"

"Never heard of the man."

I knew Nearest had likely passed some ten or twenty years before Aunt Nell was born in 1910. There was no doubt she fully understood the questions, but she didn't recognize her grandfather's name. That was hardly uncommon—to this day, I'd have to call a relative to confirm the name of my own father's father. I'd been hoping for a silver bullet, I realized. That couldn't be Aunt Nell, even with all her age and wisdom.

WITHOUT AUNT NELL'S recollection of Nearest, I felt lost. The family tree was coming along, but I was missing huge swaths of Green descendants. Nearest had eleven kids, and so far everyone I had met was from Jessie's side of the family. His branch of the tree had led me to Aunt Nell and Mammie, who had kept the story alive on her porch with her grandchildren.

Mammie was a woman of strong faith, and she used to tell her grandchildren, "We don't look back. Our blessings lie ahead." This has long been my philosophy as well, so it was easy to take this to heart.

We looked into Minnie Green's family tree and saw that she had also married a Daniel brother—James Daniel. They'd had kids and a grandchild. But that was as far as any of us could trace Minnie's tree. And both of Eli's sons, Hubert and Henry, had passed away and hadn't had children.

Then I started to follow Nearest's son George. George's branch of the tree led to a rich area of research. I learned that, by all accounts, George was Jack Daniel's right-hand man at the new distillery site at Cave Spring Hollow.

George was born sometime between 1863 and 1866, and as a boy, he worked the farm with his brothers. On July 22, 1888, he married Mariah "Missie" Whitaker; they would go on to have a large family, too. They lived near County Line until George purchased property of his own on the other side of town in 1905.

On August 19, 1905, he put a down payment on "32 acres and 100 poles" of land, which he purchased from the estate of a Black man named Phillip Reese for $550.50. George was the highest bidder at a courthouse-steps sale. The hilltop property was located on what is today called Tanyard Hill Road in Lynchburg. It adjoined Jack Daniel Distillery and was bounded on all sides by Jack and Lem's land.

There was a mortgage detailed in the deed, which George continued to pay until 1935, likely using the money he made working at Jack's neighboring distillery. He grew tobacco and vegetables.

So much of what I learned about George and his children came from a remarkable woman named Helen Butler. After Aunt Nell, she was one of Nearest's oldest living descendants. When I met her in Indianapolis, she was in her eighties. But as a little girl, she had played on that land on top of the hill. Miss Helen was George Green's granddaughter. He had raised her there in Lynchburg, and she called him Daddy George.

Miss Helen had graduated from high school in Indianapolis in 1951 and worked in the magnetic tape division of RCA for over thirty years. She and her husband Bill were an entrepreneurial pair. He managed the Skaterina Roller Rink, and Miss Helen ran the cash register. The roller rink saw the Four Tops and Patti LaBelle perform before it burned down. After that, Bill and Miss Helen formed a janitorial business. She sent her sons to Lynchburg every summer so they would form a connection to that special place just as she had.

I found that to know Miss Helen was to love her, and to love her was to understand that what you see is exactly what you get.

"Daddy George always had a bunch of white sharecroppers taking care of his land," she said matter-of-factly. "And did you know Uncle Townsend [George's son] always had a chauffeur? He kept some of his money in the bank in Lynchburg even after he moved" to Indianapolis.

Townsend never learned to drive, she said, but "his chauffeur would take him back and forth to Lynchburg."

A chauffeur to drive him almost four hundred miles to do his banking! I made a note—obviously, I would need to look more into Townsend. But Miss Helen had more surprises.

"Uncle Townsend was the first Black man to have an alcohol license in Indiana. He had the most popular pub on the main drag. Everyone played music there." A quick search proved her memory was right—Townsend Green established Al's British Lounge in 1945, adjacent to Madame C. J. Walker's theater.

I knew liquor licenses were incredibly expensive back then. I wondered if Lem Motlow could have helped Townsend with the money. Indianapolis would've been a strategic city for a whiskey maker building back from Prohibition.

"Yeah, it's quite possible," Miss Helen told me. "Daddy George was the only person who could tell Lem what to do, and Lem would listen. Whenever Lem would get to drinking too much, they'd call Daddy George, and Daddy George would go over and get him straightened out. Lem didn't listen to too many people, but he listened to Daddy George."

B UT LONG before Lem could help anybody get a liquor license, he had to face the looming threat to his own distillery in Lynchburg and the spirits business overall. The temperance movement didn't fade away with the Civil War—in fact, if anything, the surge of soldiers and veterans struggling with drink helped fuel it in the postwar years. Temperance became a populist force that swept the nation. It was fueled by organizations like the Women's Christian Temperance Union, which held that "liquor caused poverty, abuse, and ill health," and the burgeoning women's rights movement.

What became known in the US as Prohibition started at the state level. Maine, Kansas, Georgia, North Carolina, and Mississippi all had various laws on the books outlawing some or all alcohol sales by the early 1900s, and North Dakota and Oklahoma both included Prohibition provisions in their constitutions when they became states. Laws about where was dry and where was wet varied widely state to state and county to county, but temperance seemed unstoppable. In a concession to the changing mood, Jack Daniel's began running ads encouraging buyers to "ask your doctor" and drink "pure" Jack Daniel's for medicinal needs.

In 1909, Tennessee outlawed the sale of liquor. Hundreds of saloons closed overnight in Nashville alone, along with the White Rabbit and Red Dog in Lynchburg. In 1910, a law prohibiting alcohol's manufacture went into effect. Jack Daniel Distillery made plans to shut down operations in Lynchburg and convert the distillery to a flour mill for the time being. The economic effects of the distillery's closing reverberated throughout Middle Tennessee. Until now, Jack Daniel's had bought nearly all the corn grown in Moore County, and it purchased supplies and stock from Franklin, Lincoln, and Bedford Counties. Only three hundred of the six thousand people in Moore County reportedly supported Prohibition, the *Nashville American* reported.

"There have been times in my life when I thought I worked, but the work I have done in the last few days filling orders convinces me that I never knew before what work really is," Lem Motlow told reporters the day Tennessee's Prohibition went into effect. "What will we do with Jack Daniel's old-time sour mash distillery at Lynchburg? Why, we will let it stand just the way it is for future use." Lem believed Tennessee's laws would change as people saw money leave the state that could have stayed in Tennessee and filled its coffers.

In the meantime, the plan was to relocate to St. Louis, Missouri, where laws were friendlier to whiskey makers—at least for the time being.

"We cannot move the distillery and it will remain intact, together with the other buildings," Lem wrote in the *Nashville Banner*. "If it is the law, we must obey it." He wrote that he was "sorry for the good people of Moore County, our friends and neighbors. They have always profited by Capt. Daniel's enterprise."

With the distillery closed, George Green needed to start raising crops in earnest to make money. He sharecropped on Lem Motlow's property, which adjoined his own.

In 1912, George borrowed $151 from Tom Motlow at Farmers Bank, with a year to pay it back. He used his personal property as collateral, which included, among other things, two horses and a mule, as well as the two-thirds share of the crops he was entitled to as a sharecropper.

IN 1910, Jack Daniel's left Lynchburg to set up shop first in Alabama, then with a distillery and warehouse facility on Duncan Avenue in St. Louis. Large white capital letters ran alongside one side of the building reading "Jack Daniel Distilling Co.," and a smokestack belched exhaust.

The new location ran ads in English- and German-language newspapers promising to "pay your car fare to and from the distillery if you buy one gallon," explaining, "this is our method of creating a demand in St. Louis for our goods. We know a trial will convince you of the Jack Daniel merit." The residents of St. Louis may have needed convincing. When the distillery later ran out of the thirty thousand gallons of whiskey it had barreled back in Lynchburg and tried making it in St. Louis, Lem Motlow found the taste of the whiskey noticeably different. Ben Green wrote that Lem had precisely duplicated the whiskey-making process but "always said he could not make whiskey elsewhere 'exactly like' the Jack Daniel Whiskey with water from Cave Spring in the Hollow. That water is different from any other water in the whole world."

The move to St. Louis corresponded with the beginning of the Great Migration. Black Americans left the South and headed north and west in search of work, social mobility, and freedom from Jim Crow laws.

When some of George Green's adult children relocated to St. Louis, they did so alongside a massive wave of new Black residents. They found that Black life there was not only segregated but confined, with many residents living in poor, overcrowded neighborhoods with inadequate housing, and others worried for their safety.

Redlining, racial covenants, and other discriminatory housing practices at the turn of the century contributed to what would later become known as the Delmar Divide, which saw Black people living in low-income areas north of Delmar Boulevard and white people living south of it in higher-income areas. Some Black neighborhoods, like the Ville, became known for their vibrant culture, but they were also established because of restrictive and racist housing laws.

In 1917, white citizens in St. Louis rioted, angered by the influx of twelve thousand Black residents seeking work during World War I. Two days into the violence, *Post-Dispatch* reporter Carlos F. Hurd wrote that he'd seen the "massacre of helpless negroes" and that "a Black skin was a death warrant." Afterward, thousands of Black citizens fled the city. Amid the racial tensions and violence, Nearest's grandchildren made St. Louis their new home for generations to come.

They lived there when Prohibition went into effect nationwide in 1920 through the ratification of the Eighteenth Amendment, which prohibited the "manufacture, sale, or transportation of intoxicating liquors" at the federal level.

WHEN I TALKED to Clay Risen about the passage of the Eighteenth Amendment, he called it an extinction-level event in the industry. There was a tectonic shift for alcohol manufacturers across the country. The new Jack Daniel's location in St. Louis closed down just as it had in Tennessee. Once again, people were out of work. If Charles, Jessie, and Otis Green did work at Jack Daniel's new St. Louis operation, it's not clear how long they were there before it closed.

Several Green family descendants distinctly recall Otis working at the Keeler-Morris Printing Company at one point. This was a factory where they made paper, glued it together, and cut it to notebook size. The notebooks were bigger than one of today's Post-it notes, but smaller than an eight-by-ten piece of paper. Otis often brought them home for the kids to write and draw on.

Times were tense for everyone, it seemed. In 1924, the *St. Louis Globe-Democrat* reported that Otis had found his brother Charles dead outside his home—he had been shot. Charles's wife Maggie reported that a pistol they kept in the house had accidentally gone off while they were having a late-night argument. She was taken into custody, but I couldn't find any further details.

GEORGE'S SON Townsend remained a tantalizing mystery to me, although I knew he'd taken a decidedly different route than his St. Louis–based siblings. Years later, I would meet a Green descendant who knew Townsend well and filled me in.

Dr. Geri Lovelace is a project manager living in Texas. She's Miss Helen's niece, George's great-granddaughter, and Nearest's great-great-granddaughter. Miss Helen didn't have any girls, so she spoiled her niece. "She cooked whatever I liked, that type of thing," Dr. Geri recalled. Miss Helen, Geri's mother Geraldine, and her Aunt Wilma "were very close. They usually spent the weekends doing grocery shopping together."

Dr. Geri grew up in Indianapolis and spent summers in Lynchburg throughout the 1960s. Growing up, Dr. Geri always knew she was related to Nearest Green. "It was always well-known, well documented," she recalled. Miss Helen and Geraldine thought it was important for the younger generation to travel from Indianapolis to Lynchburg every summer to stay connected to their family history. They would come down for three or four weeks at a time.

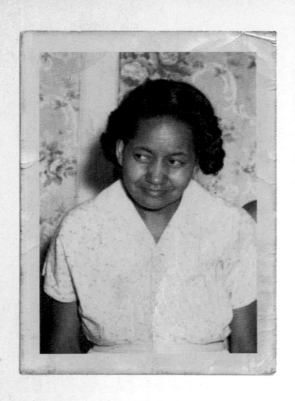

FOR MANY OF NEAREST GREEN'S descendants, this story
started on Annie Bell Green Eady's porch. Known as Mammie, she was
Nearest's granddaughter, and proudly passed down his story to her grandchildren. "My granddaddy used to make the whiskey for Jack Daniel,"
Mammie told them. "My granddaddy and his boys made the whiskey,
then Jack would come with his wagon and pick some up and take it into
town to sell." When I learned she was born on September 5, my heart
skipped a beat. Mammie, Ben Green, Clay Risen, and I all share the same
birthday—and traditionally, so did Jack. Without a known birth certificate, Jack Daniel's traditionally observed his birthday on September 5th
(until they recently shifted to celebrating for the entire month).

EVERYONE IN LYNCHBURG had a story about Elzie "Bus" Eady II. They would talk about his love for working at Jack Daniel's, his kindness to everyone, and the close bond he shared with his sibling, Sis Eady. They were thick as thieves, telling each other everything. Bus had a passion for watching golf on television, rivaled only by his enjoyment of being on the golf course. Everyone seemed to adore Bus, which is why I wish I had had the chance to meet him. He passed away on November 1, 2016, just as I was settling into Lynchburg, and I never had the honor.

WHEN I FIRST ARRIVED in Lynchburg and began researching this story, this photo was one of the only traces of Black people I could find in the Moore County Library. It shows Debbie Staples and her Aunt Geneva "Sis" Eady with a friend talking to a Tennessee State Trooper in Lynchburg. I was struck by the easy way Sis stood beside the cop car, just casually chatting with the white trooper inside. You could tell that she was equal—there was no question. *Who is this Black girl?* I thought. *I need to know who she is.*

WHEN I FIRST BEGAN introducing each family branch to the others, many were skeptical. Although they all knew they were descendants of Nearest Green, they did not know one another. The key to convincing each branch of their connection was Charles Green. Every family album contained pictures and postcards from him, sent as he traveled the world as a service member, sharing messages with all the Greens who originated from Lynchburg.

JOHN W. GREEN was Nearest's great-grandson. He graduated from Stowe Teachers College in St. Louis, Missouri, served as a clerk in the Post Office, and enlisted in the U.S. Air Force in 1949. A corporal, he was stationed at Perrin Airfield in Texas when he married Emma Lee Teague of St. Louis.

GERTRUDE GREEN-DANIEL was Mammie and Nellie Mae's mother, and Debbie, Jackie, Jerome, Jeff, and Victoria are Gertrude's great-grandchildren. Through researching Gertrude's place in a complicated and overlapping family tree, Miss Neat (Nearest's great-great-granddaughter by marriage, Juanita Dunlap) learned her family history and later helped me decipher who Nearest Green's descendants were.

WHEN I MET HELEN BUTLER, who was raised by her grandfather George Green on land that was later sold to Jack Daniel's, she was in her eighties and one of Nearest's oldest living descendants. Miss Helen taught me a great deal about the Green family and the special town of Lynchburg. "I don't know nothin' about no Jim Crow laws," she told me about her experience under segregation. "I never went through the back. The ice cream was in the front!" One of the most important things Miss Helen helped me with was identifying the Black man sitting next to Jack Daniel in the image seen around the world. "Yep! That's Daddy George," she proudly proclaimed, looking at him on the walls of Jack's old office at the Jack Daniel Distillery.

———— ⊰✦⊱ ————

J.B. MCGOWAN welcomed me into his home in Lynchburg immediately, even though I'd stopped by unannounced, and let me look through his late mother's photo album. J.B. and his twin brother, L.B., were born in 1934 and grew up in Lynchburg. The two did almost everything together, including working at Jack Daniel's, where many Black people worked in those days and where the pay—$2 an hour—was based on tenure, not race. The workplace culture would later go on to change following the death of Jack's great nephew Reagor Motlow.

THIS PHOTO of Nearest Green's grandson Jessie Green was my first glimpse into the high-society life of the Greens—high society by Lynchburg's standards, anyway. I didn't know much about the Masons, but many had told me they were a powerful group in the area and that many of Nearest's descendants were members. One of Nearest's relatives, through marriage, was a local Masonic grand master. I approached him to confirm if the insignia on Jessie Green's right ring finger was a Masonic ring and if the pendant on his lapel was as well. Although he didn't allow me access to their membership records, he confirmed that each of Nearest Green's sons and grandsons were Masons. He also shared that the pendant on the lapel signified that Jessie was a Shriner. When I asked him what a Shriner was, he said, "That means he was at the top of the Masons." Knowing there were Black and white Masons at that time, I asked if this meant he was at the top of the Black Masons. He replied: "He was a Shriner. That meant he was on top of both."

<hr />

GROWING UP IN LYNCHBURG had been "100 percent positive!" L.B. McGowan told me. He and J.B. recalled an idyllic childhood where young Black and white boys played together. "I wouldn't want to grow up anyplace else," L.B. said. He recalled "white only" bathrooms and water fountains at the courthouse under segregation and that a café called the Coffee Cup made him and other Black people enter through the back door—but once inside, Blacks and whites ate at the tables together. In other words, Lynchburg only followed the laws of the segregated South for the visiting public to see, but in private, they were friends and family.

———— ⟨✕⟩ ★ ⟨✕⟩ ————

NEAREST'S great-great-granddaughter Mamie Green sent her daughter, whom I came to know as Aunt Tee, to Lynchburg during the summers as a child. Whenever she and her Uncle Curtis went past Jack Daniel Distillery, Curtis would always say of Nearest, "You know, my great-grandfather taught him how to make whiskey." Mamie left a trove of late nineteenth- and early twentieth-century family photos after she passed away, which were incredibly helpful to me as I worked to piece together this story. Mamie loved her family deeply and was known for her big, kind heart. "She was a sweetheart," Aunt Tee said.

★

EVERY FRIDAY, I ran an ad in the Lynchburg paper looking for information. "Local Author Needs Your Help," it read. I got a call from a neighbor, who asked if the name Minnie Green meant anything to me. "That's Nearest Green's daughter. Can I come over and see what you've got?" I asked. It turned out to be a legal document; Minnie had sued someone. I hadn't gotten far with tracing Minnie's family tree, and it was amazing to see such a snapshot of Minnie's life—and exciting to see a document that wasn't a birth or death certificate or a simple line item in the census.

---⟨★⟩---

LEOLA DISMUKES, a descendent of Nearest's, and Margaret Tolley, a relation of Jack's, were such close friends that Lynchburgers referred to them as Bonnie and Clyde. Leola—known as Miss Dill—had worked for Miss Margaret, but people who knew them told me they probably hadn't gotten much work done—they'd stop every day and watch the soaps together. They were lifelong friends and thick as thieves. People in Lynchburg swear that when Miss Margaret died a month and a half after Miss Dill, it was because of a broken heart. Their photo demonstrates the friendship between Nearest and Jack's families better than words ever can.

———— ◆—✪—◆ ————

FEW THINGS brought Nearest and Jack's story to life like holding this "Jack Daniel" metal jug stencil in my hands. Joel Pitts found it with a metal detector at the Dan Call farm long ago, buried nine inches below the original distillery site. Joel pulled this piece of real, physical history—something Nearest or Jack may well have handled—from the earth, preserved and protected it, and waited until the time was right to hand-deliver it. "This is the only known Jack Daniel jug stencil in the world," he told me. "I've had it in my collection all this time, but if you're bringing this farm back to life and will be telling the story of Nearest Green, it belongs here with you."

CLAUDE EADY, pictured here, left, with Jack Daniel's brand historian Nelson Eddy, began working at Jack Daniel's in 1946 and was frequently featured in news stories about the distillery. The 2016 *New York Times* story about Nearest Green identified him as "a descendant" in a photo caption. "I'm ninety-one years old," Claude said when I reached out ahead of my first trip to Lynchburg. "I don't know that I'll still be here in two weeks' time. But if I'm still around, I'm happy to talk to you."

Claude and his wife, Dorothy, who I came to know as Miss Dot, were fixtures of the Lynchburg community. Miss Dot was a longtime teacher, and she told me that school integration in 1965 had been a "nonissue" in Lynchburg. "I didn't have any problem whatsoever with the teachers or the students or the parents," she said. "Everybody just knew everybody."

We worked out Claude Eady's family tree and found that he was related to George Green by marriage, not blood. But he and Miss Dot were instrumental in helping me meet town elders through their church and connect with Nearest's direct descendants. At the end of our first conversation, Miss Dot looked me deep in the eyes and said, "I don't know why I feel like I need to say this to you, but I am just so proud of you."

WHEN VISITORS turn off US Highway 231 in Shelbyville, they are greeted by the expansive 423-acre Nearest Green Distillery. Uncle Nearest became the fastest-growing Black-owned spirit brand of all time in 2020, and in 2023, we were the world's most awarded bourbon or American whiskey for the fifth consecutive year. With 250,000 visitors in 2023, it ranks as the seventh most-visited distillery in the world. The Nearest Green Distillery, which opened on September 5, 2019, received a congratulatory ad from Jack Daniel's in the *Tennessean*. That's the kind of class Jack himself would have applauded! We became the most successful Black-owned distillery globally after crossing the $100 million mark in sales in 2022. Thanks to the Nearest Green Distillery—and the hundreds of people who have worked tirelessly to spread its message of love, honor, and respect—Nearest's story is no longer in danger of disappearing.

"That was about as much as I could take," Dr. Geri recalled, laughing. "At the time I was going, they did not have indoor plumbing."

They took the Jack Daniel's tour often as kids and always heard stories about Nearest and his sons. Geraldine and Miss Helen would point out where George Green's property had been. Geri remembered hearing Mammie's stories about Nearest, and she inherited her mother's copy of the Ben Green book after she passed away.

In 1978 or 1979, her mom went on the tour again and discovered that Jack Daniel's had stopped talking about Nearest altogether. She called Dr. Geri.

"They white-washed my great-grandfather out of the story," Geraldine said.

Dr. Geri moved to Tennessee in the late eighties and attended Chattanooga State Technical Community College. At college in Tennessee, she did extensive research for a report on Nearest and Jack and met members of the Motlow family in the process. She knew the Daniel and Motlow families' reputation for taking care of funeral arrangements for the Greens who lived in Lynchburg. Not yet knowing that they had sold the distillery to Brown-Forman in the 1950s, she asked if they would contribute to her education. They agreed and paid for college as long as she attended in Tennessee.

She took her young children on the Jack Daniel's tour. "Okay, this is the true story," she would tell them, and fill in what they were leaving out about Nearest. Just as her mother had done with her, she pointed out George Green's land and told the kids how Nearest had taught Jack to make whiskey. She passed down "everything that I had been told," she said. "My kids have always known."

Geri's mom and aunts were close with Townsend, and she'd grown up knowing him well.

It turns out Townsend continued his grandfather's pioneering work in the liquor world—work that opened the door to prosperity and acclaim that Nearest could barely have dreamed of.

Born to George Green in 1900, Townsend spent his early years in Lynchburg before fighting in World War I. By 1931, he was living in Indianapolis, where he worked as a doorman at the Madame Walker Theater—the social and cultural center of the Black community of Indianapolis. The theater showcased African heritage—"spears, monkeys, striking sphinxes, and Moorish-style arches." It was the country's first Black-owned and -operated theater, and likely Indiana's only non-segregated movie theater.

He was married to Corina Porter, a stenographer at the Union Trust Company, and they adopted a daughter named Oreva. For decades, positive mentions of him abounded in the *Indianapolis Recorder*—pictures, quotes, praise, and mentions of his philanthropy. He was a man about town, and the vacations he took with Corina and Oreva made the society pages. In July 1937, he was lauded as the "pleasing manager of the Walker Theater." In the picture accompanying that article, Townsend appears serious but sly, bald, and in a suit and tie.

In October 1937, he was hailed as the "affable and efficient house manager" of the Walker Theater. And in 1945, Townsend and Corina opened a "swank British Lounge" at 643 Indiana Avenue, adjacent to the Madame C. J. Walker building at 617 Indiana Avenue. It was a true family operation, as Oreva eventually worked as manager of the lounge and Corina was in charge of the "food department." They received their retail liquor license and were determined to use it to the fullest, serving up Tom Collins and "invigoratin' Old Fashioneds." I have little doubt that Jack Daniel's would have been one of the whiskeys served. Townsend continued to run the lounge for another two decades; toward the end of his career, he was hailed in the *Indianapolis Recorder* as "one of the very best mixologists in the city."

Dr. Geri's high school prom had been held at the Walker Theater, close by Uncle Townsend's bar. During the dance, Geri went downstairs and stopped in to see him. She'd never been in a bar, and she was curious to see it. A teenager in a prom dress didn't cause much stir in the bar, but the sight of her brought Townsend right over.

"What are you doing here?" he asked. What he was really saying was, clearly, *Your mother's going to kill me.*

"I just wanted to say hi," she said. She wasn't supposed to be down there, but she couldn't be so close and not venture out.

Geri recently recalled with a chuckle that she was "just trying to be grown." There was no question of letting her have a drink while she was there. "He was too scared of my mother," she laughed.

In his later years, Townsend owned a gorgeous teal green Ford Thunderbird with a cream top. Dr. Geri remembered her Aunt Wilma driving Townsend around in it often. "I thought it was hers," she recalled. "She thought it was hers." But it was Townsend's, and when he and Wilma had a falling out, he gave the car to Geri's mother, who didn't have a license, so she could drive him. "And then my mother had to learn to drive," Geri recalled.

Dr. Geri and one of Miss Helen's sons looked after Townsend while he was ill at the end of his life. When Townsend passed away, she let her mother know, and she told the rest of the family.

"I don't know if it was the experience of being on the farm and seeing the whole cycle of life and death," Dr. Geri recalled. "But I've never been shaken by death. Especially if somebody's sick, I see it as they're no longer suffering."

MISS HELEN AND her family had begun to paint a much larger picture for me of the relationship between Nearest's sons, Jack's family, and the town of Lynchburg.

Miss Helen was proud of her Green lineage on her mother's side and just as proud of her father's side. That side of the family had owned a great amount of land in a place she called Portertown.

I'd heard of Portertown at least once before, back in Berry Chapel AME on my second visit to town. It was said to be a predominantly Black community right at the county line, with many people owning property and the town having its own school. The elders in Lynchburg had told me the town no longer existed.

Miss Helen said the town was not far outside Lynchburg, and that her great-grandfather donated the school. "Whenever you in Lynchburg, that's the word—Portertown," she said.

I hit the archives again.

I learned that Miss Helen's father, Odie Tate, was descended from Jarman H. Porter and his wife Martha. They were pioneers and landowners who'd arrived in Moore County in the 1800s. It's unclear whether they were brought there as enslaved people or somehow arrived on their own as free people, but they were prosperous farmers. The area where they lived was indeed known as Portertown, although I didn't find it labeled on any map. Adding -town to a family's name was just a colloquial way of saying that family owned a lot of land. Tolleytown and Bakertown, where Chuck Baker's family once lived, sat near Lynchburg, too. If the Motlows hadn't lived so close to the heart of town, there almost certainly would've been a Motlowtown.

Jarman and Martha's son Joe Porter and his wife lived in Portertown their whole lives. In August 1900, Joe provided a half acre of land for the Porter School, one of the first schools for Black children in the rural parts of Moore County.

When Odie and Annie Lee Green married, they united two Black families of great significance to the area. I learned, though, that lots of the little places named after their prominent landowning families faded away over time. That had happened with Portertown as the people left or passed away. Chuck Baker told me about a similar situation. There aren't nearly as many Bakers remaining in Lynchburg, so Bakertown, like Portertown, is known only to the old-timers now.

It was sad to think of a prosperous enclave of Black landowners, with so many ties to the Green family, just fading away with time. But I knew that's what it took for their children to become prosperous and educated. Take Miss Helen—education meant so much to her that her sons honored their parents' sacrifices on behalf of their schooling in her obituary: "Their day jobs and entrepreneurial passion enabled Miss Helen to send their children to some of Indianapolis's finest schools." Or Miss Helen's niece, Dr. Geri, who earned two master's degrees and a PhD. That Green family emphasis on education resonated with me when I considered the youngest generation of Greens I'd been meeting—those who were currently in high school. They couldn't be bothered to participate in all these amazing conversations about their ancestors, and some were getting Ds and Fs in class.

We had to do something for Nearest's descendants. It was clear they did not realize they came from such a rich legacy of excellence. Dr. Geri had told me that her grandmother Annie Lee Green had been raised to be sophisticated and proper.. Dr. Geri assumed her grandmother had gotten that from her mother, Missy Green. "White families in Lynchburg would have her come set things up" for elegant parties, Dr. Geri said of Annie Lee, because she knew the right way to set a table and so on. "She was taught to be genteel, taught to be refined. She always carried herself that way."

Education was incredibly important to the family. "It was always understood you will go as far as you can go," Dr. Geri said. "That's why I have a doctorate, because it's a terminal degree. Anything less was not acceptable to my mother."

If we could encourage Nearest's youngest family members to embrace excellence, their achievements could change the trajectory of his entire lineage moving forward.

It came to me then: we would send them to college and beyond. There was no changing the past, but knowing as young people that they were entitled to a four-, six-, or eight-year education was going to be the most transformational way to build generational wealth moving forward.

We were going to need much more money than we had. As Keith put it, we earned a nice living, but it wasn't "Let's send everybody to college" money. I was talking about making a lot of commitments, and things were moving fast.

"This math doesn't work," Keith said.

We could start a foundation and raise money through donations. Beyond that, we looked at our options. What if we sold Serenity Ranch? It was our dream home, and I never thought we'd leave it. But I was spending more and more time in Tennessee, and what we were being called to do here meant so much.

We decided to explore it and worked feverishly to try and figure out how to pay for it all. We'd also require the descendants to submit a family tree that tracked their relationship to Nearest, and they'd have to be related by blood rather than marriage. Without that cutoff point, the scholarships would balloon past any money the foundation could afford.

On the application form, we reminded descendants that neither Nearest nor Harriet could read or write, and that the scholarship was offered in order to "extend his legacy of excellence in work to excellence in education through his lineage."

I told Miss Helen that Keith and I had been asking ourselves, "Why did the Lord give me this story to pursue?" There were so many Green family members who could have done it.

"They should have," she agreed.

The foundation and scholarship would open doors that would help each forthcoming generation of Green descendants find opportunities to carry their family legacy forward.

A S I UNCOVERED George's branch of the family tree, I found relatives who the descendants living in Lynchburg never even knew existed.

I flew out to St. Louis to meet them and do more archival research. I visited the *St. Louis Post-Dispatch* newspaper morgue and the *St. Louis Globe-Democrat* collection. I spent several days researching at the University of Missouri–St. Louis Mercantile Library and Washington University St. Louis, as well as the National Archives at St. Louis. After reading about a 1911 fire at the distillery that thousands of people had showed up to watch, I then learned that it was scheduled to be razed days later to make way for the City Foundry STL development. I tracked down what I believe was a remaining piece of the building. If it was going to be knocked down, I had to see it.

Around the fenced-in backside of the building, which had clearly been a place of rest for many homeless people in recent years, I saw high windows up above my head. I jumped up as high as I could to grab a window opening and pulled myself up. Unfortunately, I couldn't see anything inside—the old, cracked windows were absolutely filthy.

To this day, I'm not sure if the building I visited was torn down or incorporated into the foundry.

In St. Louis, I found Theresa McGilberry, the elder who knows everything about that branch of the family. We bonded instantly, with me calling her Aunt Tee and her calling me Niecey.

She pulled out a metal box filled with photographs from the late nineteenth and early twentieth centuries. Her mother, Mamie, had recently passed away and left her this trove of family photos. On the very last page of a family album was an eighty-year-old article on Jack Daniel's relocation to St. Louis. It was the only article in the box. Aunt Tee told me she'd asked Mamie right before she died about any recollection of Jack Daniel's, but she'd had none. The family didn't know if they were connected to the distillery or not.

Aunt Tee was so excited to hear everything we'd learned about Nearest and to meet relatives she hadn't known she had on branches of the Green family tree.

When Aunt Tee was a young girl, she would travel from St. Louis to stay with her Uncle Curtis on his farm in Lynchburg for weeks or months in the summer. Country life was a treat and a relief. She helped out on the farm, which felt more like play than work to a city kid. Lynchburg was very special to her, and she loved her childhood summers there. She remembers Lynchburg in 1965 as a close-knit community where people walked up and down the streets and spoke to one another. People would stop at a stop sign and honk their horn and wave at you. In the country, particularly through the sharecropping system, Black people and white people lived on the same land, not divided into different parts of town. Two-thirds or more of Tennessee sharecroppers were white, and white and Black sharecroppers got to know one another well as they worked side by side. Her uncles took her to the family cemetery in Lynchburg when they visited; she was raised with a strong sense of family.

Whenever they went past Jack Daniel Distillery, Aunt Tee's Uncle Curtis would always say, "You know, my great-grandfather taught him how to make whiskey." That was the most she knew of Nearest back then.

In St. Louis I also met Mickey Murphy, Otis Green's step-grandson, who also remembered his childhood summers in Lynchburg as idyllic. He loved milking the cows and spending time with the animals—including the horse named Jack that his uncle kept. Mickey experienced a drastic change going to Lynchburg from the projects of St. Louis, where Blacks and whites lived such separate lives that he rarely saw his parents interact with white people.

Mickey remembered visiting the Jack Daniel Distillery plant in Lynchburg with his grandfather. The Motlows would quit whatever they were working on and sit and talk with Otis, reminiscing about when they were young. They'd send Mickey out to play in the lab and offices, and "they'd hang out all day together," Mickey recalled.

As another Green descendant recalled, "When people around the distillery came walking through, Reagor, Tom, or any of those guys, they'd always stop and say hello. They told us Lem did the same thing when he was alive. We ran around there and they never told us to stop. I can't quite explain it other than to say the Greens got a lot of respect around the distillery."

Aunt Tee heard a lot of family stories, too. She told me the reality of Charles Green's wife Maggie shooting him was that it had been self-defense. "If he beats you one more time, you need to shoot him," the Green family had told Maggie—and she did. Afterward, whenever the Lynchburg folks visited St. Louis, they stopped in to see Maggie. She would always have a sweet potato pie made and sliced up for the kids.

I was moved by the respect and love the family had for Maggie. They'd stood by her doing what she had to do to save her own life.

"The family looked at her as a treasure," Aunt Tee said.

She didn't know much more about it, though. "That's how we grew up," she recalled. "Kids didn't get in grown folks' conversations." If they were playing cards or whatever the adults did when the doors were closed, "we weren't allowed in the room."

For Aunt Tee, the most important part of Nearest's story was that Nearest was *not* enslaved by Jack Daniel—and that for the post–Civil War part of his distilling career, he'd been a free man. His whiskey wasn't an example of something white men stole from him. "No, my great-great-grandfather wasn't Jack Daniel's slave," she says proudly. "He did this. This was his livelihood, his work, and he was proud of it." And like me, she shares an affection for Jack Daniel. She respects the fact that he did not enslave people when so many around him did.

"I could just imagine them walking down the street together," she told me, "this tall Black man and this little short white man, thick as thieves, best friends."

BY THE TIME national Prohibition ended and Tennessee's liquor laws changed to allow the Lynchburg distillery to reopen in 1938, George Green was in his seventies. He'd spent the last three decades working the land that adjoined Cave Spring Hollow. It must have been bittersweet seeing the distillery that had both sustained and scattered his family reopen its doors in Lynchburg for the first time in nearly thirty years.

In 1935, George had finished paying off his thirty-two acres of land. This was during the depths of the Depression, when numerous Black and white families across the country were losing their land, and here was George, owning his outright.

What had allowed George to hold on to his land?

The more I looked into Farmers Bank, which is still around today, the more it made sense. Situated between Jack Daniel Distillery and

Miss Mary Bobo's, it was a "little bank," as Joel Pitts put it, but known throughout the area. The bank handled Jack Daniel's payroll and the checking and savings accounts of its employees, but not the distillery's funds. "We are, as the name says, a farmer's bank," president Tom Motlow said. They financed farm mortgages, homes, cattle, or even just a flock of turkeys.

In July 1929, Tom saw the financial crash coming that ultimately caused the Great Depression. "The collapse was overdue," he recalled. "The strange thing was that it had not already happened." He sold all the bank's assets that he could and socked the cash away.

When the crash came that October, he was ready. There was a run on Farmers Bank, as there were on countless banks across the country. The first person in line was, appropriately, a farmer.

"He had three thousand dollars saved, and he wanted it, and he was afraid I could not pay it to him," Tom recalled. "I handed him three one-thousand dollar bills." The farmer walked out grinning, and Tom turned to the next customer. Other people left the line to talk to the farmer, and word soon spread that there was no panic at the bank.

"The line in front of me just kind of dissolved," Tom recalled. At the other window, the cashier was busy taking back withdrawals. In a few minutes, that first farmer was back inside, too, redepositing his three thousand dollars.

The residents of Lynchburg "concluded our bank must after all be a safer place than some woodpecker hole," Tom said. "So the crash never happened to us."

In 1933, the federal government closed all the banks in the country for approximately one week and allowed them to reopen only after they could prove they were solvent. While Farmers Bank waited the minimum amount of time to reopen, it was famously "closed in the front and open in the back"—meaning that Tom made personal loans in cash to those who needed them.

In later years, Tom kept up his personal loans, loaning money to locals who posed risks the bank couldn't justify taking on. "It is a kind of gambling, betting on my faith that human beings are fundamentally good," he said. "I have lost that bet only infrequently."

He cited his uncle Jack Daniel's example. "I had seen him set a man up in farming or in a business, and then the man fail, but Uncle Jack would back him again and again. He would say, 'Here, take this money and try again. You'll make it next time.' Uncle Jack would not accept failure, either in himself or in his fellow man."

George Green died at the age of seventy-four, on January 15, 1941, and bequeathed his land to his children. They sold the land to Jack Daniel Distillery after he passed away over the objections of his entrepreneurial granddaughter, Miss Helen, who encouraged her mother not to sell the family land—or at least to wait and sell it for more.

Today it sits at the heart of the distillery, overlooking the entire operation.

KEITH AND I started to wonder about producing a commemorative whiskey bottle in honor of Nearest to fund the scholarship. The idea tapped into my original instincts—that inner tug I'd had to secure the intellectual property rights after learning about Nearest's life.

We talked it over and explored some options. We quickly learned there was really no middle ground between a giveaway novelty label and a full-fledged line of whiskey produced and distributed on a commercial scale. To do even a run of five hundred commemorative bottles properly—to elevate them above a vanity label slapped on a generic whiskey—would require a vast amount of capital. And honoring Nearest with a bottle meant the quality of the whiskey inside it would be critical. Bottling a high-quality whiskey in the style and up to the level Nearest would've made meant dealing with regulations, production costs, and nearly impenetrable distribution channels.

We learned that many brands entering the whiskey industry begin by sourcing whiskey—in other words, buying another company's distilled product and blending it themselves. The majority of people I knew were sourcing their alcohol from a company called MGP, and that's where everyone we talked to suggested we source introduction whiskey. But they were based in the Midwest, and there was absolutely no way in the world that we could use a product coming out of anywhere but Tennessee and be true to Nearest Green.

To be Tennessee whiskey, the product we sourced would have to be distilled, aged, and bottled within the state. It had to go through the Lincoln County Process of charcoal mellowing, and it had to happen *before* it went into a new charred oak barrel.

In most things that involve food or drink, the recipe for something is as important as how it is made. But I learned quickly that in the whiskey world, the recipe—what we call the mashbill—doesn't matter nearly as much as the processes you apply to it and the barrel you age it in. Whiskey itself is pretty simple: it's made up of grain, yeast, water, and time. To be bourbon, which Tennessee whiskey is legally categorized as, it has to contain at least 51 percent corn. More rye means more spice. Barley breaks down sugars. You can use different variations of grain and have them all turn out delicious. They're just different versions of delicious. After you combine your ratio, you've got to make a mash: ground-up grains combined with some warm water. In the old days, a distiller would have a millhouse powered by a creek on the property, similar to the original Jack Daniel Distillery No. 7 on the Dan Call Farm.

The Lincoln County Process—the charcoal mellowing method Nearest taught Jack—was critical, of course. It removes impurities without adding anything new to the whiskey. The natural carbon in the wood pulls congeners like fusel oils—by-products of fermentation that give you headaches and hangovers when you drink—out of the liquid that goes in the barrel.

The barrel you use is also essential. If you don't know where your wood came from, that means you don't know what soil the tree grew in. The soil in Tennessee creates tastes very different from the soil in

Kentucky. The soil in Kentucky is different from the soil in Indiana, is different from the soil in Texas and in Georgia and so on.

If you take regular white bread and turn it into toast, it tastes completely different. Barrels are charred for the same reason. It gives the whiskey a bit of caramelization, and the sap from the trees gives it a certain sweetness. But the sap will also taste different depending on the soil. The wood in the barrel will absolutely change the taste—I learned that 70 percent of the flavor comes from the wood. Even the place the barrel is stored in the warehouse can change the taste.

Every part of that process represented high costs. It was far more than we were prepared to think about.

I could also picture the conference rooms full of lawyers Brown-Forman would have ready to throw at us the moment we tried something like that. I was confident we'd win—our attorney Jane Shay Wald said, "Oh, I hope they bring it," and Keith recalls her practically purring for battle. She's unequivocally one of the best in trademark law, chairing the division in one of the top law firms in the country, so she knew the law was on our side. We'd worked with her for many years and knew she wasn't one to be trifled with. But I was uneasy about diving headfirst into a monumental legal fight. I'd never been in any form of lawsuit in my entire life, and I wasn't thrilled with the idea.

We went back and forth about it, asking ourselves, *Is it worth it?* Between starting the Nearest Green Foundation, buying the Dan Call Farm, and this, it would mean we were probably never going to leave Tennessee. It was a big decision, with our families back in LA, and we'd be leaving everything behind that we loved.

"I could be a whiskey mogul," Keith joked.

But the production and distribution issues were cost-prohibitive—into the millions—and beset with obstacles. A commemorative bottle would be an absolute headache, and, I concluded, basically setting ourselves up for failure.

"YOU KNOW," SHERRIE MOORE said one day, completely out of the blue, "if you ever decide to honor Nearest with a bottle, I'll come out of retirement to make sure you get it right." We were standing together in the parking area on the Dan Call Farm after one of our frequent visits.

Keith and I had no idea what she was talking about. It turned out, in addition to being a realtor, Sherrie had worked at Jack Daniel's as the director of whiskey operations, working for the company for thirty-one years. Growing up, Sherrie's family connection to Jack Daniel hadn't seemed like a big deal to her; it was just a part of normal life in Lynchburg. But she'd gone to work at the family business after college, and as she'd worked her way up, she developed a deep sense of pride in the distillery.

We were shocked to learn all this. Beyond that, we were skeptical. Was she a spy? Was she only saying that to get information out of us about our plans? In Lynchburg, it was hard to know who to trust. Uneasy, we brushed it off and changed the topic.

Sometime later, Sherrie brought it up again on the phone. I still didn't know how much to trust her or what to think, but I knew by then how much she loved whiskey and missed being in the business. It was an interesting idea and a moving offer. The revelation of her career at Jack Daniel's was serendipitous in a way that made me certain this wasn't a coincidence. I've always believed there are moments in life so perfect, so bespoke, that only God could have tailored them. These are divine appointments, and in retrospect, this was surely one.

For now, the idea was there.

CHAPTER

IN THE meantime, I was fully absorbed in my research and interviews. That tends to happen with whatever I'm working on. And I was still heavily involved in Grant Sidney and my investments. I've always done many things at one time. Working on multiple things at once is better, most of the time, than having to zoom in and do one thing at a time. This is true in my life as a CEO, and it was especially helpful with unraveling Nearest's story. I let him become essentially a second full-time job and Lynchburg a second home.

Keith was working in LA, and Stephani came down to Tennessee with me sometimes. But often, I'd travel down and research by myself. Thank goodness for Chuck. I ate his food almost every day. I'd go into Barrel House BBQ every few days and get a rack of ribs from Chuck to take home and eat on my own.

Ever since I was a little girl, I've loved exploring new places. Mundane things become magical when you're in a new place with new accents, new ideas, and new ways of doing things. Unlike at home, where I could catch myself not really looking at the ocean or some other source of beauty I'd become a little too accustomed to, staying someplace new made me pay constant attention—which let me truly see.

I found that what defined a good life in LA wasn't necessarily the same as in Lynchburg. Most people lived into their nineties and even their hundreds, and their definition of success was an old-school one: You worked at the same job your whole life. After thirty years, you retired with a pension. Then you got to sit on the porch with everybody else, whittling and gossiping, with no set time to be anywhere on any given day, except church, for the next thirty years.

The whole town was like that. Everybody wanted to talk, and everyone was so happy to be heard. As I interviewed folks, I relied on something I'd learned about myself from my past books: I'm an intentional observer. I listen closely, and the things people say and do make a big impression on me. Sometimes they stay with me for years. Being an intentional observer makes me a strong learner.

I was constantly having conversations and listening closely—with Chuck, Miss Neat, Miss Dot, Joel, Christine, Aunt Tee, Miss Helen, whoever could connect me to more information about Nearest.

LYNCHBURG IS THE kind of place where people have crates of papers stashed in their attics and huge family Bibles in their living rooms—items that have never seen a scanner or been available on Ancestry.com. Stephani and I combed through everything from country archives and local museums to dusty attics and damp basements, tracking down old files and taking oral histories from more than a hundred Green and Daniel descendants.

Every Friday I ran an ad in the Lynchburg paper soliciting information from local families who might have documents they'd like to share. "Local Author Needs Your Help," it read. I started getting phone calls at all hours from different families' descendants. Sometimes

I'd wake up in the morning to find documents related to something I was looking for waiting on my front windshield. People would want to show me photos they found in their basements or faded legal documents. Once I got a voicemail from a neighbor to the Dan Call Farm who asked if the name Minnie Green meant anything to me.

"That's Nearest Green's daughter. Can I come over and see what you've got?"

I'd long been looking for anything beyond the census and word of mouth that proved Minnie lived. It turned out to be a legal document; Minnie had sued someone. My neighbor's wife used to work at a courthouse in the area and still had several boxes of historical legal documents she'd rescued from one disaster or another in a box in the basement. It was amazing to see such a snapshot of Minnie's life—and exciting to see a document that wasn't a birth or death certificate or a simple line item in the census.

I'D OFTEN GO to Miss Neat's house in Tullahoma to study her family trees. Miss Neat lived in a brick house on a quiet street. She'd come right to the front door and lead me into her living room, which was beautiful and cozy. In a glass case on the far wall, she kept dozens of Black figurines she took around to local schools to tell historical stories.

We pored through records. There was no record of Dan Call owning people, but renting enslaved people was a common practice in the South before the Civil War. If someone couldn't afford to purchase an enslaved person, or if they needed one with a very important skill (like distilling), they could legally lease a person. In Tennessee in 1860, only one in four white Tennessee families owned people, meaning 75 percent of white families didn't. Does that mean they didn't use slave labor? Absolutely not. A sizable chunk of that 75 percent *leased* enslaved people from enslavers. I also didn't find it odd that no written agreement was uncovered since Dan Call, like all the distillers other than Jack, was a Freemason. I'm certain they did a great deal of handshake agreements within that Masonic lodge.

Lease arrangements of enslaved people were typically for a year, but it could be by the month, week, and even day. The lives of enslaved people were terribly uncertain, and they were constantly separated from their families. Enslaved people whose labor was leased did all kinds of work. Some were field hands, some built infrastructure, some worked in tobacco factories, and, yes, some were distillers. Many, like Nearest, were highly skilled.

Miss Neat pointed out that one of the census records listed Maryland as Nearest's birthplace, and with that possibility in mind, we started to investigate how Nearest might have come to Lynchburg.

From 1827 to 1855, it was illegal to import enslaved people into Tennessee. However, what enslavers could do is go to other states, buy enslaved people there, and bring them to Tennessee *for their own use.* Moreover, Tennessee's ban on the importation of enslaved people was full of loopholes, and many still managed to sell them there even before interstate trading became legal in 1855.

Tennessee was smack in the middle of the journey enslaved people made from the tobacco South (the mid-Atlantic regions like Maryland and Virginia) to the cotton South (Mississippi, Alabama, Louisiana). Gangs of men, women, and children in groups sometimes numbering into the hundreds were marched on foot on a monthslong journey that was often in the blistering summer heat.

I pulled tax records for all the small distilleries and warehouses operating in the area at the time. I thought perhaps Nearest had started out as an enslaved person to one of the distillers closer to County Line, like Tolley & Eaton or Hiles & Berry. These weren't permanent structures like we have today—many distillers moved locations annually to access a better water source or be closer to a train station. I thought one of the best ways to trace Nearest's movements would be to follow the distillers'. But we still couldn't find him.

Importantly, it was illegal for an enslaved person to sell alcohol. So Nearest couldn't bottle up what he himself made, walk through Lynchburg, and hand it out.

Neither of us was able to find out anything about Harriet beyond her maiden name, either. Harriet was a Flack, and the Flack family was based in Fayetteville, to the south of Lynchburg and closer to the Alabama border. But Harriet herself seemed to have appeared out of nowhere and then disappeared again. Outside of knowing she was the mother of Nearest's eleven children, I didn't know anything about her. I tried to tell myself that knowing her maiden name was enough. But Harriet was just as responsible for the family living on as Nearest was. She'd been pregnant or breastfeeding for some fifteen or twenty years.

Much like with Nearest, records for Harriet—primarily her adult children's death certificates, filled out by record-keepers with varying degrees of education decades after her own death—show iterations of her name. I found her listed as "Harret Flock," "Harriet Flax," "Har. Flock," "Harriet Unknown," and even "June Flack." She probably grew up enslaved in Tennessee, but beyond that, I knew little else about her life.

It's possible that Harriet and Nearest had the same enslaver, at least by the time the records show them together on Call's Farm. Another possibility is that her enslavers were brothers Elijah and Thomas Flack—early settlers of Lincoln County who were originally from North Carolina. The brothers lived in Petersburg—about twenty miles from Lynchburg—and both owned enslaved women in Harriet's age range. Elijah was a large landowner who likely left his enslaved people to his children when he died in 1852, as they do not appear in his estate sale records. Elijah's son Alvis Flack, who lived in Lincoln County, directed when he died that all his enslaved people be sold except for three "reserved for the use and benefit of my wife." An enslaved woman named Harriet was among them—Harriet Flack, it would seem. Flack's wife Susan may have rented Harriet to Dan Call herself or sold her to someone else who did.

After emancipation, Harriet moved closer to town with Nearest and their children, where she kept house. By 1880, they had settled in the County Line area just north of Lynchburg with nine of their eleven children. The 1880 census is the last record we have of her.

Perhaps Harriet was a woman of faith with a larger community around her. Perhaps she had friends and found joy in motherhood. Call was seen as benevolent, furnishing married enslaved people with a little house, some pigs, a cow, and a garden plot. But I think about their small cabin full of children, cold in the winter and hot in the summer, with the men always busy at the still. It would have been an isolated place, at best, for Harriet to spend her life. And it's entirely likely she knew she was going to be forgotten. I couldn't let that happen.

CHAPTER

WHEN WE walked the property of the Call Farm together, Ed McGee was able to point out the exact footprint of the original distillery and gristmill. Their ruins were still standing, sunken into the ground, when he bought the property. The stillhouse was tiny even in its heyday, by all accounts. Nearest and Jack weren't making massive quantities of whiskey out there at that time, but what they were making was the best.

Ed would often give his recollection of events, and Ophelia would chime in—"That's not true. That's not what happened"—and give her own version. Ed was knowledgeable about the history of the land, but it had all been passed to him through oral history and some educated guesses.

Ed and his father stumbled over Nearest and Jack's gristmill while they were digging a pond for his cows. He hired people to remove the two millstones from the ground, but each of them weighed two thousand pounds. It took a lot of effort to pull the first one out.

"After we saw how heavy the first one was, I said, 'Leave the second one,'" he recalled to Keith and me. "Just fill it in."

They used the original limestone from the gristmill to fortify the pond bed and let the water from the spring flow directly into it.

The property is rich with these springs. Around the side from the main house is the kitchen. If you keep going straight, there's a spring box—a little structure to protect the spring from dirt and leaves—that still has water beneath it. Another just like it sits behind the house. Ed told me that moonshiners used that one during Prohibition and even into Ed's day. They had a little distillery back there to make moonshine. Ed told them, "If you get caught, I didn't know you were here."

ELSEWHERE ON THE FARM, the renovations were in full swing. We got the fence installed, drained Ed McGee's pond, built a small road, and installed a pipe underneath it to divert the natural spring. We also excavated the big, white limestones that had lined the now empty pond and relocated them around the property. If you walk it today, you'll see a few sitting near the house. But we never found the second millstone. We dug and dug and dug. We brought in experts with radar equipment to scan underground. Eventually I had to make the call that it was getting too expensive. We had no idea where it was, and it had been some forty years since Ed McGee last saw it. At two thousand pounds and covered with water, we concluded it must have sunk deep into the ground and kept sinking. It's still down there to this day.

We had architects who specialize in restoring and rebuilding historic homes come out to the Call Farm. Many of these homes built around the same period of years are very similar. We were able to reconstruct the original blueprint. The architects showed us the layout of the original house, with the boys' room off the stairwell and the girls' room, which you could only access by going through the parents' bedroom, on the other side of the floor. Based on the blueprints, we were able to reinstall a staircase near the front of the house that had been removed.

At one point, the men who'd been working on the roof came into the house very excited. "Ma'am, we think you have a third chimney right there between them two walls," they said, pointing between the living room and kitchen. They asked for permission to carefully remove the walls. Just as they suspected, there was a chimney made of stone, where the large belly stove once stood. The only thing keeping the nearly two-hundred-year-old chimney intact was that it had been smashed between two walls. We watched as the workers began to number each of the stones as quickly as possible before the thing came crashing down. Once they were all numbered, the men carefully dismantled it and then rebuilt the entire thing stone by stone.

We pulled up the old shag carpet to reveal the original wood floors. We removed the faux wood paneling on the walls to reveal hand-painted wallpaper with roses. We also tore down the brick dairy building and the barns that weren't original. We restored everything as accurately as possible to how it was when Nearest and Jack lived on that property.

Many of the Green family believed that Nearest and his family had lived in the large white guest house at the entrance of the property. We had the architects pull back layers of paint and Sheetrock to reveal what was once a dogtrot cabin—two disconnected rooms that share a connecting roof—but we were met with disappointment for the second time.

"We're sorry," they said. "There's nothing original here" other than the main beam that ran the length of the house, connecting the two halves. "Everything else has been replaced." The guest house had nothing to tell us. Dan Call and his family had lived there when they moved to the property, before the main house was built.

An archaeologist from the University of Kentucky who came to examine the property believed that the way the foundation stones were positioned indicated there were three slave cabins on the back of the property, past the pond and near the spring. Nearby were pipes which would have transported water to the distillery and gristmill.

While we excavated, I took over the big front room of the farmhouse, which was believed to have been Dan Call's parlor, and executed my earlier vision of a research room. I gathered the documents I'd found, mid–nineteenth century maps, pictures of Nearest's family, and other artifacts. I laid out evidence I'd brought back from my research excursions to Washington, DC; College Park, Maryland; Atlanta, Georgia; St. Louis, Missouri; Indianapolis, Indiana; and Nashville, Tennessee.

Stephani helped me construct what she'd taken to calling the "crime scene," a giant wall of photos, documents, maps, and a massive family tree, all connected. Her dad, a police officer, had taught her to think as an investigator, and she brought that mindset to untangling the mysteries of Nearest's life.

The old house was well-made but drafty. It didn't have much cell or internet signal—it's basically out in the middle of nowhere—but we had it outfitted with a desk, shredder, and safe. Maps and photos and documents covered every surface, including the walls.

It was "a whole crazy-woman setup," in Keith's words.

I remember walking the property and remarking to Keith that I couldn't believe buying the Call Farm had worked. Some random people from LA swooped into town and purchased the childhood home of Jack Daniel? That was almost corporate malpractice.

These people are asleep at the switch, Keith thought.

CHAPTER

THE MANAGEMENT of Brown-Forman was familiar with the various members of the Daniel and Motlow families as an on-and-off presence in their world. Jack Daniel's is a big, active brand, and there were lots of occasions for these folks to reach out and indicate they weren't as happy as they could be about a new ad or bottle. The company was sensitive to their vocal critiques. I know now that Mark was getting a lot of pressure from shareholders and the executive team.

"What's happening?" they would ask. "We keep hearing about this woman down in Lynchburg." There was a general *Have you shut her down yet?* sense behind the questions, he recalled.

I knew the folks at Brown-Forman had been waiting for me to get in touch, and I was pretty sure they knew I'd talked to a great number of people in Lynchburg. They'd assumed I'd be coming to them next, but I didn't want them changing the narrative for the purpose of their brand image. That's not what Nearest's story was about.

My plan was to finish my research and write my book. I'd ask Nearest's descendants if there was anything they wanted me to say to

Jack Daniel's, or anything that they wanted Jack Daniel's to do for them.

Then I'd give Jack Daniel's an advance copy of the book but warn them no changes would be made. I would not require Brown-Forman to act. I would solely share the history I uncovered, and it would be up to them to decide if they wanted to tell the full story of Nearest Green. My plan was to use my public relations skills to share the story with the world. I'd be telling one story from the home of the original Distillery No. 7, and they'd be down the road telling an entirely different story, if that is what they chose.

I later learned the company had tried telling portions of the story at least a few times during the 2000s. They even featured a photo of Debbie singing in the 2015 Squire calendar with the text, "Her family's musical heritage goes back to Mr. Nearis Green, a well-known country fiddler. He was also the distiller at the Reverend Call's still, where Jack learned to make Tennessee sippin' whiskey. Debbie proudly carried on both Green family traditions. She works down at the distillery and sings. Of course, most agree, she's got something to sing about."

But it added up to small gestures and false starts. "We just didn't realize how big a story it was," Nelson said. When it took off in the *New York Times*, his reaction was, "Oh my goodness, we need to do some greater diligence on this and rush back and start looking at things with a new lens." I sympathize, I do. But I really wish they'd done some of that work before the *New York Times* carried the story around the globe. It was a terrible, decades-long mistake not to see the value in Nearest and Jack's story. And it had real consequences—for Brown-Forman, for Lynchburg, and for Nearest's descendants who remained at Jack Daniel's and were denied the truth for many years.

CLAY RISEN, who grew up in Nashville, later shared that he'd had a hard time getting a sense of the weight of the Nearest Green story for

Lynchburg residents. "You hear people talk about, 'Well, we all knew [Nearest's story],'" Clay said. But "no one celebrated it. No one talked about it as anything special. And why was that? One way to read that is, 'Oh, it's because it was normalized. And it was understood that Black people make a contribution to the community.'" On the other hand, Clay suggested, it might be read as, "'Yeah, that's something we don't talk about because we don't like the implications of it.'"

Clay later told me it's often hard for outsiders (like me) to understand that these "bitter ironies or weird nuances about race relations are just taken as part of the water in the air" in the South. The ironies of having people like Nearest play such a pivotal role in Southern culture are "well-known and utterly uninteresting to a lot of people," Clay said. For many of them it's, "Well, that's the way it is."

The *Heritage of Moore County* book was a wonderful repository of history, and there were more Black people collected within its pages than I'd found through any other source. I learned what life had been like after the Depression, through World War II, and into the civil rights era through its residents' own words. A member of the Bobo family wrote about the way Moore County was "racially segregated during the late thirties, forties, and fifties," but that there was "a very good relationship between the blacks and whites."

He went on to list a great many people whose names had become familiar to me, including quite a few of Nearest's descendants or members of their families—Sis Eady, Hyram Daniel, Clinton "Possum" Daniel, L. B. and J. B. McGowan, Dill Dismukes, Hubert and Henry Green. Sis had worked at Holt's appliance store; Hyram Daniel was the Farmers Bank custodian; Possum Daniel was the blacksmith. Hubert Green was in charge of the cemetery, and Henry was employed at Price's Service Station.

Other people fondly recalled watching the Black baseball team play on the weekends. The team was full of talented players and often won their games against other Black teams from Shelbyville or Tullahoma. They wore red hats and socks and unofficially called themselves the Jack Daniel's team. Plenty of white people seemed to watch both the Black and the white teams, which traded off weekends at the high school field. "There were enchanting Sunday afternoons spent watching the Black community's baseball games," a white man named Bill Copeland recalled.

"I remember 'Ham' Daniel was playing third base," a white man named Frank Larry Majors wrote about a Sunday game when he was seven or eight years old. The batter hit a line drive, hard and fast, and Ham didn't have time to turn to catch with his gloved hand. "He just leaped into the air toward the baseline and caught it with his bare hand. I've never seen anything like it before nor since," Majors recalled.

As time went on, Blacks and whites alike moved away for better job prospects. As modernity encroached, electricity and automobiles arrived, and family farming became less sustainable.

The first official school for Black children in Lynchburg was a church. Highview School was established on land deeded to the Moore County Board of Education in 1928 by a group of Black trustees that included Possum Daniel. It started as a one-room schoolhouse in 1928, heated with a pot-bellied stove, and with an outhouse a few yards away. Students walked to school—some for miles, and some just a few blocks from Elm Street.

Miss Dot said students missed out on some things—there weren't opportunities for sports or choir—but she was proud of the education she and her fellow teachers provided. In 1950, a series of improvements and additions began—a new classroom, a stage, a kitchen, a cafeteria, bathrooms, and an office were all built in just a couple of years. Gas heat arrived in 1957, and a house for the principal was added. In the late 1950s, Jack Daniel Distillery donated money for a gym.

Around the same time, outlying communities began sending their white students by bus to Moore County High School in Lynchburg. Miss Helen recalled walking to school in the thirties and forties with the other Black children along the dirt road. When the bus carrying white kids from outside Lynchburg went past, "They would throw apple cores and other things out the windows at the Black kids," she said. She remembered keeping an eye out for the bus and hiding in a ditch with the other Black kids until it passed by.

When Black students graduated from Highview School, which went up to the eighth grade, they couldn't attend Moore County High School in Lynchburg, even though it sat only a ten-minute walk away from Highview School on Mechanic Street. They had to find ways to get to Fayetteville, Shelbyville, or Pulaski to pursue a high school education. The bus hadn't been established yet, and determined pupils had to travel to stay with family near the school or attend only when they were able to get a ride. Most of Lynchburg's Black high school students went to West End High School in Lincoln County.

I knew, of course, that there was no individual city in Tennessee that could have chosen not to be segregated. The schools, the courthouses—any public building—remained segregated. I found a local history pamphlet called *From 1810 to 2010: Black History & Contribution in Lincoln County* that explained how school integration eventually came to be: "No one had attempted to integrate the Lincoln County High School system," so the school board chose not to comply with *Brown v. Board of Education* when it was decided by the Supreme Court in 1954. Eleven years later, three young Black men attended Lincoln's white Central High School, kick-starting integration across two counties. Black Lynchburg students studying in Fayetteville were transferred to Moore County High School, and a year later, the final class of students at West End graduated, and the school closed.

Jo Anne remembers there being a lot of concern around the school integration. "That was a big thing," she said. "Are they going to be accepted?"

But just as Miss Dot recalled, everything went well. Elementary school integration followed a year later. Oscar McGee was a young boy when the schools were integrated, and he remembers it as a bittersweet time. "It was sad leaving Highview," he recalled. But going to the new school wasn't too strange. "We knew most of the kids anyway. We worked in fields with them and everything."

"It was basically a nonevent," John T. Bobo told me. "It was nothing, because we'd all grown up together in that small village."

THERE WERE two consistent locations that came up whenever I asked about the Lynchburg elders' experience with segregation: the drugstore and a café called the Coffee Cup. Both catered to out-of-towners coming to the county seat to visit the Moore County Courthouse.

"Black people knew that you didn't sit on the stool at the drugstore," Miss Neat recalled, "so I never attempted to do anything like that." She remembered a girlfriend who did, only for the druggist to tell her to get up because it was a white-only establishment. "But we could go to the back door and order whatever we wanted," she recalled.

Miss Neat and her friends would walk down from Dog Row on Sunday afternoons to get ice cream at the Coffee Cup. The Black kids knew they had to go through the back door, but it was really great ice cream, so they put up with it. The only other Black people who really went to the Coffee Cup were Jack Daniel's workers on their lunch break. They would come over in the same truck, and the white men would go through the front door as the Black men filed in through the back.

"They ate the same food, came back out, got in the same truck, went back to work," Miss Neat said, just as J. B. McGowan had told me. "We just knew what was expected."

Miss Dot concurred. "Everybody treated everybody nice," she said. "We just knew that there were certain places that we didn't go and sit down."

But there were apparently exceptions. When I asked Miss Helen about her experience with Jim Crow laws at the Coffee Cup, she proclaimed, "I don't know nothin' about no Jim Crow laws. I never went through the back. The ice cream was in the front!"

"How'd they treat you when you went through the front?" I asked.

"Like everyone else," she said. "I got my ice cream and paid my nickel."

When I heard about an experience Mickey Murphy, Otis Green's grandson, had at the pharmacy, I realized it might've been something particular to being a Green in Lynchburg.

Mickey and Otis went into downtown Lynchburg while Mickey was visiting from St. Louis. Mickey, age six or seven, wanted some ice cream and wandered in by himself. He sat down at the counter to order.

"I guess people got excited about me sitting on the stool," he recalled. "The lady said I couldn't sit there."

That didn't make any sense to Mickey. Then a discussion broke out behind him.

"Do you know who that is?" a white man asked.

"No, sir, I don't," the waitress said.

"That's a Green boy," the man said. He told her Mickey was Otis Green's grandson.

"I got my ice cream," Mickey recalled. He'd been confused by this memory his whole life, but he told me learning more about the Green family's role at Jack Daniel's made it make a little more sense.

I also found a pattern as I interviewed folks: Black people who went through the back door in Lynchburg during Jim Crow days did it because they felt they were supposed to. Whenever someone told me, "Well, you knew your place," I'd ask *how* they knew. Invariably, their parents had told them to do it.

What I found unique about Lynchburg in the first half of the century was that I didn't hear of consequences for those who chose not to abide by those customs—people like Miss Helen, who just told me, "Well, I didn't pay too much attention to any of that," and people like Mickey Murphy, who were unaware. The Greens didn't take nonsense from anyone, Mickey said, and they were treated with respect for it.

I even heard a story about Stella White, whose sister worked at the Coffee Cup. One of the white men who worked there said something to her that she didn't like. Stella chased him down the street with a broom—and the whole town laughed.

When I found out Stella was a Black woman, I was amazed. Absolutely nothing happened to her. Other places in the South—and surely in quite a few places in the North—she could've been killed.

What the hell is this town? I thought.

CHANGE COMES SLOWLY to a place like Lynchburg, and things remained as they were for a long time. But in the sixties, mass media reached even the tiniest towns. Images of marches, protests, and sit-ins elsewhere changed the perceptions of Blacks and whites alike.

Jo Anne remembered watching the TV news and learning about the Black students at Tennessee State University and Fisk University demanding change in nearby Nashville. "If they weren't talking about it on the television, they were talking about that on the radio," Jo Anne said. "That was big news. Everybody was tuning in and seeing how the change was going to come about."

Black kids coming of age in the 1960s and 1970s were told, "Don't make waves" by their parents. But the waves rolled in from outside Lynchburg. After President Lyndon Johnson signed the Civil Rights Act of 1964, Jim Crow laws that segregated public spaces were overturned nationwide. When Jo Anne and her friends heard the news, they did what we all would've done: they sat at the drugstore counter and asked for an ice cream soda.

The staff served them, "but you could tell by the looks and all that they did not want to," she recalled. Jo Anne and her friends were elated anyway and spread the word—Black people could sit at the counter, order, and listen to music while they were getting their prescriptions filled.

But within a year, the counter was gone. "They thought it would be better to just remove it," Jo Anne said. It was an old-folks' way of dealing with things. Rather than embrace change, they eliminated the issue.

These two places serving sodas and ice cream, after all, were not trying to appeal to the locals; their focus was on out-of-towners coming to do business at the courthouse. And out-of-towners had no interest in the Lynchburg way of life.

Perhaps the process of turning people's hearts is best done on an individual scale. Jo Anne recalled another instance when she and her mother were driving home from the small store in Lois one summer when they saw two little white boys walking and eating ice cream that was melting in the sun. The boys were each about six or seven years old, and Jo Anne and her mom knew them; everyone knew everyone else.

Jo Anne's mom pulled over and rolled down the window. "Would you like to ride?" she asked. "We go right by your house."

"Yes, ma'am," said the older one.

They hopped in the back seat and chattered endlessly.

"Are y'all in school?" Jo Anne's mom asked.

"Yes, ma'am," the oldest said, with his face between the seats.

"Are you ready to go back to school?"

"No, ma'am," the oldest one said. "We don't want to go to school. They said we got to go to school with those n———s."

Jo Anne was upset. She asked her mother to put the boy out of the car right away. But her mom ignored her and dropped them off near their house. Clearly, they didn't even understand what the word meant; otherwise they wouldn't have gotten in their car.

"Thank you, ma'am," the boy said as he got out.

"You're welcome, hon," her mom said. "When you get home, tell your parents that some n———s let you ride so your ice cream wouldn't melt."

She drove off toward home.

"A child don't know nothing," she told Jo Anne firmly. It was the boys' parents and people like them who were the problem—people who taught their kids there were deep differences between the races, that they couldn't come together. "When you can get past those people," her mom said, "things will start to change."

That wasn't fast enough for Jo Anne. She couldn't wait to get out of her parents' home, become involved in the Civil Rights Movement, and join a sit-in.

After a little while, Jo Anne wondered aloud what the little boy might have said to his parents.

"I hope he told them exactly the way I said it," her mom said. "Just that gesture of me being nice enough to help him get home without his ice cream melting, that right there might speak something to the parents."

That moment showed Jo Anne her mother's heart. "She saw people as people, God's children," Jo Anne recalled. "I didn't feel that way as much as my mother did." She and her friends "didn't feel so nice about everything that was going on. We wanted to get involved."

But the memory of the boy with the ice cream cone stayed with Jo Anne her whole life. "At that time, I guess, I would have been a great rebel because I wanted to get really involved and make things change," she said recently. "And I see that there is change, but as long as we've got people with the mind that there's a difference and they teach their children that, it's never going to be a perfect world."

ON NOVEMBER 10, I organized a group of Nearest's descendants at a Church of Christ in Nashville. It was the largest group of descendants I'd gathered at one time so far, and I was so excited to meet with them. I was hopeful that a new branch of the family—George Green's branch, who lived in the Nashville area—would yield new information about Nearest. Keith and Stephani joined us, and as before, I brought a team of videographers with me to capture the conversation.

"Let me share with you what I've learned about your family and your ancestor Nearest," I said. "And you tell me what you guys already knew through oral history and anything you might have." As it turned out, I knew everything they knew and so much more.

I was able to tell them things about their family they'd never known. As I spoke, people started crying. Nearest's legacy brought them together in that church and made them bigger, collectively and as a family, than they'd been as individuals when they walked in. They finally felt seen.

We also announced the news that we were starting a foundation that would give every descendant of Nearest Green a full ride through college. They were thrilled!

I told the assembled group that I hadn't talked to Jack Daniel's yet. "They will take my calls," I said. "But as Nearest's family, is there anything you would like to see Jack Daniel's do?"

At that, everyone was quiet at first. They looked around at one another like they were waiting for something. I got the sense they'd discussed this among themselves already. One man raised his hand.

"We think Nearest deserves to have his own bottle," he said. The family members surrounding him nodded. "His name should be on a bottle."

I knew that was extremely unlikely to happen. Jack Daniel's seemed to have backed far away from Nearest after the rocky reception of the *New York Times* piece. By that point, I'd been on the Jack Daniel tour four or five times, and not once did a tour guide even give a nod to him in any capacity. They'd ignored the acknowledgement requests of the Green descendants who worked there. They had failed to recognize the value of the Call Farm. They had also failed to value Nearest's name—literally! The trademarks we'd filed for Nearest's name were now jangling loudly in my brain. Even if Jack Daniel's wanted to make a bottle, they wouldn't have been able to put his name on it without going through me. But I also didn't trust them to do it right or well. I knew they'd never capture Nearest's legacy properly, because they didn't fully understand it in the first place. Anything they tried would be a one-off—a limited-edition run—not the kind of lasting recognition Nearest deserved.

I also had a good understanding of what it would take to make a bottle—a real one, with proper Tennessee whiskey—and a brand that both deeply honored Nearest Green and stood a chance at breaking into distribution channels. And I heard Sherrie Moore's words run through my mind again: *If you ever decide to honor Nearest with a bottle, I'll come out of retirement to make sure you get it right.* I knew we could do what Jack Daniel's wouldn't.

"We'll do it," I told the family. "We'll raise the money."

Sitting beside me, Keith was startled. That was definitely not the plan.

Keith said to me once, years ago, "Sweetheart, sometimes your thinking and speaking are one action." That was definitely the case here.

He recalls me telling Nearest's descendants that he worked at a movie studio and we'd be able to raise the capital for a bottle, and then thinking, *Oh Lord,* that's *not enough to fuel a whiskey company.*

But I told them we would raise the money. I hadn't expected to say it; but I just knew that I had to try.

The room erupted in surprised and happy chatter. No one seemed to doubt that we could do this. No one asked for specifics. So much had already changed and come to pass that, in that church, anything seemed possible.

AFTER THE MEETING, we got in our car but didn't leave the parking lot. This was all coming together by the design of hands much greater than my own.

Keith was in the passenger seat. I think he was a little shell-shocked. I'd just committed to a room full of people that we would find the money to produce and bottle whiskey with their ancestor's name on it. The instant I'd promised it, I knew I'd be asking all our friends and family to invest—and we'd *definitely* have to sell Serenity Ranch. Plus, I was plunging us into an industry we knew almost nothing about, and although I wouldn't look at it this way, I knew Brown-Forman would see us as direct competition to one of the biggest spirits brands on the planet, Jack Daniel's.

But Keith and I never fight against each other. We fight *together* to solve the problem. We're indefatigable partners, and we work together on everything, even when we're on different pages.

I felt my book's publication day move considerably further away. I'd still be telling Nearest and Jack's story of love, honor, and respect— it was just going to look far more at home on a bar than a bookshelf at first.

I called Sherrie from the parking lot.

"If you come out of retirement, I will raise the money, and we will make this happen."

PART
TWO

⟨ ★ ⟩

NOVEMBER 2016

THROUGH

DECEMBER 2017

31

THE IDEA of a master distiller is a pretty modern one, and Jack Daniel's helped elevate the job into one the whiskey industry takes seriously. Jimmy Bedford, who was Jack Daniel's master distiller from the late 1980s through 2008, took the title from whiskey-making to celebrity. "He traveled the world as something of an ambassador for Jack Daniel's," wrote the *New York Times*. "He led tasting seminars, signed bottles and appeared in television commercials and print advertisements."

Early on, a PR person walked into Jimmy Bedford's office and saw he'd put framed photos of some of his predecessors up on the walls. They arranged them artfully and snapped a photo that became part of Jack Daniel's history. The collectors' market did the rest.

Jack Daniel's put out a line of master distiller bottles that sell for hundreds of dollars and a complete boxed set for north of $1,000. The series honors six men, beginning with Jack. (A bottle honoring Frank Bobo, who was master distiller from 1966 to 1988, came out in October 2016, right as I was beginning to unravel the mystery of Nearest. He was the first person I met who'd worked at Jack Daniel's to just flat out say, "Yeah, we've always known that Nearest was the first master distiller. That isn't a question.")

After the church meeting in Nashville, Keith and I found ourselves on different pages. He thought that Jack Daniel's should produce a limited-edition bottle for Nearest that would be part of their master distiller line. *The family just wants his name on a bottle*, he recalls thinking. *Why wouldn't we sell them the IP and have them do that?*

He was thinking strategically, which he's great at. He figured we'd sell our trademarks and the Dan Call Farm, right the historical wrong, make a pretty penny, and go back to our lives in LA.

But after that day with George's family in Nashville, I saw what a new company could become—a living legacy, a physical space, a gift for future generations. I started raising money right away. My calculations showed we'd need a bare minimum of $3 million to get Uncle Nearest started, so there was no time to waste.

When friends asked him about this later, he said, "Fawn is responsive to circumstances faster than I am." This is true. I *had* to do something. But I understood Keith's position, too. He thought it was all too much at once. We were pouring an insane amount of money into the Call Farm, our travels to and from Lynchburg, and my other business ventures. We were still learning what it would take to keep up the Call Farm, and now we'd be pairing it with raising money to start a company. I was also sending my book editor chapters regularly. I'm accustomed to splitting my attention between multiple projects. I might even say it's one of my superpowers. But looking back on everything I was juggling at once, it's still hard for me to believe I was doing *that* much at one time. I should have been exhausted, but I don't recall feeling overwhelmed at the time. To the contrary, I was full of excitement. But in hindsight, I'm not sure how I maintained my composure.

Keith would fly into Nashville on a Thursday night red-eye, land on Friday around 5 a.m., rent a truck, and make his way to Lynchburg to join me. If he had Friday meetings, he'd have to arrive on Saturday and then leave again on Sunday night or at the crack of dawn on Monday morning.

"I took these crazy flights," he recalled. "It was exhausting."

I missed him, and I missed sharing the historical discoveries with him as I found them. For months, I'd been telling the Green descendants that I was going to write a book. I still was—but on top of it, now I was also pivoting to an industry I didn't yet understand.

IN DECEMBER, I made first contact with Jack Daniel's. I met for several hours with Steve May, a Jack Daniel's executive who oversaw the visitor experience—meaning he was one of the people charged with being the keeper of Jack Daniel's story. He spoke candidly, telling me that while it didn't make business sense for Jack Daniel's to formally change their story to include Nearest, they also had no intention of hiding Nearest's contributions, or his sons'. They welcomed anything the family and I deemed right in terms of honoring Nearest. I wrote to friends that afternoon, "They want to see Nearest and his sons honored, they just don't want to be the ones to do it." Steve even offered access to Jack Daniel's archives. "Now, it's just up to us to do it right (and BIG)," I wrote.

About a month later, I emailed Steve a follow-up request about accessing the archives, hoping the leadership team would allow a researcher in to look for documents and take photos. Instead, Brown-Forman requested that I meet with the historian of Jack Daniel's, Nelson Eddy. This wasn't what I was hoping for—rather than the archives, they were referring me to a publicist. They were trying to spin me!

I insisted on having my publicist team meet with Nelson first and vet him to see what his true objectives were. If they were going to send me to their publicist, I was going to send them to mine.

AROUND THIS TIME, Debbie, Jackie, their cousins from Tullahoma, and I made a plan to see the movie *Hidden Figures*. It's a great movie, and we had an amazing time. We were in the theater cheering, fist-pumping, and crying.

Afterward, in the lobby, I said, "When we make the movie about Nearest and Jack, it has to be like this." Just as the main heroes were African American, and they had an ally in Kevin Costner, our story also honored the legacy of an African American and his ally. "Our movie has two heroes." Sadly, I later learned from the talent agency that packaged the movie deal that the Kevin Costner character wasn't real. He was an amalgamation of many people who were allies. After more than fifteen years as the spouse of a studio executive vice president, I knew that was Tinseltown's way of saying, "We made him up!" So, I guess our movie would have two heroes, but both heroes would actually be real.

Two weeks after having such a great time at the theater, I realized I couldn't remember the names of any of the women that Taraji P. Henson, Octavia Spencer, and Janelle Monáe had played. The whole point of going to see *Hidden Figures* was to learn who the hidden figures were, and we all left only knowing the actresses we were already familiar with before going to the theater in the first place. Entertainment was never going to be the way we cemented Nearest's legacy across generations.

The reason we all know about Johnnie Walker, Jim Beam, and Jack Daniel is because we constantly see their bottles and say their names. They're the Mount Rushmore of whiskey. Putting Nearest's name on a bottle really was the only way to carve him into that mountain beside them and make him a hidden figure no longer.

I KNEW I WANTED us to make whiskey the same way Nearest did. But as I threw myself into learning about the industry, I found there was an extraordinarily steep learning curve. Part of that is because the modern spirits industry was born after—and complicated by—Prohibition. After the ratification of the Twenty-First Amendment, states worked to ensure that single ownership of the production, distribution, and sale of alcohol was either impossible or extremely difficult. This resulted in a three-tier system that meant producers could only sell to wholesale distributors, who in turn sold to retailers. Distributors have a lot of power in the spirits industry, and that's how it's meant to be. Literally—it's federal law. They're far more than a middleman; they are the most powerful of all three tiers. They buy spirit brands wholesale, then sell them to retailers all over the country. This keeps alcohol regulated and controlled as it's transported, stored, and resold.

Distributors are massive companies, but you've likely never heard of them; unlike distilleries, they aren't household names. They tend to either be regional—focusing on the South or the West—or extremely large, with operations in dozens of states. Most distribute spirits, wine, and beer, which all have different regulatory requirements. Distributors have small armies of sales reps who travel throughout their markets, giving them an outsize influence on the success (or failure) of a new brand. Because there are few distributors, it's hard to break in. Many are owned by third- or fourth-generation Italian or Jewish families and date back to the end of Prohibition. They often give retailers—bars, restaurants, liquor stores—incentives for taking one brand over another, almost universally a brand by one of the giant spirit conglomerates. The industry is specifically set up so that the big guys work with the big distributors to make sure that every new brand that comes in either sells or fails.

Before we launched Uncle Nearest, those were the only two options.

But I knew that I wanted to build a different kind of company. I didn't want us to be bought out by Brown-Forman or any other spirits conglomerate. And I knew the fastest way for a brand to die in this industry was to stay small.

Uncle Nearest was going to be something new. Each time I talked to the Green family, I felt like I owed them something. And it wasn't just the Greens—I wanted to do something for all the Black people in Lynchburg, for everybody who'd been responsible for preserving their history on their church bulletin boards and the walls of their fellowship halls.

Black people had gotten the short end of the stick when it came to spirits. Uncle Nearest could change that. Throughout the course of my research, I'd learned that, for centuries, the coastal region of West Africa—integral to the slave trade—had a long history of alcohol brewing and consumption. West Africans regarded drinking as a collective activity, one that was regulated by temperance and etiquette. In the wetter regions of West Africa, wealthy lords maintained groves of palm from which they drew sap to make alcohol. In the wooded uplands, people made mead out of honey, and farmers in the drier areas brewed millet beers from grains or palm sap. Alcoholic drinks tended to have a low alcohol percentage, almost always below 10 percent.

Eventually, Europeans brought new spirits to West Africa. This alcohol was distilled as opposed to brewed. As European enslavers took power, they began to use alcohol as currency. Unlike textiles and firearms, distilled alcohol had a dual purpose as currency and controller. If Europeans were threatened by a tribe, they'd use alcohol to subdue them, and in time, a network developed that made liquor, money, and slavery dependent on one another.

Spirits were a part of the transatlantic slave trade. Liquor didn't spoil, and it kept captives quiet. I often think about those enslaved Africans on the barbaric ships of the Middle Passage. Some 12.5 million people were enslaved, and two million died in the Middle Passages alone; 388,000 made it to the shores of the United States, which was the farthest distance away from Africa in the Atlantic slave trade. The only way anyone could survive that journey was to be the strongest of the strong—mentally, physically, emotionally, spiritually. Whenever I walk into any room, I do it with the strength of those ancestors.

SINCE NEAREST isn't around anymore, we can't ask how he got started making whiskey or how he learned to use charcoal to mellow it. But we know, according to the National Museum of African American History and Culture, that "charcoal filtration can be seen across enslaved communities that produce illicit alcohol, making it incredibly likely that Nearest's mastery of technique was a result of the generational, and far too often unacknowledged, skill of enslaved people."

When people say Nearest came up with the recipe for the Lincoln County Process, I'm like, "Nah. Scratch that. Didn't happen." Because that recipe was floating around before Nearest was even born. When folks give credit to Nearest for inventing charcoal mellowing in general, I have to correct them on that as well.

Filtering whiskey to improve taste and safety was a common activity, and there were lots of methods. Many of the same things that had been used to filter water over the millennia were tried—charcoal, yes, but also chalk, sand, cloth, paper, and other materials. Those methods go back at least as far as ancient Egypt and made their way with enslaved people from West Africa to America.

In the 1770s, a South Carolina woman named Mary Pearson recorded a process that filtered corn mash through hard sugar maple by filling a tub with a blanket, covering the blanket in sand, and covering the sand with eighteen inches of charcoal. The filtered spirit made its way through the charcoal, sand, and cloth through holes in the tub. An 1809 book published in Harrisburg, Pennsylvania, called *The Practical Distiller* was a how-to guide for making gin, brandy, and whiskey. Author John Wyeth advised using "finely beaten maple charcoal and burnt brick dust" in flannel. In a chapter on clarifying whiskey, Samuel McHarry of Lancaster, Pennsylvania, recommended a similar method: two inches of ground maple charcoal or brick dust would leave behind "scarcely any taste or smell of whiskey." I probably wouldn't have been a fan of all the brick dust. By 1829, distilleries throughout Tennessee were using charcoal to filter whiskey in a variety of ways. "This method appeared at the dawn of distilling in Middle Tennessee," wrote Chris Middleton of Whiskey Academy.

So this process predates Nearest by centuries, but there was great significance to him perfecting it—with no formal training, no ability to read and write, with primitive equipment, and while enslaved. People miss the magnitude of that accomplishment.

THE BIGGEST PROBLEM we faced in doing things Nearest's way is that whiskey needs to age, and we were in a hurry. We needed to establish a brand, make Nearest's name known, and get to the market fast. Most brands are able to go to market focused solely on offense. We were coming to market and also had to consider defense. We knew Brown-Forman would not simply allow us to enter the market they dominated. We'd have to kick, scratch, and fight our way onto every shelf around the world. In an industry where the maker of a product is not allowed to sell directly to the consumer of the product, and the third-party wholesalers are bought and paid for by the big guys, it would be no easy task. We'd have to enter the market like a Tasmanian devil: moving too quickly and in too many directions for anyone to slow us down, no matter how great their power.

In those early days, close friends believed in us so much they wanted to wire money without seeing a business plan. Keith was so nervous that unbeknownst to me, he kept highlighting their risks.

But I knew if Brown-Forman chose to sue us, it would have damaged them greatly. I could just imagine the headline: "Jack Daniel Sues Uncle Nearest, Namesake of Its 'Hidden Ingredient,' the Slave Who Taught Jack How to Make Whiskey." From a PR standpoint, I knew it would have been an absolute disaster.

WHISKEY IS ALL about chemistry—altitude, temperature, humidity—but it is also about time. Once we secured the whiskey-filled barrels, we needed to taste each one, choose those with the best aroma and taste profile, and then blend the product. Most people don't know that you can distill the exact same thing and still have every barrel of whiskey taste completely different. And bottling has to happen quickly. If you leave whiskey in its barrel for any real period of time after you've done your sampling, the flavor can change. The whiskey is still interacting with the wood and pulling flavors from the barrel.

Through brokers, I found a distillery offering sourced Tennessee whiskey that was made most like Nearest made it when he was alive. We kept our plans for a bottle very close to the vest, but I knew it was only a matter of time until Brown-Forman would know what we were working on. The trademark filings for Uncle Nearest and Nearest Green with the US Patent and Trademark Office were public, as were the bottle label filings with the Alcohol and Tobacco Tax and Trade

Bureau, the legal governing body for alcohol. Brown-Forman had some two dozen trademark attorneys employed or on retainer, and I knew they'd spot the public filings sooner or later.

I felt like I'd been living a story somewhere between the movies *Spotlight* and *Concussion* since I started researching Nearest's story. Brown-Forman had lots of avenues available to them to slow us down once they found out. They could shut down our barrel supply or throw their weight around and hire our distilling partner to distill a large amount for them instead. They had armies of attorneys they could use to try to intimidate us into halting the product before it ever made it to market. But I wasn't worried or anxious. I understood the facts while knowing I was secure in the protection of God's care and the comfort of Keith's love. My heart was safe.

Although it was a goal that would take years to come to fruition, we decided to distill our own bottle early on. We were a tiny brand—and tiny is an understatement. It would have been easy to choke our supply lines in Tennessee. We knew we'd better plan to distill our own whiskey as soon as we could, or we were going to be up a creek, should we grow to a size that Brown-Forman was uncomfortable with us reaching.

AFTER HEARING FROM my publicists that they believed that Jack Daniel's historian, Nelson Eddy, had his heart in the right place, I invited him to my research room at the Call Farm on March 17 and showed him what I'd learned about Nearest. I could tell that in his heart, he really was a true historian. He was so excited to see all that we had found and welcomed the outside voice amplifying Nearest's story. I was pleasantly surprised.

Nelson later recalled thinking, *It's wonderful when you have somebody who's done research, shared it with you, and is speaking to issues that she's uniquely qualified to speak to.*

I didn't take that for granted. And I didn't expect a similar reaction from the leadership at Brown-Forman. I always knew I would talk to them eventually, but I planned for that to come after the book was written and done.

Nelson briefed Mark McCallum thoroughly: Nearest Green had taught Jack Daniel how to make whiskey. He had overseen every step of Dan Call and Jack's whiskey operations. Nearest had been the first head stiller, not Jack Daniel, and his descendants had kept the connection alive for generations. Jack Daniel's began at the Call Farm, not the current Cave Spring Hollow location. Earlier attempts to tell Nearest's story and honor his family were commendable, but they had fallen far short of the mark. He told Mark I'd built a case through both research and an oral history of the Green family tree.

"You know what?" Nelson told Mark. "This is real."

He also told Mark I was scheduled to fly to New York the following week to meet with Clay Risen at the *New York Times* building. For better or worse, I'm a pretty transparent person. All you have to know is what question to ask me. Nelson asked the right questions, and I shared with him what I planned to share with Clay.

Nelson was more vague on the details when it came to connecting Mark and me. "There's someone I want you to meet," he told me. "He's an Australian guy, and I think he would be open to learning what you've just shared with me." He didn't mention Mark's name, or that he was the president of Jack Daniel's and the chief brand officer of Brown-Forman.

MEANWHILE, Keith had stopped discouraging friends from investing and started telling them we'd lay the groundwork, get the business off the ground, and sell before things got too risky. Cementing a legacy means going BIG, and no independent company in the spirits industry had ever succeeded at BIG. A few independents had done well—Tito's Vodka is a great example—but no person of color or woman had even gotten close to what I was talking about doing. Keith thought our goal should be to sell to Brown-Forman. He was on board with raising money, but he figured the longer we held on, the more it would cost, and the more we had to raise, the greater the risk would be of our friends and family losing money.

Before he launched his career with Sony, Keith had a background in California politics. Through that world, he'd grown close with the late Michael Berman, a top adviser in the California political world. Over the years, Michael became an invaluable mentor and trusted friend.

Michael's great talent was working with data. In the 1970s, he took demographic data that had been painstakingly collected for voter records and used it to target mailed campaign material about specific issues on a micro level. Slate mail had an enormous impact on California politics and became such standard operating practice for campaigns today that it feels strange to remember a time when it was otherwise. Later, Michael deployed his deep knowledge of voting patterns and the population as an expert—albeit a partisan one—in redistricting, which was done every ten years with the new census.

Michael studied our plans and found them to be a massive risk. Nothing about what we were proposing looked like a safe bet, from our inexperience in the industry to the direct and gigantic obstacle posed by Brown-Forman. And the spirits industry is volatile and fraught with hazards no matter what experience you bring to the table. Despite his qualms, Michael was instrumental in helping us raise the $3 million we needed. I believe Michael—who, in addition to politics, was so skilled at blackjack that he'd been banned by casinos—saw it as a calculated risk.

I wasn't afraid of failure. I don't believe in failure; it doesn't exist unless you give up before you succeed. But I did fear losing other people's money, and I knew I'd spend the rest of my life working to make sure I paid every single person back if that happened. Michael knew that about us. He didn't believe in the brand; he believed in us. And because he believed in us, he made a large initial investment and, just as crucially, encouraged others in his network to do the same. Not only was he our first investor, but he secured our first six investors, each investing significant amounts. Because of him, we were able to raise the funds to take the brand to market.

CHAPTER

33

"I THINK YOU may have a certain idea about Brown-Forman and who we are," Mark McCallum said over the phone in his gentle Australian accent. And he was right. I'd had scenes of intrepid reporters and crusading doctors playing in my mind whenever I thought about what our first encounter might look like. "I want to be able to come and share with you in person and personally who we are and how we see ourselves."

That's not at all how I expected the president of Jack Daniel's and the chief brand officer of Brown-Forman to begin our call. For months, I'd prepared myself for a fight.

But Mark was patient on the phone. He knew I was headed to share my research findings with Clay Risen at the *New York Times*, and despite his mild manners and soft-spokenness, I sensed some urgency in Mark's request. "I'd like to meet with you this week, if you'd be open to it," he gently prodded.

I agreed to meet with Mark two days later, before I flew out to New York, on one condition: I wanted him to make a special stop at his distillery. I knew he'd have to drive past it to reach me at the Call Farm.

"There are three Nearest Green descendants that work there," I told him.

I wasn't sure Mark knew that. In fact, I wasn't entirely convinced that any of the people at Brown-Forman in Louisville knew that Jack Daniel's actually had Nearest's descendants working there. There was a big disconnect, because the Brown-Forman executives in Louisville didn't come to Lynchburg often. I think some of them saw it as a backwoods little town. It's definitely a pain in the neck to get there from most places. In Brown-Forman's own words, "You don't just happen by Lynchburg, Tennessee. To get there, you really have to want to go."

Besides, none of the Green descendants have "Green" as a last name. For two of them, their last name is Vance; the third's last name is Eady.

"Everybody knows who they are," I said to Mark on the phone. "All you need to do is walk in there and ask to see them. And I want you to shake their hands. Let them know that you know the significance of their ancestor. Let them know that you appreciate what their ancestor did. Then come and see me."

Mark did as I asked and met with Debbie, Jackie, and Jerome in the employee community room at the back of Jack Daniel Distillery on March 24. He arrived in a tailored shirt, a black leather jacket, spotless black leather shoes, and pressed jeans. In contrast, the siblings were dressed casually, wearing their Jack Daniel Distillery shirts and jackets. I hadn't given them a heads-up that he'd be coming. I didn't want to undermine the significance of the visit by letting them know I'd made it a prerequisite of our meeting, and it was important to me that he received their most authentic feelings. They sat around the conference table and met privately, just the four of them.

"I've got to believe they were terrified," Mark recalled. "They didn't know me."

Debbie remembered thinking, *We can't blow our cool, because we got work.*

She started out telling him how they'd tried to tell Nearest's story and been told not to and accused of lying. She openly expressed all her anger and disappointment, never mind that she worked in bottling and he was the president of the brand.

Mark wasn't prepared for the level of pain and anger. He'd expected to hear that they'd been "passively rebuffed," or "ignored by management at the distillery," and "most probably just not followed up on." He was deeply struck by how hurt they were.

Jerome got frustrated and took over telling the story. The meeting went on for at least an hour, with raised voices and tears. It was brutal.

Mark got a clear picture, too, of the incredible love the three of them had for Lynchburg, their family's home for generations, and for Jack Daniel's. He clearly saw that the brand was more important to them than it could ever be to an "occasional steward" like himself. "They loved that brand."

At some point, they all took a break to make coffee, and Mark used the opportunity to take a breath. He was trying to think of what he could commit to immediately that could help, but he held off.

Before he left, Mark told them he would make things right—although he "didn't know how to quite yet."

A FEW HOURS after he'd arrived at Jack Daniel Distillery, Mark made it to the Call Farm. He'd texted to let me know he'd be late. Knowing where he was coming from, I certainly didn't mind.

At first he didn't even walk through the threshold of the door—just kind of poked his head in and looked at Keith and me.

"I hear you know more about Lynchburg and Jack Daniel's than I do," he said.

I'm pretty sure that was true.

"I don't ever want to go through something like that again," he went on. "I don't ever want to experience what I just experienced. Tell me how we make this right."

That was definitely the right question. I invited Mark into the research room, where my findings were spread across several large tables. He could have no doubt I'd done the work. There were copies of original IRS ledgers; Department of Treasury assessment books; direct tax commission books; a copy of an incredibly well-preserved diary of Jack's last living sister, written in 1899; original paychecks from Jack Daniel's descendants to several of Nearest Green's children and grandchildren; the metal "Jack Daniel" bottle jug stencil; more than a hundred original letters to and from Jack's descendants; a copy of Jack's original will; copies of original receipts and deposit slips for monies given to Jack's siblings and descendants by Jack; a three-hundred-page Supreme Court case that involved every major distiller from 1867–1871 in Lynchburg; and thousands of additional documents.

We talked for hours. I told him everything I knew about Nearest, and we discussed ways to lift him up without causing harm to Jack. It was a good conversation, but it was complicated. I still didn't know how much I could trust Mark, and he still didn't know I had started working on a bottle to honor Nearest. I didn't know exactly what he had said to Jackie, Debbie, and Jerome, either.

For his part, Mark remained cautious. He wrote me back later that night, mentioning he was emailing from his front porch, sipping on a little Jack at the close of a very long Friday. "I'm not sure if my head is spinning or my imagination is just sifting information," he wrote. "My 'true north' right now is to deliver on my commitment to Debbie and her family as soon as possible. I'm not yet sure how best to do this, but very much appreciate your and Keith's thoughts."

Mark asked for time to process, which I was more than happy to give. He wrote that he was looking forward to finding "the most helpful way to add our voice to the story of Nearest and his vital connection to the story of Jack Daniel the man, Jack Daniel's the brand, and Lynchburg the town. And maybe even America the country."

AFTER THAT MEETING, Nelson and I began to trade historical information. He searched for every mention of Nearest Green he could find in the Jack Daniel's archives, and we worked together to find indisputable proof that Nearest was Jack's first master distiller.

The first document Nelson gave me was an issue of *Tennessee Historical Quarterly* that named Nearest as the first head stiller, based on information provided by the Motlows. The other was a letter from former master distiller Frank Bobo to the Field Testers, a group quite like the Squires but considerably easier to join. Bobo's letter named nine head distillers before him, including Nearest.

There was also a 2001 insert celebrating Jack Daniel's 150th birthday in Brown-Forman's annual report that said:

Jack learned the trade that would be his life's work and the mellowing process that would become his signature from Call's master distiller—a slave named Nearest Green. [The photo of his son sitting beside Jack Daniel] says something about his importance to the operation. It also says something about Mr. Jack.

At this point, I had told no one at Jack Daniel's that I was thinking of doing a bottle. I assumed one of two things: either their attorneys had already alerted them of the trademarks or bottle labels or, if their trademark attorneys were asleep at the switch, they still thought I was just an author working on my book. But they'd find out eventually. I knew Nelson couldn't keep helping us for long without finding out about our plans to launch a whiskey brand. Later, Mark told me he kept asking Nelson for updates on what I was doing. "He was my spy," Mark said.

I knew that, so I was always very careful with what I shared with Nelson. I liked him a great deal, but I also know quite well how the game of business is played.

THE PRELIMINARY steps I'd taken back in July 2016 meant much of what we needed to put Uncle Nearest, Inc., into business was already done. I brought on Katharine Jerkens as our senior vice president of sales and marketing in December 2016. A California native, Katharine and I had worked together at the Viceroy Hotel in Santa Monica, where I had overseen event production and she was a sales manager. Later, I'd brought her in as the vice president of sales of the struggling business I'd invested in, in the hopes she could help me turn it around. When the founders of the company turned on her instead, I knew this would be a better fit for her enormous gifts and talents. I also knew I could trust her to hit the ground running with me.

There were so many components to figure out in a short period of time. Of our tiny but mighty three-person staff, only Sherrie came from a spirits background—and a very different one at that.

At some point I noticed a pattern: people weren't calling Katharine and me back. I'd reach out to a bottler or distiller and hear nothing. Katharine mentioned she'd been calling people for three or four weeks without being able to get anyone on the phone.

It turned out Sherrie was also not receiving calls back as she reached out to vendors. I had the dream team to help me build the foundation for this brand, but we couldn't get anyone to answer us.

At one point Katharine had even reached out to two people she thought were women, based on their gender-neutral names. *Finally, women,* she thought. She emailed and emailed, but they didn't respond. *These two chicks won't even respond to me.*

I had a hunch about what was going on: no one had really talked to women in this industry before. It was a boys' club run by middle-aged white men, with many distributors family-run for a long time. At times, it felt impenetrable. I decided to test out a theory. I asked Katharine and Sherrie both to send an email that listed the people they were trying to reach and what they needed from them. I forwarded the list to Keith.

"Babe, I want you to call all of these suppliers and tell them that Uncle Nearest is yours," I said.

With every single phone call, Keith either got through immediately, or he got a call back by the end of the day. And each call turned friendly at some point. "Do you golf?" they asked Keith. "Do you like beer? Let's get together at a bar."

That's the way this industry has always been. Even the nonresponsive folks with the gender-neutral names turned out to be men who did, in fact, respond to Keith.

It would've been easy to feel pissed off. Instead, I was invigorated. It let me double down on sales, marketing, and PR and not be concerned about corks and bottles.

I've found a good mantra for life and business is never having a plan B. Plan Bs only distract from plan A. Backup plans involve investing time and energy in *not* being successful.

"We just powered through a lot of that," Katharine recalled. We didn't let it slow us down—if one person didn't respond, we went on to the next, and the next. "Nothing was ever in slow motion. We were never at a standstill."

I love being underestimated, and their attitude allowed me to build the company under the radar. We allowed everyone to think Keith was the brains behind the operation and I was just the historian and author.

WE WERE ALL learning in real time as things came together. Where would we warehouse our product? How would we have it shipped out? Which states were "control markets," meaning the state buys alcohol, distributes it, and controls its sale, and which were "open states" where private businesses occupied those roles? We were still learning which states allowed the sale of liquor in grocery stores versus liquor stores and which prohibited selling alcohol on certain days of the week.

The great thing was, we'd already assembled a strong branding team for the ill-fated company I'd invested in that the founders rejected. Like Katharine, they were also perfect for this. As a matter of fact, I invited every person and company I'd attempted to bring into that business venture to join me on this journey instead.

I also brought Evette Martinez in as my executive assistant to continue the work I'd begun with Stephani, whose father was ill. I missed her terribly, but after so much time enmeshed in Nearest's family, she was called to be back with her own.

I'd known Evette since she was eighteen, when I first hired her as my executive assistant. When that business faltered, I remained a mentor and we'd stayed in touch. In 2017, she had a job in a hospital that wasn't letting her use any of her gifts. She'd been praying for three months for a different path.

"I have a project," I said in an impromptu February 2017 call. "It's confidential. I need a right-hand girl. Are you ready?"

I suggested she pray about it, but she knew right from the start that it was the right place for her.

"Lady, I don't need to pray anymore," she told me while chuckling in her signature laugh I've always loved.

I sent her a video we had made in the research room, telling Nearest's story as we showcased the farmhouse and featured the smiling faces of Juanita, Oscar McGee, Joel, Claude Eady, Miss Dill, and Margaret Tolley. "Jack Daniel's descendants to Nearest Green's descendants to the distillery and everyone in between wanted to tell the story," I said in the video. "They just didn't know how."

Evette took in the family tree, the photos, the documents, everything I had so far spread across big tables. At first glance it reminded her of the main character's room in the film *A Beautiful Mind*, with documents and Post-it notes pinned up on the walls, connected by red string. In this case, though, the red string that connected all the pieces of this history was in my brain, and I needed help getting it out so we could all follow the story.

Evette was immediately all in. She put in her three weeks' notice and started working with me. She remembers sending the video to her then-co-workers with "tears running down my face to see the magnitude of this new project that I was blessed to be a part of."

When we hired Steven Henderson, based in Portland, Oregon, as our first salesperson, Uncle Nearest became five people strong. We worked remotely across states and time zones, a group of dedicated people who knew how to move quickly and adapt in the face of any obstacle.

Our small group kept things supersecret and under wraps as we sourced product, bottled it, found distributors, and handled logistics. Our team's friends didn't know what any of them were working on, just that we were working feverishly, all hours of the day and night. We called it "the UN project" among ourselves, as a code word. We wanted to be completely ready to go, with no interruptions, before the word went out. As an upstart independent whiskey company, we knew we'd need momentum and surprise to introduce Nearest to the world outside Lynchburg and make the biggest splash we could.

We were working hard on design, branding, and advertising for the bottle. For our initial expression, we used an artist's sketch of the Call farmhouse on the top of the label. I knew I didn't want any of our marketing to make people think of Uncle Nearest as a new brand. I wanted them to feel like it was an old brand they'd just learned about, because Nearest's story has always been here.

In 2017, the spirits industry—especially whiskey—was still marketed almost exclusively to white men. No one in bourbon or American whiskey in general was really marketing to anyone outside this pool beyond a few half-hearted attempts at observing Black History Month and similar occasions. These efforts were both inauthentic and underfunded, making them ineffective at best. The companies doing a better job tended to be those outside the bourbon space—tequilas, cognacs, and so on.

The way I always look at who a brand is targeting is to ask, who are you spending money to bring in?

In 2024, thanks to Uncle Nearest and the work we've done to reposition bourbon in the market, no one would look at bourbon and say, "That's a white man's drink." But in 2017, that was absolutely the way it was.

Here's something that's true no matter what industry you're in: it's the disruptors who move things forward. Institutional actors nearly always catch up eventually, copying the changemakers with more money and resources. But for a minute, they're behind. It takes someone from the outside to really bring change.

So many times, people's reaction to me was, "That's not the way this works."

And my whole thought process was, *Well, this is an industry that has stayed almost completely white and male in terms of leadership and ownership for over two hundred years. So clearly, this industry wasn't built for me.* The way things worked was going to have to change.

I FLEW TO New York to meet with Clay. He interviewed me for an article that would run months later, in the summer. Since his 2016 article introducing Nearest to the wider world, he'd thought a lot about the gaping holes in the history of whiskey-making. But he'd also moved on to other topics. Journalists rarely get the chance to revisit past stories, so when my PR firm in Nashville reached out to him and said, "You've got to meet this woman; she read your story and now she's doing all this work on Nearest," it was too good of an angle to ignore.

Most entrepreneurs in most industries come up with a product and hire a PR firm. They're excited and enthusiastic about their product, and they want everybody to report on it. What I tell new entrepreneurs in the consumer goods business all the time is: that's not enough. A bunch of behemoths run this industry, and they spend hundreds of millions of dollars on marketing every year. The only thing that levels the playing field is getting consistent and nonstop earned media—that is, genuine news and social media coverage, not paid advertising.

If you want sustained newspaper, television, and radio coverage, you have to be continuously and incredibly interesting. My press strategy is to identify eight or nine things per year that I believe will be a captivating story to viewers, listeners, and readers, then make those true stories come to life. Telling a story people would genuinely care about was exactly what I was able to do with Clay.

We met in the surprisingly cheerful *Times* cafeteria on a sunny day. It had massive floor-to-ceiling windows overlooking midtown

Manhattan and the Empire State Building and a bright red carpet. I spread out some of the artifacts we'd found at the Dan Call Farm, and I could tell, as I showed them to Clay, that he was blown away. He saw what I saw.

"Stencils, nails, the sort of ephemera that many people might ignore underfoot but that she understood held almost totemic value," Clay later wrote. "Green himself might have touched them."

He seemed to understand, from that first conversation, that I was the real deal. I had a good sense of the land, I had filled out corners of Nearest's story, and I had asked hard questions.

"It's easy to assume that anyone who digs up a character from the past will plaster them on a bottle," he would later write. "But Weaver didn't want to use Green to promote whiskey. Rather, she wanted to use whiskey to promote Green—and the idea that enslaved Black people were also a part of the story."

Within two weeks of Mark visiting me at the Call Farm, Nelson arrived with a new script fully integrating Nearest into the official Jack Daniel's materials. Soon after, in a letter to Jack Daniel's employees, Mark wrote that Nearest "was Jack Daniel's first head distiller, or what's more commonly known today as a master distiller. . . . We weren't fully aware of the unique role he played in the history of our distillery until recently. And for that, we have Ms. Fawn Weaver to thank." He also met with dozens of Jack Daniel's employees to talk about building Nearest into the tour and otherwise getting his story out there.

Some of the family remained skeptical. Dr. Geri Lovelace remembered all too well that Nearest had been cut out of the tour for decades. She'd read Clay Risen's 2016 story and wondered where things were going to go from there. Now, as then, she didn't fully believe Brown-Forman's efforts were genuine. "Not after all the years of the way they had done things," she said. It seemed more like "trying to cover their behind."

But I give Brown-Forman a lot of credit for acting swiftly and saying, *We made a mistake. Let's correct quickly, because it's the right thing to do.* I've never seen any major corporation move that fast on anything.

CHAPTER

35

WHILE THINGS with Uncle Nearest were revving up, I continued my work on the Nearest Green Foundation. Beyond its educational goals, the foundation planned to build a memorial park and rename a street in Lynchburg to Nearest Green Way. We purchased a four-acre parcel of land in the heart of Lynchburg to establish the Nearest Green Memorial Park and began working with some of the most high-profile Black artists in the country on a planned art installation. I wrote to colleagues that the beautiful space on Lynchburg's main drag "was obviously waiting for us, as nothing else explains it being available." I loved the idea of visitors touring Jack Daniel's, grabbing a bite to eat at Barrel House BBQ, and walking over to the memorial park to learn about the friendship between two men that shaped an entire town.

We were also working on improvement projects to clean up and maintain Highview Cemetery and Annie Bell Green Eady's house.

Although I never got to meet Mammie, I loved everything I knew about her—from our shared birthday, to the meals she'd cooked for the men in her family who worked just down the street at the distillery, to the oral history she'd passed down to her grandchildren. After she passed, her house fell into disrepair. The front porch, where so many Greens had eaten lunch and listened to Mammie's tales, was crumbling and covered in moss.

Keith and I hired a crew to keep it up. The porch where Mammie kept Nearest's story alive will always be preserved.

In the meantime, Evette and I kept building the family tree, contacting members of the family, working on the foundation, and establishing restoration projects.

From Tennessee and around the country, I sent a constant stream of info to Evette in California as I learned it—names, birthdays, anything we could add to the Green family's genealogy. I took notes on napkins and texted her photos. They all added up to a gorgeous, expansive, and ever-growing family tree.

Katharine remembers me calling her often with what I'd learned. "There was discovery all the time," she said. "There's always something new."

Evette's own kids frequently found her at the dinner table on her laptop late at night, trying to pinpoint exactly where everyone fell on the tree.

"The vibe was absolutely incredible," Evette recently recalled to a friend. "I don't think Fawn ever slept."

"I WAS ONLY EVER down in Lynchburg in the distillery three or four times a year until I met Fawn Weaver," Mark recently recalled to a friend. "Then I had to be there a lot more."

Given the extent of the foundation's plans for Lynchburg, Keith and I kept Mark McCallum in the loop. But we hadn't yet laid out our plans for a bottle. I assumed he already knew—in fact, I couldn't imagine a scenario where he didn't. I thought he was waiting for me to bring it up directly in order to address it.

I was dead wrong.

During a meeting at the Call Farm with Mark and Nelson, as well as their chief diversity officer they'd brought to meet me, it was time to unveil our work.

I brought out a box that looked like a leatherbound book, with *The Story of Uncle Nearest* written on it in gold. When Mark opened the book, he saw an illustration of Nearest as artist Raymond Bonilla had imagined him based on photos of his descendants: standing tall and confidently in his still house with his head held high. He wore a handsome blue shirt, suspenders, and a hat and held up a glass of his whiskey to the light to inspect it.

Mark turned the page and saw the empty cutout where our distinctly shaped bottle of Uncle Nearest would be nestled. This was a mockup of the sales presentation we planned to launch later that year.

Mark was clearly shaken. He looked like I could have pushed him over with a feather. I realized I had inadvertently blindsided both him and Nelson.

This was not the response I expected. I'd fully anticipated them both to say, "Yes, our attorneys informed us of this months ago, but we were just waiting for you to share your plans."

Mark said he needed a moment, stepped outside, and went for a walk.

Oh my God, they're going to launch a product, Mark remembers thinking.

He understood the IP and business implications almost immediately. But with a twinge of sadness, he also realized that the most natural avenue Jack Daniel's had to recognize Nearest—and the most straightforward avenue he'd had for honoring his commitment to make things right—had been closed off to him. Launching major products and carrying them around the world was what Jack Daniel's did best. Debbie, Jackie, and Jerome had worked there long enough to see that many times over, and to set their hopes accordingly.

When he walked back in, Mark had one main question: "Why didn't you let us do this for you?"

I was struck by how genuinely surprised he was. Brown-Forman had been stubbornly oblivious to the importance of Nearest's story and the outrage of it being allowed to fade away. They'd had more than sixty years to proclaim Nearest their first master distiller, to secure the trademarks, to put Nearest's name on a bottle. His reaction baffled me, because their attorneys were clearly asleep at the switch. And it saddened me, because I never would have shared the news with him this way if I'd known that he didn't know yet. I would have shared it in private, one-on-one. I would not have gutted him that way. By then, Mark and I had developed a friendly, helpful relationship. Neither of us fully trusted the other, which was to be expected, but I genuinely liked him as a person. I believe he would've said the same about me.

Mark went back to Brown-Forman headquarters to tell them we were launching a competitive brand. The story I was going to tell, the book I was going to write, the movie Keith and I might make—these had all been bad enough, to his mind. Now, suddenly, they had to worry about us impinging on Jack Daniel's intellectual property with a competing bottle of whiskey—and figuring out where their IP ended and ours began. *Another little hand grenade thrown into the hole*, he thought.

There were all kinds of IP boundaries to worry about: what the product would be called, how it would be promoted, what we'd say about it, and so on.

Brown-Forman's lawyers told Mark right away that he had to get things codified between the two companies. At Uncle Nearest, we were thinking, *Are they going to oppose our trademark? Are they not?* And internally at Jack Daniel's, they were deciding, *Do we oppose them? Do we not?*

One of the main reactions we got was, how could you market this story without including Jack? I was very clear with Brown-Forman that I saw Nearest's story as a standalone one that wouldn't infringe on their trademarks.

Mark's main job became getting us to sign an agreement that would let both companies use the name "Nearest Green" on products. I remember thinking, *That makes no sense. You're a massive conglomerate, one of the most powerful in America.* If we let Jack Daniel's sell products with the name Nearest Green, how would anyone know about or find Uncle Nearest? More importantly, why would distributors, who have a long history of prioritizing the big guys over independents, take on our brand if their biggest client were to sell a bottle representing the same legacy? Jack Daniel's lawyers called it a coexistence agreement. Privately, I called it a *non*existence agreement, because signing would squash everything we were setting out to do.

Keith thought some of what Jack Daniel's proposed in the coexistence agreement was very craftily written. He would play a little dumb in his negotiations with Mark. "If you had this, wouldn't you have more market share than we do? So wouldn't you be able to crush us?" That kind of thing.

Keith and I have always been partners in every sense of the word. Even though his full-time role was with Sony, he took the lead on all conversations with Brown-Forman so I was able to focus on ensuring that when we brought our brand to market, it would be the most well-researched of any brand the spirit industry had ever seen. I knew people would try to pick this story apart left and right. It had to be flawless. There could be no holes. I also knew I lacked the level of patience Keith has for nonsense. And this *non*existence agreement was just that.

Had I been the one negotiating with Brown-Forman, the answer on the coexistence agreement would have been a quick "Absolutely not" and we'd have been done.

Keith, on the other hand, negotiates for a living with leaders from countries who don't give straight answers. My negotiation strength is saying exactly what I will do, requiring the other side to do the same, and then giving a definitive yes or no immediately and moving on. Keith's tactic is to just let people talk. He might've been a little unsure about uprooting our lives to start a whiskey company, but he's the master of not saying no and not saying yes. When he negotiates with China or Japan on Sony's behalf, he lets things go back and forth. This was normal for him.

Each time the Brown-Forman people came back with a new response, he'd basically say, yeah, this doesn't really make sense for us, but let's keep the conversation going. And they kept coming up with new drafts, back and forth and back and forth.

"I rewrote elements of that coexistence agreement probably a hundred times over a period of a year and a half," Mark recalled later. "It was the bane of my life."

WE DECIDED to launch our first bottle, Uncle Nearest 1856 Premium Whiskey, in mid-July.

We would highlight the local Tennessee grains used in the mashbill and the charcoal mellowing process Nearest Green helped perfect over 160 years earlier. The whiskey was a natural caramel color with a deep golden hue, and it tasted amazing. We named it 1856 for the year we believed Nearest perfected the Lincoln County Process, the foundation of Tennessee whiskey. Our plan was to anchor a multi-million-dollar marketing campaign in two cities known for their love of craft whiskey cocktails—Portland, Oregon; and Nashville, Tennessee. Nearly every penny Keith and I raised in the friends and family round would be dedicated to PR and marketing. I would do the job of ten people to keep employee overhead low—a lesson I'd learned the brutal way from overextending myself during my first outing in entrepreneurship. Just one of those jobs was overseeing every aspect of the marketing, including our social media and concepting our commercials and advertising campaigns. I was—and remain—strategic about this, crafting and implementing marketing built around PR strategies I came up with at least six months in advance.

We'd also be launching through e-commerce channels, and Portland was home to one of the top boutique digital marketing firms in the country. If you wanted a bottle of Uncle Nearest the minute it came on the market, you'd have to buy it in-person in Oregon or online, and our digital marketing team there made it as easy for as many consumers to find us as possible. One week later, you could buy it in Tennessee. Our strategy was to add another state or two every month after that, with the goal of being in every state within two years.

Launching in Portland was purely practical. It would've been too hard to keep Uncle Nearest under wraps in Tennessee, but Portland was on the complete other side of the country. It's a vibrant and creative town with an incredible craft spirits market and a plethora of mixologists, bartenders, bar owners, store owners, and restaurant owners. We invited them, our friends and family, the Oregon Liquor Commission, and as many members of the press as we could get to the largest whiskey launch in the Rose City's history. We lined up our first distributor and worked with a food and beverage PR agency in Portland to craft a campaign that would introduce Uncle Nearest to the world on July 19, 2017.

I let myself walk into the situation with absolute abandon, certain in my knowledge that Nearest and Jack both wanted this story to be told. They both wanted Nearest's legacy to be cemented. And I had the great honor of being the one who was chosen to do that.

It was a fabulous party, with Uncle Nearest cocktails poured over ice cubes engraved with "1856" and delicious hors d'oeuvres. Keith's family was there; my sister was there; Katharine's husband flew in. We were blessed to be joined by so many of the people who'd loved and sustained us along the way.

"It was a really, really fun night," Katharine recalled. "We'd been working so hard to get there, it was like a wedding. It was really,

really fun to finally be there and to tell everybody what we'd been doing."

At one point I turned over a crate and climbed up on it to speak to the crowd. It was the first time I'd spoken publicly about the brand, and the first time I wore one of our signature "Honor" T-shirts before a group. (The circle with three stars that stands in for the first *o* is an homage to the Tennessee state flag.) I raised a glass and said a toast to Nearest, and to Jack. From our very first moments, we were raising up legends. After all, as one of our signs told our fans, "By the creek behind the preacher's house, Nearest Green turned water into gold."

The next day was exhilarating. Boom! The brand was here. The secret was out; the "UN project" was done—Uncle Nearest had arrived!

One week later, we had our Tennessee launch and went national with our first TV appearance. Our focus in Portland had been on the food and beverage industry, but in Tennessee, we concentrated on unfolding Nearest's story to the world. In Nashville at the end of July, we had an even bigger party. More cocktails, more press—but more importantly, members of the Green family and a lot of the people I'd come to know and love in Lynchburg.

AROUND THIS TIME, Keith received an inquiry from a Black executive within the Food & Beverage department of commercial banking at Wells Fargo. He was genuinely excited about Black owners entering the industry, having seen so few during his time in the business. However, he had numerous warnings for us. One evening, over dinner while he visited from Atlanta, he sternly advised us not to cross paths with Brown-Forman. They have the capacity to crush you like grapes, he said.

He made it clear he wasn't representing Brown-Forman—just sharing his perspective based on years of watching them dismantle potential competitors. He said they had a tendency to initiate lawsuits without hesitation and urged caution.

We were confident in our formidable legal team, I said—and more importantly, in my unwavering commitment to the mission I had embraced. Neither fear nor concern would sway me, I said.

Still, he said he'd keep his ear to the ground for us.

A month later, Keith and I were together in California, enjoying a rare break in my schedule. At 5 a.m., Keith's cell phone rang.

"They're coming for you!" the voice on the phone said. We both struggled to wake up and understand. It was the executive from Wells Fargo calling.

"They're coming for you!" he said again. He sounded panicked. He had a close friend within the Brown-Forman leadership team, and they'd just left a meeting where a decision had been made to enlist a journalist to target us. "They've found someone who's delving into your background, your businesses, personal life—everything." It would be a damaging piece, with no trace of Brown-Forman's fingerprints. "They've set this plan in motion," he said. "It's now the journalist's responsibility to do the dirty work."

Keith relayed all this to me. My answer was easy, and exactly what he expected it to be.

"I have absolutely no concerns," I said. "I'm an open book, and there's nothing about me that I haven't already shared in my books, press interviews, or public speaking engagements. So next time, could he kindly wait until 7 a.m. to express panic over something?"

SHORTLY AFTER OUR launch in Nashville, the story Clay Risen had written about my research and the start of the whiskey brand ran in the *New York Times*. Once again, they chose a bold headline: "When Jack Daniel's Failed to Honor a Slave, an Author Rewrote History."

This was a moment I'd been preparing for since March. This time the pissed-off people online seemed to fall into two main groups: Black people who felt I messed up the narrative by defending Jack Daniel as one of the good guys, and Jack Daniel's enthusiasts who felt I was undermining the value of their collectibles.

Babe, I'm sure you already know this, but you and Clay Risen share the same birthday, Keith texted me one day.

I didn't know that. I immediately stopped what I was doing and searched "Clay Risen" online. He didn't have a Wikipedia page, but Google showed he was born in 1976. *There were a lot of people born in 1976; that's not a big deal*, I thought.

Then I saw another web page that gave his exact birthday: September 5, 1976. The exact same day as mine. I remember gasping inwardly. *Someone much greater than us is pulling puppet strings on this.*

Everything made sense—all the coincidences and strange things that had fallen into place up until now. I knew we'd all been chosen to tell the story, rather than making that choice ourselves. That's when I knew we were the five—the five keepers of Nearest's story.

It's the coolest thing, Katharine thought when I told her about it later. *It doesn't even make sense. You just know there are other forces at work.*

CHAPTER

37

I**N THE** spirits industry, capturing consumers' attention isn't enough—our primary focus has to be catching the distributors' eye. If they aren't willing to present a brand to restaurants, bars, hotels, retail stores, and everywhere else people buy alcohol, the product can't be sold. To grab their attention, you need three things: a flurry of press coverage, significant and consistent marketing spend, and a substantial presence on the ground.

I hired a small team of salespeople whose charge was to hit the streets and make sure that people knew the significance of our bottle: that we were telling a story, and that unlike most of the stories behind American whiskey brands, ours was undeniably true. I also channeled a lot about love from my dad into how to tell that story. He wrote amazing songs about love, and he made a study of love in other people—how it works, why it sometimes fails, and why some people seem to come by it so naturally. This story was about a different kind of love and friendship, one that transcended race and lasted through generations, and I knew that had to come through with every bottle we sold to cement Nearest's legacy.

I also channeled a lot of what I'd learned about business, and how to operate within an industry that is rigged against independent creators, into all my daily efforts. I set significant goals for our team and for myself. Understanding the distributor tier's rightful allegiance to the spirit conglomerates who pay their bills, I told our team, "If we fail at any of these goals, it cannot be because of the distributors." I'd heard so many founders of independent brands in the spirits industry blame their lack of market penetration and growth on the distributor tier. "That will not be us," I told our sales team. "If we fail to meet our goals, that is on us, not on them. Until we have grown to be large enough to pay some of their bills, we must look at them as high-priced FedEx. Our job is to sell Uncle Nearest and make sure everyone knows the significance of Nearest Green. Their job is simply to drop off what we sell."

The team posed the question, in liquor stores, restaurants, and bars, about whether they had any whiskies or bourbons representing someone who wasn't a white man. People tended to just look over the bottles one by one, taking in Jack Daniel, Johnnie Walker, Jim Beam, Elijah Craig, Colonel E. H. Taylor, Blanton's, Pappy Van Winkle, and so on until they realized they really were all white guys. "Holy cow, this entire time," they'd say. My team would tell them how enslaved people had been integral to every bit of the whiskey-making process, from manufacturing to barrel-making to charring to filtering, and not one bottle on any shelf represented them—until now.

I charged Katharine with landing top distributors in every state— something that had never before been achieved by an independent brand in its first ten years, let alone in the time frame I'd set: two years. But Katharine took on the challenge and made it personal, and she did it in less than two. She knew we were going to make history together.

Katharine and I, along with Steven Henderson, zig-zagged the country doing sales presentations for the salespeople within the distribution companies responsible for selling our brand. Everyone we shared our goals with in that first year saw it as an impossible quest, but the three of us didn't believe in the impossible.

"We're talking thousands and thousands of miles between the three of us," Katharine recalled. "Traveling everywhere to ensure that as we got distribution somewhere, we were in that market." We trained people, visited bars, and partnered with mixologists. We did everything we could to introduce ourselves and get Uncle Nearest out there. It was a true start-up mentality. "Your sleeves are rolled up and you're everywhere, every day, just trying to tell your story," Katharine said.

On Fridays, each distributor would have their salespeople come into the office for trainings by suppliers, like us. On any given Friday, Katharine, Steven, and I would be in different cities, presenting to the distributors' teams of salespeople.

"It was literally divide and conquer," Katharine remembered. "Who can go here? Who can do this?"

We attended general sales meetings where dozens of brand representatives, including us, vied for the salespeople's attention. These were long days filled with pitches from various alcohol companies and product samplings—a surefire way to put anyone to sleep. During these journeys across the country, sharing the Uncle Nearest story, I became accustomed to receiving standing ovations in rooms that were almost always 98 percent made up of white men. They would approach me afterward, praising it as the best general sales meeting they'd ever attended, and express gratitude for keeping them engaged. After all, a full day of continuous alcohol product pitches and samplings could easily lead to fatigue.

The general sales meeting in Louisville, Kentucky, followed a similar pattern. The room was packed beyond capacity, and at the end of my pitch, the crowd erupted into thunderous applause. This reception pleasantly surprised me, considering that they also represented

Brown-Forman, whose corporate offices were just a few miles away. As I left, the enthusiasm from the salespeople encouraged me, and I informed Katharine that I expected significant growth for Uncle Nearest in Kentucky.

Later, I learned that following the standing ovation and the congratulatory gestures, after I had left the building, one of the leaders in the room stood up and uttered just four words: "We sell Jack Daniel's."

But we didn't know that yet. Instead, without delay, we hired a salesperson for the Kentucky market to work closely with the distributor and act as the boots on the ground for Uncle Nearest. Richie had a background at Jim Beam and knew many industry players in the region. But he struggled to elicit responses from their sales teams, who were mostly ignoring his calls, emails, and texts. This behavior was perplexing. Nevertheless, I reminded the team we couldn't blame the distributors if we didn't meet our goals.

Richie rolled up his sleeves and put in tremendous effort to grab the distributors' attention, but it seemed futile. This treatment was a common challenge faced by most new independent brands, so we knew how to handle it: we would do the work ourselves. Richie went door-to-door, conducting tastings and stocking shelves whenever he could. He persisted in his efforts, emailing and calling the distributor reps multiple times just to get product dropped off at accounts that he'd sold into.

Noticing a trend, I asked him to create a spreadsheet detailing every point of distribution we had and who secured it—him or the distributor. He meticulously compiled this data, which revealed a surprising fact: in 18 months, the distributor had secured only one point of distribution, while Richie had secured 169 out of 170.

The same distributor represented us in other states, and would continue to, but I knew what I had to do in Kentucky. One of my firm convictions upon entering this industry was not to allow anyone or anything to instill fear in me. No one was too big for me to hold accountable. While we might have been considered the underdog at the time, I approached every situation as if we were already a major player.

I asked Katharine to email Kentucky and let them know we were terminating the contract.

Anyone familiar with the industry will tell you that is not a common move. Most new distributor contracts for independent brands are unfavorable and restrictive. Fortunately, we had excellent attorneys who carefully reviewed every contract, understanding what the major players included in their agreements. We'd fought for as many of the big guys' rights as possible. I knew we could exit the contract, though it would undoubtedly be a hassle.

The distributor pushed back when Katharine communicated our decision. So, instead of engaging in a drawn-out back-and-forth, I made the phone call personally.

"We're ending our agreement," I said. "Your team has made no significant progress in 18 months, despite personal commitments made to me during the general sales meeting." The distributor argued that his team had secured 170 points of distribution, which was a commendable number for an independent brand in Kentucky, according to his assessment. Their rationale was that people in Bourbon country preferred Kentucky bourbon.

"Your team is lying to you," I said. "Richie secured 169 of the 170 points of distribution your team is claiming." The call grew heated, so I proposed an alternative. "How about you allow us to exit without resistance, and we'll switch to a regional distributor? One with a fraction of the sales force you have and covering only Louisville, rather than the entire state. After ninety days, I will report back to you on our progress. Then we'll know for sure if your Kentucky team has been providing inaccurate information."

We promptly made the transition, and within ninety days, our new Louisville distributor had secured over five hundred new points of distribution. By year-end, Kentucky had become one of our top eight states.

During an in-person meeting between Katharine and the original distributor's leadership team, they asked, "When can we expect to be released from the penalty box in Kentucky?"

"Funny you should ask," Katharine said. She presented the report on Kentucky I had asked her to prepare, fulfilling my commitment. As they reviewed it, their eyes widened in astonishment.

"What the hell were our guys doing in Kentucky?"

That's a valid question, Katharine replied.

AS SHE AND STEVEN got out into the sales world, Katharine asked me to do more and more press. "Everyone needs to know the woman behind this," she told me. It was never my intention to be as public-facing as I am. I'd hired a spokesperson early into the process and it was him, not me, who was quoted in each of our early press releases. But when the press reached out about the story, they never wanted to speak to him. They consistently asked to speak to me instead. I never consciously chose or approved it. I actually pushed back against it for as long as I could. It certainly wasn't how I'd led or managed any company before. My preference was strategizing from behind the scenes. But Katharine and Steven recognized something happened when I stepped in front of the camera: the world listened. The story was growing, and the interviews and the press kept coming—everything a start-up could ask for and more. Uncle Nearest was unique, and in being entrusted with telling Nearest's story, it had become intertwined with mine.

"From that moment on, the strategy never changed," Evette recalled. "It was placed upon her."

CHAPTER

38

THAT SUMMER, every member of the Green family received a black invitation with gold foil letters that read, "Join us as we honor the best whiskey maker the world never knew."

Five generations of Green descendants RSVP'd yes to return to their ancestors' hometown. They drove or flew into Nashville, and on August 12, 2017, nearly a hundred descendants boarded two buses to Lynchburg. They were nervous but excited. There were elders, teenagers, and little kids, cousins and nieces and nephews galore.

This was the first time all the branches of the Green family had come together. Most didn't know one another, and some didn't know the others existed. "Watching them discover each other's existence was so beautiful," Evette said. "There was so much love and honor and anticipation of meeting everyone."

Miss Helen's doctor had warned her she didn't have long to live and shouldn't travel, but she made the trip to Tennessee anyway. At eighty-six, she was a matriarch of the family, and everyone treated her like royalty.

We started the day with lunch at Miss Mary Bobo's, where each descendant was given twelve cards with previously unknown facts about Nearest Green. "We had food and just—fellowship," Aunt Tee remembered. "That's the word I want to use. It was like a fellowship."

Then we drove to the Call Farm. It was a rainy day at first, and we had to be careful in the mud and soppy grass. But then the sun came out, and it was a glorious day there on the farm.

Each family member walked through the research room and saw the family tree we'd spent months putting together containing each of their names, birth dates, locations, ancestors, siblings, and children. We encouraged them to correct errors directly on the oversized document.

Then I led everyone to the spring, where I'd put up a white tent alongside the exact place where the original Jack Daniel Distillery once sat and where Nearest Green made his famous whiskey for Distillery No. 7. Hundreds of family photos dangled from string lights with clothespins, along with birth, death, and military certificates, too. They stretched from one tent corner to another so everyone could walk around and examine them closely. There were large photos of Nearest's children and grandchildren printed on canvas and mounted on wooden frames. We printed another copy of the family tree on a huge poster board and hung it for everyone to take a good look at.

The photos and records helped them see how each branch of the family was connected. The cousins all friended one another on Facebook and started a family page so they could keep up with what everyone else was doing. A bartender made Uncle Nearest–based cocktails. People posed for photos in front of their ancestors' photographs, and they all crowded into a big family shot toward the bottom of the spring, a short distance from where the original gristmill once stood.

A lot of the Greens tasted the spring water. Some people filled their water bottles. Others took off their shoes and socks and dipped their feet in the stream. "Somebody's going to always do that," Aunt Tee laughed.

Visiting the Call Farm made a big impression on Jackie, Debbie, and Jerome. They hadn't spent time there as kids, but they knew its significance. They took in the spring and the road that Jack and George would have traveled by horse and buggy. They walked the ruins of the slave quarters where Nearest and Harriet and their children lived.

Their grandmother's stories became real. "What she had been telling us," Jackie said, "it was like we could see it."

It was beautiful, Debbie thought, and being there made it easier to picture Nearest at work. Long after the event, Aunt Tee remained struck by the bedroom with the stencils on the wall.

"Meeting the descendants and seeing the families united, it was incredible," Evette said.

Many of the family members met Keith for the first time that day, too. He got to know them all, moving from table to table in a blue polo as I did the same in my Honor tee. I was so glad for Keith to see the family like this and get to know them as I had. Preserving and amplifying Nearest's story through a whiskey bottle made so much sense and had so much power when you could see his descendants walking where Nearest worked.

"I felt like we were trusted very early," Keith recalled. "Before we deserved to be trusted, to be honest, and embraced almost like being introduced to the family."

We gathered around big round tables that had mason jars overflowing with daisies and black-eyed Susans. Everyone got a bottle of Uncle Nearest 1856.

Since the launch, I'd discovered I'd greatly undershot the cost of getting shelf space in any bar, restaurant, or retailer. We needed to raise more money—quickly. But every person we personally knew who had the ability to invest already had.

"I've had a hard time raising the money," I told the family. "It's a risky venture. If you know anyone who might want to invest, please let me know. But either way, I commit to do whatever it takes to keep bringing these bottles to the market."

No one took me up on that, although that was to be expected. Many of them didn't know people in a financial position to invest, and this was an extraordinarily risky endeavor being led by someone who had never been in the whiskey industry before this brand. I imagine their thoughts were similar to Keith's and mine when we began, not wanting to be responsible for losing friends' or family money.

Despite this vulnerable moment, we were excited to share something we had been successful at achieving. We announced the names of the Nearest Green Legacy Scholarship recipients who'd been granted full scholarships to college that fall.

After that, the family members held up glasses of Uncle Nearest 1856 high in the air.

"Here's to the teacher and his student," I toasted. "Here's to the mentor and his mentee. Here's to Jack, the man by which none of us would even know this story if it were not for his success. And here's to the greatest whiskey maker the world never knew, Nathan 'Nearest' Green."

With that, nearly every living member of the Green family raised their glasses and said, "Cheers to Nearest!"

Six hundred miles away, we later learned, deadly violence had occurred the same day between white nationalists and protestors in Charlottesville, Virginia. "It was this beautiful moment where all these Greens were meeting each other, many of them for the first time," Katharine said, "and then this was happening, parallel, hours away." The juxtaposition on social media of our loving, happy photos—made possible by Lynchburg and its unique past—and the photos out of Charlottesville was stark.

WHILE WE HAD the honor of Miss Helen visiting us in Lynchburg, I accompanied her on a tour of Jack Daniel Distillery. It was a glorious day as the tour guide fawned over her for two full hours, understandably honored to be in her presence. Miss Helen led the bus driver up to the top of the hill, where she grew up, and shared with them that this land once belonged to her family. The Jack Daniel's tour guide and bus driver had no clue. As we approached Jack's old office, she told the tour guide, "I heard folks say there's a picture of my granddaddy here. Show it to me. I can tell you if it's him. He raised me."

After we were led inside, I guided Miss Helen's wheelchair over to a prominent image on the wall—the photo from the *New York Times* article with a Black man sitting next to Jack.

"Take me closer," she told me. I pushed her wheelchair a couple feet forward and stopped.

She raised up ever so slightly from her wheelchair, "Yes, that's him!" she proudly exclaimed with a smile. "That's Daddy George." When Aunt Nell hadn't been able to identify the Black man in the photo, I had lost hope that we would ever be able to say for sure who he was. Miss Helen—maybe the only person left alive who still remembered George's face—had just confirmed what I'd been aching to prove.

To finally recognize the face of George Green was like getting a glimpse of Nearest himself. It was a monumental moment for the project. *We're literally rewriting a part of American history*, I texted Stephani.

CHAPTER 39

THE CONVENTIONAL wisdom for starting a spirits company is to start local, sell into bars and restaurants, and expand once you're successful at that.

"There were times where I felt like I was kind of getting this proverbial pat on my head," Katharine recalled. "There has not been a lot of disruption in this industry, truly."

But we didn't have that kind of time. We were in make-it-or-break-it territory, so we decided to ignore traditional advice and go national right away. Nearest needed to be known everywhere; Oregon, Tennessee, and a trickle of other states just wasn't enough. We pushed the boundaries and made some mistakes, but we succeeded.

By the end of the summer, a little more than a year after I first read the *New York Times* article in my hotel in Singapore, Uncle Nearest had arrived in stores all across the country. We were digging deep into our pockets to fund our purchases of mature Tennessee whiskey, in addition to crafting our own. The product we made in-house wouldn't be ready for sale for at least four years, which meant the bills kept mounting for a product we were at least 1,408 days away from monetizing (not that anyone was keeping count).

We were on a relentless quest for financial partners. Investors were now keenly interested in us—but in exchange they wanted equity, or ownership of a percentage of the company. I refused to allow this until we were nearly running on empty, though. Our valuation stood at $25 million, which sounds substantial for a new company—but it was actually pretty modest when you consider we needed to raise approximately $10 million. Raising too much money in exchange for equity early on would mean being stripped of control over our own enterprise, and that was a nonnegotiable no. So Keith and I continued funneling every penny from his job and our collective investments into the venture. We personally secured loans from banks, leveraging our individual credit scores. But the company had only a one-year track record, so it remained a high-risk investment.

While we looked for financing alternatives, we learned that virtually every major bank had a specialized beverage lending department, primed to assist start-up spirit brands.

Could there be a more thrilling start-up spirit brand than Uncle Nearest right now? I thought.

Keith was still positioned as the figurehead of Uncle Nearest so we could make strides in the industry while it started to get used to the sound of women's voices on the other end of its business calls. He met with Gregory Webb, a consultant who had previously navigated the start-up landscape in this industry and had connections with various banks' beverage lending departments. Gregory was extremely confident that Uncle Nearest was destined for greatness and believed the banks would vie for the opportunity to back us.

Gregory made a flurry of calls ahead of the annual National Beer Wholesaler Association's convention and trade show in Las Vegas. Despite the beer-centric focus that drew most of the thousands of attendees, many of the nation's spirits wholesalers would be there, networking their way through Caesars Palace. Armed with a persuasive pitch deck, Gregory began setting up meetings between Keith and representatives from nearly every major bank. Their beverage lending teams had requisitioned conference rooms for these pivotal pitch meetings.

Wearing his best suit, feeling excited, trepidatious, and just a bit anxious, Keith arrived at the first room. He and Gregory were immediately met by bad news: the meeting had been canceled.

Before they could reach the second meeting, that one was canceled too. It kept happening, again and again, all day long. There was clear interest among the junior level of bankers who'd set up the meetings, but the senior people who made the decisions kept deciding not to proceed.

The last bank Keith was slated to meet with was also the one with the largest beverage lending department—an ideal partner for Uncle Nearest. Keith and Gregory watched a horde of bankers enter the conference room. Keith prepared himself to make what could be the pitch of a lifetime.

But the door swung open, and a man stepped out to deliver the crushing news—this meeting was canceled, too.

Gregory insisted he and Keith wouldn't leave unless they were allowed to pitch the brand. The banker relented and agreed to hear the pitch himself.

They sat together at a coffee stand and, nestled beside some slot machines at the edge of the casino floor, Keith made the Uncle Nearest pitch. But the banker did very little listening. Instead, he worked on his phone nearly the entire time—texting, emailing; basically doing everything he could that didn't involve looking Keith in the eye or paying attention to his pitch.

Finally, Keith gave up. Deflated and likely on the verge of internal tears (he's not the public crying type), he went back to the hotel room and called to tell me about the day. So many doors had slammed in our faces. We both felt an ominous sense of being locked out. With our options nearly exhausted, we clung to each other through the phone line, finding solace in each other's words.

It would have been easy to be disheartened by this kind of rejection by institutional investors and private equity funds. In retrospect, it was simply too soon to expect results from an event like that. But I remember feeling that if ever there was a moment that required divine intervention, this was it.

It turned out to be a blessing in disguise.

Here's what happened instead: our longtime attorney Ross Burningham introduced me to John Eugster, an investment banker who stands out against the backdrop of conventional venture capitalists. John became a strategic partner from day one, and he helped us find early investors like Curtis Gardner, Minott Wessinger, Devin Johnson, and Larry Wert, who grasped the import of what we were doing and whose mindset matched our mission.

John's group found more investors, and I got to know them, hosting groups at the Dan Call farm and introducing them to everything I'd fallen in love with in Lynchburg. Some people came into the investment with the mindset that we'd have to sell Uncle Nearest to Brown-Forman eventually—a highly profitable outcome—but over time they've come to share my position that we're forging a different way forward and needed their help to build Uncle Nearest into a great American brand for generations to come.

Corporate leader Mark Pacchini and Craig Leipold, owner of the Minnesota Wild hockey team, joined me for one of those investor tours. As Mark has reminded me every year since, I told their group, "If you don't believe in God, you will by the end of this tour."

And by the end, they did. There were just too many things that had happened exactly as they needed to happen; something greater was at work here.

We've continued to attract more investors than we needed every time we've done an equity fundraising round. And we've now built a whole coalition of individual investors who share our vision—and we've found they tend to network closely. They've helped us establish a nationwide presence in hotels, restaurants, and airport lounges that is astonishing for an independent spirit brand.

IN OCTOBER 2017, Keith and I learned that white supremacist groups were applying for permits and demonstrating in lots of towns, basically trying to provoke another Charlottesville. They picked Shelbyville and Murfreesboro.

Business owners in Shelbyville started putting up signs to let the "White Lives Matter" rallygoers know they weren't welcome here. That made me really happy to see. Keith and I were celebrating a friend's birthday weekend in Sonoma the day the rally was supposed to happen, and I was keeping an eye on the clock and refreshing my phone for updates. It was covered widely on the news.

Oh my gosh, I hope this isn't another Charlottesville, I remember thinking.

The Shelbyville square had filled with a crowd of protestors. The town had arranged things so the two hundred or so white supremacists had the space they were legally allowed to occupy, but there were barricades keeping them and the Shelbyville protestors, who were nearly all white and wildly outnumbered them, separate and across the street from one another. As the white supremacists began filing into town later than anticipated, a protester taunted them over the microphone. "Some master race," he said. "Can't even show up on time."

As the white supremacists' featured speaker tried to give a speech, the protesters began playing a recording of Martin Luther King's "I Have a Dream" speech on a loudspeaker. They never let the guy talk;

they just kept cranking Dr. King's volume higher and higher. They never let him get anything out.

The white supremacists were supposed to get back on their buses and head to Murfreesboro, where even larger crowds of protestors were waiting for them, but they wound up canceling the whole event. I was a continent away in California, scrolling through my phone, going, *Yes! They were not expecting what they got in Shelbyville!*

Some folks in Lynchburg worried about a proposed rally materializing in town, but everyone knows white supremacists aren't welcome in Lynchburg. I loved the towns' responses, and I remain enormously proud of both.

A S MISS NEAT recalled it, I had a vision of raising a monument for Nearest and Harriet at Highview Cemetery the very first day we met.

Vision became reality on December 2, 2017. It was a hot, hazy day, but a group of us gathered in Highview Cemetery, behind Berry Chapel AME. We erected a large iron sign identifying HIGHVIEW CEMETERY, established circa 1891, along with a monument to Nearest. I wanted visitors to be able to see Nearest's name from Jack's resting place and to know the cemetery by its name, rather than the Black or colored cemetery.

For the dedication, we put down gravel and hay bales, set up rows of metal folding chairs, and wrapped a bright red ribbon around the cemetery fence. Attendees were invited to come early and decorate friends' and family's gravesites.

When we gathered, the monument itself was covered by a heavy tarp. We had a big buffet lunch set up inside the church for the family. Most people dressed casually—jeans and tennis shoes for walking through the cemetery grounds—but others wore their Sunday best.

"It was so much excitement going on," Aunt Tee recalled recently. "People in and out, going inside, getting something to eat, coming back outside, and sitting there waiting for them to unveil the monument."

Miss Helen came down from Indianapolis. Aunt Tee came down from St. Louis. Descendants flew in from all over, and we brought the out-of-towners in from Nashville on coach buses.

Debbie, Jackie, Jerome, and Victoria attended, along with John T. Bobo, whom we'd met at Celebration during our very first days in town, and his ninety-seven-year-old mother Marie. Miss Neat was there, of course, and Joel Pitts and Miss Dot and Claude Eady. Jo Anne Gaunt Henderson joined us and took lots of pictures.

A sizable Jack Daniel's contingent came to pay their respects. Mark McCallum stood toward the back of the crowd beside Larry Combs, the general manager of Jack Daniel's global supply chain. Melvin Keebler, Jack Daniel's assistant general manager, and Jeff Arnett, Jack Daniel's master distiller, were there. Numerous of Jack Daniel Distillery employees who lived in Lynchburg joined us, too. It felt like nearly the whole town was there.

We gathered everyone in with a song from the Believer's Faith Fellowship praise and worship team. Once everybody was seated, with many standing in the back and along the sides, Jo Anne shared a brief history of the cemetery.

"Many of the people buried here are our family members, but before they died, they were the citizens of this Lynchburg community," she said. "They were business owners, homeowners, and above all, respected people of the community." Nearly every Black person in Lynchburg who'd passed away since 1891 was buried there.

"A little whirlwind and ball of thunder blew into town and turned this small Lynchburg community upside down on a great mission," she said, recounting my search for Nearest's burial place. "I want to thank

God for placing this vision on her heart and guiding her here at this appointed time."

I took the mic, wearing one of the T-shirts we'd had made for my niece Brittany's celebration of life, featuring a favorite photo of her paired with the reminder to "Live for Today." It felt like she was with us, and she was at the top of my mind.

Hope was what I'd needed in that moment more than anything else, I said. I had to grieve Brittany, but I'm not really the grieving kind. I'm a "catch me if you can" kind of person when it comes to grief. Instead, I work. My need for work and hope, and not to grieve, is what put me on a plane and sent me to Lynchburg. It fueled everything I did.

I was near tears as I spoke. The racial divide in our country at that moment was also very present in my mind, with nonstop news cycles seeming to set race relations back by decades. I was so proud of the region's reaction to the white supremacist rallies just a couple of months earlier.

"The love, honor, and respect of Nearest and Jack flourished here, and let me ignore all the noise from the rest of the country and focus solely on the positive relations between Black people and white people in Lynchburg."

Our joyous gathered crowd was briefly silent. All you could hear was the faint sound of gravel crunching underfoot. After all these years, God's charcoal was still working in my spirit—and now so was Nearest's.

We recognized some of the oldest descendants among us. I asked Miss Helen, Nearest's eldest descendant, and Joanne Woodson, Dan Call's eldest descendant, to come forward and cut the ribbon. I saw tears running down Joanne's face as she sat in the front row. Both were in declining health, and I was so honored to have them there. After that, I asked the Green family members to come forward and surround the memorial.

Mammie's grandson Jeff Vance, in a red velvet jacket, thanked everyone for coming out to honor his ancestors and all the Black pillars of Lynchburg. Then he pulled the heavy tarp down, revealing the monument.

Everyone cheered.

"It was just breathtaking," Aunt Tee said. "Everybody was in awe."

The monument towered over the crowd with the deeply etched letters spelling out GREEN visible from the cemetery gate. In a style reminiscent of their son George's grave, Nearest and Harriet's monument has two columns. They flank an urn labeled Sugar Maple Charcoal, to honor his contributions to the Lincoln County Process, and we had laid fresh sugar maple charcoal inside the inner cylinder to honor Nearest. These words appear at the base of the monument: "Father. Husband. Mentor. The Best Whiskey Maker the World *Never* Knew."

A pastor prayed over the cemetery, and then the quiet was broken and the ceremony turned to a happy celebration and family reunion. We played music over tall speakers. Everyone was eating, talking, laughing, and enjoying one another.

"It was a day of awe and honor," Evette recalled. "There was so much love."

As we mingled, I was glad to finally meet Melvin Keebler. He'd worked at Jack Daniel's since the early 2000s, and he was the first senior-level Black person I met in the whiskey industry. Melvin was from Selma, Alabama, and served in the Navy aboard a nuclear submarine in his pre-whiskey life. As the general manager for technical services and whiskey maturation, he oversaw nine different departments at Jack Daniel's—everything from engineering and maintenance to barrel distribution and data analytics. Over time he also took on diversity and inclusion.

"The Green family is just as much a part of the history at Jack Daniel's as Jack and the Motlow family," Melvin said. "I don't know of a friendship or a collaboration that is as long-lasting to an industry."

To his point, nowadays, when a Jack Daniel's aficionado stands at Jack's grave and looks into the distance, they'll see Nearest's marker, too.

When you go by Highview today, it's a beautiful spot on a country road, peaceful as it ever was, with a still, small pond just beyond it. Even if it isn't Nearest and Harriet's final resting place, a great many of his family are there, comfortingly close to the church they loved.

Brittany would have loved that day. It was for her, like everything I do, but it was also for Nearest, for Harriet, for all the Greens—past and present. I surveyed the scene, looking around at all my Lynchburg neighbors, friends, and so many who helped uncover the truth and made me an honorary family member. They'd graciously allowed and helped me replace my grief with meaningful work, whether they knew it or not. Each and every one had contributed to making sure Nearest would never be forgotten.

PART

THREE

⟨✦⟩

DECEMBER 2017

THROUGH

PRESENT

CHAPTER

41

B Y THE end of the year, we'd spent a million dollars on bill-boards and digital ads. Stores sold out, and customers went online to buy the product. In the process, they learned our story and became unofficial ambassadors—retelling our story all over the country. We were selling faster than we could bottle!

Keith and Mark continued to negotiate the coexistence agreement, but they agreed to navigate things on a case-by-case basis in the meantime. Mark encouraged his organization to voice their concerns to him if they felt Uncle Nearest did something that went against the IP interests of Jack Daniel's.

Predictably, emails came flooding in. *We saw they did this. We saw they did that.*

The US sales and marketing team for Jack Daniel's was big—probably a thousand people strong—and they did not like what we were up to. Many of them had struggled with the news that we were launching what many of them believed to be a competing product. They were even competitive with other Brown-Forman brands internally. In meetings they referred to them as SOBs—Some Other Brand.

So being told to be nice and share shelf space with Uncle Nearest didn't go over well with them. It ran counter to their company culture.

They "didn't look at it the way I was looking at it," Mark McCallum recalled of the salespeople deep in the organization. They "looked at it as undeserved competition." And they wanted us to fail.

"Some thought the company couldn't risk letting an outside brand—run by a Californian, nonetheless!—redefine part of the Jack Daniel's story," Clay Risen later reported for *Bourbon+*, a whiskey enthusiasts' publication. That captured it exactly.

For one thing, we heard that Jack Daniel's folks were testing and analyzing Uncle Nearest at their distillery. They were trying to figure out what was in the bottle. They were looking for regulatory compliance mistakes.

Keith found this out through some complicated web of actors, beverage industry guys, and others who knew spirits, then made some calls to confirm it. *The world is so small*, he thought. *People always talk*. And in the end, it was just business. It actually made a lot of sense—why *wouldn't* you test your competitor's product if you had a lab at your disposal and knew what you were doing?

I knew we were making our Uncle Nearest to code. But I didn't like the idea of anyone at Jack Daniel's messing around with our product.

Lynchburg residents and frequent visitors were restive, too. There was talk of a Squires' boycott of Barrel House BBQ as word of Chuck Baker's support for Uncle Nearest spread.

Chuck—himself a Squire—took the whole thing in stride. "You got people who grew up here their whole lives," he said. "Jack Daniel's is the only thing here, really, industry-wise. It's fed a lot of people for a lot of years. There's people that are just diehard."

Chuck loved being a Squire and didn't let the negativity get to him. "The best thing about being a Squire is all the other Squires," he likes to say—and he means it. He's met Squires from all over the world and made more friends than most of us will get to in a lifetime.

It's hard for anyone to pass up Chuck's "grilled cheese on crack" long enough for it to register as a boycott, so I was never worried about Barrel House BBQ. And as John T. Bobo says, "You've got redneck idiots in all consonants, shapes, and sizes wherever you go." The whole episode just made me appreciate Chuck, himself a self-proclaimed redneck, all the more.

Mark had a strategy to bring around the naysayers that mostly seemed to involve having me talk to Brown-Forman—talking to the executive committee, the board, the employee resource groups, and so on. As he put it, I'd be 90 percent of the content, and he'd be the "top and tail" of the sessions.

I was happy to do it but decided only to talk with the Brown-Forman folks about history and leave the business discussions to Keith. I didn't want the things that were happening on the business level to influence how I shared the story—or what I told the press. I wanted my role to be completely pure and focused on the historical record. Keith did the best to protect me from what the Jack Daniel's people were doing to try and harm our company behind the scenes so that I could protect Jack Daniel the man. At that time, most people didn't distinguish him from the brand named after him—the brand his family hadn't owned for some sixty years.

And it seemed to work. Hearing me speak about Nearest and the legacy of friendship between him and Jack had a real and observable effect on the skeptics.

SEEMINGLY EVERYONE IN Lynchburg takes immense pride in Jack Daniel's, even folks who don't work there. They feel like Jack Daniel's is their own. I get it. I fell in love with Lynchburg too—the one stop light, the little library, the barrel tree at Christmas—but it's not my town the way it is theirs.

Nearest had moved to County Line. Maybe it would be good for us to give Jack a little space, too.

At any rate, it was becoming clear that our time living out of suitcases in Lynchburg was naturally drawing to an end. Keith and I needed a real home. His parents had relocated to Murfreesboro, about an hour away from Lynchburg and a college town that's home to Middle Tennessee State University. Keith's mom told me she'd known we weren't moving back to California since the moment she'd looked in my eyes as I shared with her the legacy of Nearest Green. Keith is her only child, and at the time she was hoping grandbabies would be on the way soon, so she and Keith's bonus father sold their house in California and bought a house in Tennessee, sight unseen.

As we began to look to the future, we realized we couldn't build a distillery at the Call Farm—the land was too sloped for barrelhouses, and although it was big, it wasn't nearly big enough for what we had in mind.

Besides, Lynchburg was Jack Daniel country. Jack built that town. As Katharine later said, Jack Daniel's had "spent more than a century and a lot of marketing dollars putting Lynchburg on the map," and we respected that.

And we weren't going far. Keith and I had come to love the town of Shelbyville, sixteen miles away, where we'd stopped on our very first day in Tennessee.

It had a neat history, too. During the Civil War, parts of Tennessee had been conflicted about joining the Confederacy. Eventually, Tennessee joined the Southern cause, despite supplying more soldiers for the Union than any other Confederate state. Lynchburg had been solidly Confederate territory, but Shelbyville was among the dissenters.

An October 8, 1862, issue of *Harper's Weekly* dubbed Shelbyville "the Only Union Town of Tennessee."

A Union soldier quoted in the article said, "Shelbyville stands alone in the rebel States true to the Union. . . . Shelbyville is like an oasis to a traveler in a great desert."

That's how Keith and I felt, too. We savored the idea of getting out of Lynchburg and relocating to a town where we could go to the grocery store or church without everybody recognizing us.

It had been wonderful to be in such a small, tight-knit community when I was doing research for the book, but now I was building a business. Shelbyville was far enough away from Lynchburg for peace of mind, but close enough that I could still drop in on Berry Chapel AME, pick up BBQ from Barrel House, or say hi to Miss Dot. When Keith and I found a beautiful home halfway between Shelbyville and Lynchburg, it seemed like fate. It's right about where I began to wiggle and hope for a restroom on our first day in Tennessee. Today, our house is positioned so that fifteen minutes in one direction is Nearest and fifteen minutes in the other is Jack.

The woman who originally had this home built asked the fire chief how long it would take for his firemen to reach her home if it caught on fire. The chief said, "Your house will burn down before we get there." So she hired the architect behind several famous projects in Nashville to build her home out of solid concrete, every bit of it. After years of being concerned about my research being burned, it's finally safe.

Keith and I are definitely Shelbyvillians now. I absolutely love it here. I love the people. Our living room has a floor-to-ceiling window that looks out over the rolling hills. In the distance, on the next hill over, sits a pretty white church with a steeple. Lucy, my sweet dog who came with us from the Call Farm, has the run of the place. We named the property Still Point because it's our still point in a turning world.

KEITH AND I were also incredibly lucky to find a new home for Uncle Nearest at Sand Creek Farms. Set on 270 acres, it had originally been a historic walking horse farm. Like many other large horse farms in the Shelbyville area, Sand Creek had been a place dedicated to breeding, training, and preparing the horses for shows and competitions. Its beautiful fields full of horses were a popular landmark.

We'd been eyeing a property with existing whiskey-making facilities along a dead-end road on the south side of Lincoln County. But every time we drove between Lynchburg and Murfreesboro to visit Mom and Pop, this beautiful property would catch my eye. The land was stunning, right on the highway between Nashville and Lynchburg, and I could see the vision immediately: We could rework the hay barn into a 3,500-barrel single story rickhouse. A three-hundred-foot former horse barn could be converted into the Nearest Green History Walk. The six-hundred-seat sales arena could be reimagined as a private concert venue for country music artists.

I called John T. and, of course, he knew the owner. In fact, he was the same person who'd sold us the four acres for the Nearest Green Memorial Park in Lynchburg, and John T. represented him. The plan had been to build a residential community on the land, but it turned out there were too many springs running belowground to make the soil conducive for building foundations. What would have been a building disaster for him would be perfect for a whiskey distillery in search of underground springs. Within a few months, John T.'s client put the property on the market, and we made an immediate offer.

We made big plans for a distillery, tasting room, and music venue with a bar whose length would break a Guinness World Record. We wanted to grow one hundred acres of corn and name it the Field of Dreams.

This was going to be so much more than a simple distillery. It would take years, but we'd work to make it happen. It's been that way ever since I started FEW Entertainment as a young woman and made being successful in business my dream. Most of my dreams are those I've picked up and adopted as I went.

Nearly every Tennessee distillery during the time Nearest was alive was built on a farm, so it made sense to keep horses and cattle. Plus, I've always loved horses. I couldn't turn down a chance to have a few dozen of them around.

Three months after we first saw the place, I stopped by Chuck Baker's BBQ in Lynchburg and asked him to meet me at the farm the next morning. Chuck joined me, Keith, and a few other folks out at Sand Creek Farms. In order to buy the land and turn it into a distillery, we needed to get a unanimous vote from the commissioners to rezone the area.

I wanted to build for Shelbyville and its residents what Jack built in Lynchburg. I wanted to build something that would become Nearest's, something the people of Shelbyville felt belonged to them, too. "We needed to lay down our roots," Katharine Jerkens recalled.

We walked into the kitchen area, with its large commercial hood vent. The space had obviously been used as a kitchen before. I looked at Keith. He looked at me. And then we turned to Chuck. We just knew at that moment—we had to create a second Barrel House BBQ at the Nearest Green Distillery at Sand Creek Farms.

It was a wonderful full-circle moment. Chuck was ambitious; he'd told us that first night—back when we were afraid he was going to kill us in the woods—that he wanted to expand his business. And now we'd be expanding together. We'd be bringing a little bit of Lynchburg to Shelbyville, and our good friend would be coming, too.

ONE OF THE first things I planned for the distillery was a non-alcoholic speakeasy, Philo + Frank's, named for and built in honor of my father Frank, a teetotaler until he passed away, and my mother Philomina, who is still one to this day. When I started Uncle Nearest, my mother said to me, "I'm so proud of you, and I love what you're doing for that man and his family, but I sure do wish he made lemonade." Years later, she said, "So I guess I'm forever going to be known as the whiskey lady's mom." She's enormously proud of me—has been my entire adult life—but the role that spirits play in my life remains a disconnect for her.

With that in mind, Philo + Frank's pays tribute to the women of the temperance movement as well as those who led the suffrage movement. Their social reforms improved the lives of women and children and changed the world.

From the beginning, I knew I wanted everyone at Uncle Nearest to know they were working toward a higher calling. So we ditched the idea of "drinking responsibly" and instead encouraged enthusiasts of Uncle Nearest to "drink honorably." When we raise a glass of Uncle Nearest or something nonalcoholic, we celebrate all those who came before us and paved the way. It isn't just about what is in the glass (although, if I'm putting something to my lips, rest assured it must taste quite good), it is an act of celebration and a reminder of our great freedoms.

To me, drinking honorably acknowledges that imbibing simply mirrors and amplifies what's already in our hearts. I love to see people sit down to drink, and I love to join them—but I won't do it on an empty stomach, and you're not going to see me drunk. I appreciate drinking as something that lowers inhibitions. And a lot of us need our inhibitions lowered! So I certainly don't consider drinking a vice. I have to imagine if Jesus's first miracle had taken place in a corn-growing region like Tennessee, he would have been turning our limestone-filtered Tennessee spring water into whiskey instead of wine.

AROUND THIS TIME, the actor and *Westworld* star Jeffrey Wright reached out to me. After he read Clay Risen's original story, he'd saved the photo of George Green and Jack Daniel on his phone. The rural South is part of Jeffrey's DNA. His grandfather Boo had been a southern Virginia waterman, a crabber, an oysterman, a farmer—and a whiskey man. Boo's mother had taught him to make moonshine, and Jeffrey remembers his grandfather selling fifty-cent shots.

Nearest's story struck Jeffrey as a "secret chamber" of American history—the kind of nuanced story that large brands are reluctant to face and delve into. He savored the knowledge that Jack Daniel's, just like the rock-and-roll it's so often associated with, "has its origins in Black hands." He marveled at the nature of the story—that Jack Daniel had not only worked alongside an enslaved man and formed a "familial bond" with him, but was in fact mentored by Nearest. "It defies our contemporary, shallow understanding of what life might have been like at that time," Jeffrey said.

So he found himself pulling Jack and George's photo out every time he went to a bar, telling every bartender he met about Nearest, and toasting with them to their new understanding.

One day he stopped into a Valencia, California, bar after a day of filming on *Westworld*. This time when he told the story, the bartender already knew it—and told Jeffrey something new: "There's a bottle of this now. There's a woman behind it, and she's based here in LA."

Jeffrey reached out to see how he could be involved as an investor or voice of the brand. At the time, I thanked him and said I'd just finished a round of funding and wasn't looking for additional investors at that time, or a voice, but the moment I set out to do another round of money raising, he would be my first call.

CHAPTER

42

THE QUESTION underpinning everything I was doing was: If Nearest Green could have owned his own distillery, would he have?

I believed the answer could only be a resounding yes. So did Victoria Eady-Butler, Mammie's granddaughter and a fifth-generation descendant of Nearest's, who joined the company as a shareholder and became our master blender. She started out administering the Nearest Green Foundation, but we all soon discovered she had whiskey in her blood.

When it was time to add another expression to our portfolio, we wanted to get a member of Nearest's family personally involved. Uncle Nearest 1884 Premium Small Batch Whiskey would turn out to be lighter-bodied, 93-proof, and aged a minimum of seven years. We named it in commemoration of the year we believed Nearest may have last put his own whiskey into barrels before retiring. The bottles would be curated and signed by Victoria, his great-great-granddaughter.

She lived in Nashville but had grown up in Lynchburg in the 1970s hearing her grandma's stories about Nearest with Debbie, Jackie, and Jerome. "I had the absolute best childhood," she said. "Growing up in

Lynchburg, I would not trade it for anything in the world." She had especially fond memories of high school, where she had plenty of friends—Black and white—whom she remains close with to this day. Chuck Baker was several years behind her in school and remembers being wowed by all she accomplished. She was a cheerleader, acted in plays, and was named Miss Moore County High School 1979, making her the school's first Black homecoming queen.

"That was never an issue," Victoria said. Lynchburg was special in her eyes. "Black people and white people would gather all the time" and for every occasion. "The only time that there was separation—and it's still much like that today—is Sunday morning at church."

In college at Middle Tennessee State University, she found Black people and white people kept themselves much more separate. She had a great college experience otherwise, but it was startling after what she'd grown up with in Lynchburg.

Things were so harmonious that some barriers only became evident in hindsight, after they were broken. Victoria's girlfriends liked to go swimming, and she wanted to join them. None of her relatives swam—back then, some people still believed that Black people don't swim by nature—but she learned how and loved it. She went swimming every day and even became a lifeguard. Eventually, Mammie told Victoria she was the first Black person to swim in the public pool in Lynchburg.

"No one told anybody not to," she said. "They just didn't do it."

Victoria had known since seventh grade that she wanted to go into law enforcement. Her grandmother hoped that might evolve into becoming a lawyer or a judge in the mold of John T. Bobo, whose family she knew well. "The whole town was proud of him," Victoria recalled. Mammie wanted Victoria to attain that kind of status and accomplishment. There had never been a Black judge in Lynchburg, and Mammie wanted Victoria to be the first.

"She always thought I was the kind of gal to lead people and guide people," Victoria recalled. Plus, "she always said I'm bossy," so it would be a good fit.

Victoria didn't want to be a judge, but her grandmother was right: she is a natural leader. She spent decades as an analytical manager at the Department of Justice before discovering her place in the whiskey world.

We'd met her at the college graduation of her niece, one of the foundation's scholarship recipients. It was a beautiful day of celebration, and the whole family turned out to watch her earn honors from the University of Tennessee Chattanooga. Keith and I were graciously invited to join them. We'd gotten to know the entire family intimately but somehow never managed to meet Victoria despite all the time spent with her siblings Debbie and Jackie.

After the ceremony, Victoria shouldered aside some relatives and walked right up to me. "Excuse me," she said to her siblings. "Since y'all haven't introduced us, I'm going to introduce myself!"

We all went to brunch afterward, and Victoria and I sat together. I learned about her more than thirty-year career working as an analytical manager for the Regional Organized Crime Information Center (ROCIC) in Nashville. They work on making sure different law enforcement agencies share information and coordinate across jurisdictions to combat organized crime. For the majority of her tenure, she'd led and supervised a team of criminal and forensic analysts.

Victoria didn't know anything about making whiskey back then, although she liked drinking it. Her go-tos were Colonel E. H. Taylor and Maker's Mark 46, and she somewhat pointedly didn't drink Jack Daniel's.

She had experience leading and managing people. She'd dealt with the judicial system and inside politics of local, state, and federal agencies. She had gravitas and presence, and she knew how to speak to the press.

From that first conversation, I knew Victoria was the Green descendant I'd been looking for. Despite their love and enthusiasm for the raising of Nearest's profile and their cheerleading for the distillery, none of Nearest's living family members had an interest in taking up that line of work. Whiskey-making can seem sexy from the outside, but it's hard and dirty work. When I asked Green descendants if they were interested, the response I generally got was: *Let us get this straight. We can be doctors, lawyers, whatever we want to do—you're paying for us to go all the way to our PhD—and you want us to come run a still? I don't think so.*

Modern Black Americans, on the whole, don't want to go into jobs where our ancestors had no choice about being there. You're generally not going to find us in the tobacco, cotton, or whiskey industries. And a lot of Black folks from religious backgrounds also don't necessarily want to work in spirits.

But Victoria was game. I took her to the temporary, nondescript distillery Uncle Nearest was working with in Columbia, Tennessee. We had graduated from sourced whiskey and were now distilling our own product and growing alongside a valued production partner. This was a working distillery; there were no tours, no folksy charm or whimsical history, and no tastings—just business. It was a clean, secure place to distill, blend, filter, and store our barrels.

We went to work in the lab, outfitted with a big metal worktable, scales, and a refrigerator. Victoria stood before the massive table full of samples—some thirty-odd dram glasses of whiskey from different barrels.

"It was nerve-racking," she recalled, "but it was a thrill, kind of a rush to do this."

Victoria took her time, and Keith and I watched her relax into the blending work as her nerves subsided. She clearly stopped thinking about the room she was in and the rest of us in it as she focused her concentration on the samples before her.

Blending is an art, and Victoria took to it right away. She worked the liquid around her palate slowly and deliberately, trying to engage all her senses. She paid attention to the sensation on her lips, in her nose, and on her tongue. There were no amateur mistakes here.

We knew right away, watching her, that we were seeing something truly special happen before our eyes. And when I tasted what she'd blended, I was completely sold. We all had a lot to learn about whiskey and the business ahead of us, but sometimes you can just tell.

The awards and sales that rolled in for Uncle Nearest 1884 backed me up: gold, double gold, Best in Class.

Victoria was hooked, and she threw herself into her whiskey education. She read widely and consulted with industry experts. She became a certified executive bourbon steward through Stave and Thief, which teaches students everything from grain, barrels, and warehouses to what the legal components that define bourbon and whiskey are. The course takes months, and the certification test, held in-person in Louisville, Kentucky, is hours long. "Victoria gave her all to a gift she didn't even know was within her," Evette recalled.

"This is work," Victoria said, describing the disciplined thought process she's developed. "I'm looking for a burn. I'm looking for the flavors that I pick up, whether it be caramel or butterscotch or stone fruit." She compares blending to cooking, with her samples spread before her: How much of this one? How much of that one? She blends until she gets it just right.

I asked Victoria to blend for us again, of course. This time, she walked into the lab as if she'd been born for it. She had full creative power—I didn't even taste her second expression until it was bottled. Victoria knew exactly what she was doing.

THE ONLY complication about hiring Victoria was that her siblings were still working at Jack Daniel's, and Jack Daniel's was still trying to figure out how to put out a Nearest Green bottle of their own. They wanted to call him "Nathan" to distinguish their bottle from ours.

"They *can't* do a Nathan Green bottle," Victoria told her siblings. She knew Uncle Nearest had the IP on Nearest's name locked up, in every variation including misspellings, and a Jack Daniel bottle would never come to fruition.

"Yes, they are," the siblings said. "We've picked out the designs."

The situation was prickly. Keith and I were putting literally every penny we had, tons of money from friends and family, and even more money from accredited investors we'd sold on the idea into Uncle Nearest, not to mention every ounce of our energy. Debbie, Jackie, and Jerome were waiting for a horse that had already left the barn and wasn't coming back. I suspect holding on to that hope was easier to live with than admitting Jack Daniel's broke their hearts.

When Uncle Nearest first came out, they'd been excited and supportive. But as they continued to be told by the Brown-Forman leadership team that they'd have their own bottle to celebrate, they began to distance themselves from the brand made to honor their ancestor. Brown-Forman convinced them that they'd be the better steward of their ancestor's legacy because—as Mark shared with us, and others within Brown-Forman shared with them—we didn't have experience, and they were the most experienced in the world at taking a bottle to market. What they didn't tell them is how most consumers cannot name even one of their prior master distillers who have their own Jack Daniel's bottles. If you know Mr. Jess Motlow, Lemuel "Lem" Tolley, Jess Gamble, and Frank Bobo by name, you are probably an avid Jack Daniel collector or live in Lynchburg. I didn't tell them that Uncle Nearest was already on track to sell more bottles than all their Master Series bottles combined. With the nonstop press interviews I was doing to share with the world who their ancestor was, Nearest Green already had more name recognition than all the men in their Master Distiller Series combined.

The other hundred or so descendants continued to back Uncle Nearest. But the three siblings at Jack Daniel's were caught between a rock and a hard place, because they were loyal to the company that had employed them for a combined one hundred years. I understood the tough spot they were in. There were a lot of behind-the-scenes things I didn't tell them, because they loved Jack Daniel's and because my unyielding respect for Jack extended to Brown-Forman, even during times when they didn't deserve that level of grace.

I didn't tell them that the reason Mark had gone to talk with them was because I'd made it a prerequisite for meeting with me. I didn't tell them that Jack Daniel's had only showed them designs for a Nathan Green bottle because they thought I'd be foolish enough to sign a coexistence agreement that would have put us out of business. I didn't tell them I believed the reason they continued showing Debbie, Jackie, and Jerome designs for the supposed bottle they would create was an attempt to drive a wedge between the Green family and Uncle Nearest.

KEITH AND MARK MCCALLUM were still sending versions of the coexistence agreement back and forth. At one point, Keith asked how many bottles Jack Daniel's had in mind for the supposed Master Distiller bottle honoring Nearest.

Oh, it's just going to be a small run, they said. Maybe a hundred thousand cases.

A hundred thousand cases is 1.2 *million* bottles. Now, for Jack, that really is a small run. But it would be a massive wave that could swamp and drown Uncle Nearest.

It couldn't happen.

Keith had kept me out of the negotiations until now. But this was something he couldn't ignore. He had to loop me in.

I immediately shut down all the coexistence talk. I think that's the day Brown-Forman figured out that there was more to all this than an author in over her head and a new nuisance brand on the market. I was a businesswoman, and I was making the whiskey space my own.

Today, Mark calls the coexistence agreement "the dumbest thing I ever did."

But I felt terrible that Debbie, Jackie, and Jerome weren't getting what they wanted.

Their brother Jeff Vance texted me, concerned, in March 2018. A good friend who'd been in distribution for over fifteen years had been told by reputable distributors that Jack Daniel's was coming out with its own bottle to honor Nearest. That meant it made no sense for distributors to gamble on us.

They're trying to create a Nathan Green bottle, but Uncle Nearest is here to stay, I told him.

When they do make that bottle, I know they don't plan on making it a permanent item, he texted. *Surely, they are not trying to confuse consumers on what they are buying??*

But they were. I would not allow that to happen, I said. I assured him that although I was new to this industry, I was not new to business, and there was zero chance that bottle would ever see the light of day.

In order to be sure we could honor Nearest using his chosen name, the name his children and grandchildren had known him by in life, I had to do something I'd never planned: put a "Nathan Green" bottle into the marketplace. I needed to secure the trademark and, potentially, gear up for the fight I'd always expected. The "Nathan Green" bottle was a limited edition, with a very small run and for a single bourbon society. We sold a handful in the US to secure the trademark here and sold the rest outside the country.

THE ONLY CONTENTIOUS conversation I ever had with Brown-Forman was when I was asked to join a Zoom call with Jeff Arnett (Jack Daniel's master distiller at the time), Melvin Keebler, and a recently appointed head of marketing for Jack Daniel's. The call was supposed to be about working together to help diversify our industry, so I understood why Melvin was on the call. It was confusing to me that Jeff was there, but I like Jeff so I welcomed his inclusion.

Moments into the call, though, I learned it wasn't about diversifying the industry but to pressure me into allowing the Nathan Green bottle to be made. The new head of marketing, who clearly didn't have the background on the bottle, put an image up on the screen of the Nathan Green bottle they had mocked up.

For the first time, I saw the bottle they'd been using to confuse the distributors and telling Debbie, Jackie, and Jerome they'd be making. But really, all I saw was red.

The marketing head began by telling me the bottle had been in the making before I came to the story.

My response is unprintable. Let's just say it was in French.

"We've been aging whiskey in the warehouse at the top of the hill for four years for this project," he said.

"You never even thought about a bottle for Nearest until I came along," I said, raising my voice. "You didn't even know that warehouse was on George Green's land until I shared that with you. His family sold it back to the distillery. And you keep lying to Nearest's descendants, causing confusion and unnecessary tension by having them continue to work on this bottle with you."

I don't lose my cool very often, but I was letting them have it. Until now, they'd only seen my historian side. On that call, they were seeing the businesswoman you do *not* want to attempt to back into a corner.

"I know without question not a single barrel in there was ever for a Nathan Green bottle," I said. I turned to Jeff Arnett. "Since you're on the call, you can clear this up. Who were you laying that whiskey down for four years ago?"

Jeff, of course, confirmed they were just normal Jack Daniel's barrels, not whiskey barrels planned for any special bottle.

When I got off the call, I was so furious that I nearly called Debbie, Jackie, and Jerome. I was ready to tell them the whole story behind that bottle. But I prayed first. Thank God. My goal from my earliest moments in Lynchburg was to raise up the legacy of Nearest without harming the legacy of Jack. If I'd made that phone call and they'd chosen to leave Jack Daniel's, that would have harmed Jack's legacy. I didn't want the poor decisions of the current generation of marketers impacting the overwhelmingly positive relationship the company had built with the Green family. It was important that they continued to love the company that so many of their ancestors before them had loved.

It's the only time Jack Daniel's has ever seen me angry, and the nonsense stopped after that. *They needed to see it—an angry Fawn, I guess*, I remember thinking.

MARK REMEMBERS THE making of the Nathan Green bottle differently. His recollection is their team had a bottle mocked up, with a bottle shape and a label. "It was just too small an idea." As much as Debbie, Jackie, and Jerome wanted to see it come to fruition, it wouldn't have done justice to Nearest's legacy. "I think it was probably wanted more by the Green descendants at the distillery, not by the broader Green descendant group," Mark said.

By the time the siblings learned there would be no Nathan Green bottle, there was no one to blame but Uncle Nearest. It looked like we intentionally killed the Nathan Green bottle when in fact the Nathan Green bottle never had a chance. To this day, the three Green family members who work at Jack Daniel's are the only ones who refer to Nearest as "Nathan," a name no other family member has ever called him.

Still, though, the siblings were glad Jack Daniel's was listening to me and taking my research and documentation seriously.

"Thank God," Debbie said recently. She recalled the scene from the movie *The Color Purple* where Sofia's character, played by Oprah, says, "All my life, I had to fight." The siblings had been fighting their whole lives to get Jack Daniel's to tell Nearest's story.

"People would've been still saying it's not true," Debbie said.

Jackie felt that if anybody was going to tell Nearest's story, it should be family, and she was disappointed that it took my outside voice to prod Jack Daniel's into formally recognizing Nearest. Even so, "I'm proud somebody's speaking his name," Jackie said, "and everybody all over the world knows."

"Now that everyone else knows his contributions to the company, it's been amazing," Jerome said, "but it's also been bittersweet" because their grandmother couldn't be here to see the world finally recognize what she'd known about Nearest the whole time.

That bittersweetness manifested in other ways. Once the story became widely known, nothing in the siblings' lives really changed. They didn't get different jobs or raises. They had more to talk about, and now it was encouraged rather than suppressed, but otherwise no one treated them differently.

Victoria, on the other hand, has become famous. When she walks into a room, everybody knows her, and there's a line waiting to meet her and take pictures with her. When it was announced that she'd be doing a bottle signing at Lax, the top liquor retailer in Washington, DC, the owner wasn't prepared for the number of people who showed up. He'd had celebrities like 50 Cent and P. Diddy come and do bottle signings at his store. But he'd never seen a crowd like the one that showed up for Victoria.

"She's the biggest thing in whiskey since Jimmy Bedford," I told the owner.

"I see!" was his response.

In contrast, Debbie, Jackie, and Jerome said they were ushered out by Jack Daniel's every now and again to lead a tour, talk to the press, do some kind of special event, and then were sent back to the bottling house and the warehouse.

I just can't figure out why Brown-Forman did not make some decisions that could have honored and substantially improved things for Victoria's siblings. I do my best to apply grace, but I will admit that I am still confused by this. What Jackie, Debbie, and Jerome wanted was not difficult and would cost them nothing more. I shared with them what I thought they could do, things as simple as making Jerome a Tennessee Squire—something I'd been told he'd always wanted—and was told that wasn't possible because it's against the rules for employees. I don't understand the background to that rule, so I say this with no judgment, but can't we change that for the Greens? It seems to me their ancestor did more than enough to warrant an exception.

When Soledad O'Brien interviewed Debbie in 2018, she asked if Debbie felt special when she walked through the distillery gates.

"And I said no," Debbie recalled. She still doesn't. Debbie and Jackie are both adamant that this story isn't about any of us alive today. It's about Nearest and, by extension, their grandmother's legacy. And she doesn't feel that's there yet.

Debbie retired in 2023 and is emphatic that the company never mistreated her or her siblings. "I loved my job," she said. "I stayed here forever."

But what she's missing is the feeling that her great-great-grandfather's accomplishment mattered.

"How come I don't feel that? How come I never felt that? How is it that nobody in our family ever felt that?" Debbie has said. The descendants of the Daniels and the Motlows feel that every day. They're part of the fabric of Lynchburg, the essence of the place—and a consequence of 150-odd years' worth of mythmaking. "But that's just the way the world is," Debbie said. "I don't expect anything."

To know she feels this way, when Jack Daniel and his descendants went out of the way to make sure her ancestors were honored, breaks my heart. I'm absolutely certain it would have broken Jack's.

Until recently, Jackie, Debbie, and Jerome didn't talk to Victoria about Uncle Nearest. They would just sit around and talk about Jack

Daniel's. Victoria wanted them to be proud of her work, but she was determined not to push it.

My approach through all this has been not to respond or try to change Debbie's, Jackie's, or Jerome's minds. I know I'm not blood family. I know my presence complicates their lives—although I like to think it's in a positive way, overall.

Victoria and I remind ourselves that some things, like good whiskey, just take time.

CHAPTER

44

UNSURPRISINGLY, ONE of Uncle Nearest's biggest early challenges was with distributors. When you're starting out in the alcohol business, it's hard to get distributors to care about your products. They'll give you a hope and promise that they're going to move products for you. But when we used secret shoppers who tried to purchase our spirits in stores where they were supposed to be, they came up empty. In several instances, when they requested Uncle Nearest, they were given Knob Creek instead. Keith and I also had this experience personally. It's something that I still find utterly confusing, since our bourbons taste nothing alike—but it did make me wonder if the distributor for that brand had given that switcheroo order to bartenders across the country. It just seemed to be too much for coincidence. Distributors compete with one another, and some large brands sometimes suppress sales. (This is an illegal practice, but practically speaking, it happens all the time.) The public was trying to buy Uncle Nearest but was being presented with an empty shelf and other whiskies to choose from instead, even when they had plenty of our product in their warehouses.

The outcome of all this back-end maneuvering is your brand will have low sales and you'll have to worry about retail outlets dropping you, followed by the distributors, then investors losing confidence in your leadership. This is different than when you voluntarily pull back sales to drive demand or because your supply can't keep up.

We were able to overcome the obstacles of the distributors by effectively decentralizing their power. Where most small spirit brands work with one or two distributors, we racked up a network of seventeen different distributors across states and regions. It's a lot of extra effort and a ton of relationships to maintain, but it meant no single distributor had the power to make or break us, or even slow us down for any real period of time. I dubbed this the "Nobody Puts Baby in a Corner" strategy. As we grew, we were able to compare each of their sales numbers and prod the ones that weren't measuring up.

We had more general annoyances. There were people we worked with who took a needlessly paternalistic approach to what they clearly saw as our little whiskey brand. Some white guys who went on and on about "the Black community" in a limiting way. We understood early on that our whiskey is for everyone who likes to consume premium whiskey. But Keith and I are Black, and Nearest being the first Black master distiller was integral to our story, so everybody in the spirits industry thought we were only focused on a singular demographic.

Keith sees these years—the grit in between the growth—as a testimony of faith where we pushed through all this. I agree with that. He remembers thinking at a certain point, *We have all the elements. We got our labels. We got bottles. We got whiskey. We got this. We can do this thing.* Eventually we reached a place where we had positioning and presence, and industry partners wanted our business. We've been fortunate not to have allowed any of the many setbacks to actually set us back. In bad circumstances, my reaction is to pray, think through strategically what we should do, and then act.

ONE SUCH TIME came while I was showing *CBS This Morning* reporter Michelle Miller and her segment producer around Sand Creek Farms. "Just two weeks ago, these were all horse stalls," I said as we walked through our massive construction project. We'd come a long, long way from the first time Michelle had interviewed me about Uncle Nearest in 2017.

Just as we were about to shoot a segment, Katharine called me. She was upset. For the previous six months, she'd been working to secure a military broker for Uncle Nearest. The US military is a large and loyal buyer of spirits, and its more than 1,000 bases overseas meant partnering with them would be a crucial step in expanding internationally. One of the top brokers was intrigued; after extensive meetings and negotiations, they had agreed to represent Uncle Nearest.

But they also represented Brown-Forman, which brought them substantial revenue. Katharine assured them of our respectful relationship, but they needed clearance to proceed.

Brown-Forman had shut down the broker's request with, "You sell Jack Daniel's." They came back to Katharine to tell her they couldn't represent us based on their relationship with Brown-Forman.

I couldn't believe Brown-Forman was throwing yet another grenade our way—and right before I taped an interview for a national morning news show watched by millions.

As soon as I got off the phone with Katharine, I called Mark. He'd warned me that the presence of individuals within the company who wanted to see Uncle Nearest fail meant there might be incidents he couldn't prevent, but he'd promised to do his best to resolve them.

I told Mark I stood by what I'd said this whole time: At no point would I jeopardize the legacy of Jack Daniel, the man, while raising up the legend of Nearest. Most people conflated Jack Daniel the man with Jack Daniel's the company, so I would not speak out against Brown-Forman with negative words in the press.

I said this because I'm a radically transparent person, but I also wanted to demonstrate to Brown-Forman that I posed no threat to Jack's legacy. I wanted the message to circulate within the company so the people there who were plotting against Uncle Nearest's success wouldn't be able to use safeguarding Jack's legacy as an excuse. I wanted them to fully grasp that they could not break my resolve; my commitment to this cause was unwavering. There's a saying that the times you get to know a person the most are when they're drunk or under attack—some of the only times our characters are truly revealed. By withstanding their body blows without going down, I wanted to make our detractors reconsider how many rounds in the ring they really wanted to go with me.

No matter what you do, I will remain steadfast, I thought. *This mission will remain unchanged, and I will complete the work I set out to do.*

It took them years to understand this at Brown-Forman, but Mark understood it earlier than most—which let us develop a profound mutual respect.

I told Mark I was growing impatient with these incidents. He apologized and made it his mission to identify the responsible party.

In the meantime, we had to film the segment. I didn't share any of this inside baseball with Michelle, but it was clear there was more to the relationship with Brown-Forman than I was letting on. She asked me about Jack Daniel's.

"They were solidly behind you in this discovery mode of who Uncle Nearest was," she observed. "You're their competition now, aren't you?"

I laughed, hard, and said I didn't consider myself competition whatsoever. "When we go out into the marketplace, we're selling Uncle Nearest, but we are talking about Jack in a way that makes you want to drink Jack Daniel as well," I said.

Thank God for grace; it guided me to stay true to this purpose, even in moments of frustration and disappointment. The redirection worked, and the interview went on. But Michelle clearly took my words with a grain of salt.

In the end, Mark found the responsible party at Brown-Forman and had them contact the military broker to clarify that they'd been expressing a personal opinion only. But the damage was done, and the broker was wary. They deemed it too risky to proceed, and six months of effort went up in smoke. We had to start a whole new search for a military broker.

WE PLANNED TO release an Uncle Nearest commercial that would air shortly after the Super Bowl in February 2019. For the first time, Uncle Nearest needed a voice. I'd told Jeffrey Wright he'd be my first call, and he was.

Jeffrey had never been to Tennessee, but he was quick to hop on a plane and join us. We started filming early in the morning, but he took time to walk the land first, going to the spot where Nearest's still had been.

He was moved by the natural beauty, the generosity of the land, the stone foundations of the structures. It struck him as almost sacred. He sat on the little stone bench—like a pew, he said—beside the spring and took it all in.

"My mind was just racing," he recalled recently. "Within that story of slavery is something much more complex about the relationship between Black and white in our history. It's this incredibly rich portrait of who we are, and who we were."

It only took one day to film. It was overcast, and the mist hanging over the hills lent a bit of mystery to the Call Farm. And we didn't just film a commercial. That wasn't going to be enough to do the story justice. Instead, we created a ten-minute film that captured the sweep and importance of the story and honored Nearest, Jack, their families, and Lynchburg.

Once we rolled the cameras, the story unfolded alive around us. Jeffrey captured everything perfectly on the first take, and the director and I both told him he nailed it, but he insisted we do take after take. He knew the importance of telling this story and, perfectionist that he is, felt that one take just wouldn't do it justice. In the end, the final version of the film was the first take.

"This is a special home on a special piece of American land," Jeffrey said to the camera. "Surprised it's still here. This isn't a set. We're in Tennessee, in the hills above Lynchburg."

The film captured the timeless quality of the land and told Nearest's story. It followed Jeffrey walking across the field and through the rooms of the farmhouse. We dedicated the film to Nearest's descendants and concluded with the photos I'd been surrounded by at the Call Farm—Charles Green in his uniform; Francis Eady and her friends at a punchbowl, clearly celebrating; a young Sis and Debbie chatting casually with a Tennessee state trooper; John Green standing proudly before a military plane; and one of my favorite photographs: Mammie as a young woman, in a white dress, surrounded by her family as she stands in her wallpapered kitchen with a grocery haul on the table before her. They're clearly preparing for a big gathering—on the table are mounds of dinner napkins, paper plates, bags, boxes, and jars of food. It's a scene of abundance and love. About half the group are looking at the camera, but the rest—including Mammie—are caught in a candid moment. Mammie's looking off to the right with a wry smile, like someone's just told a joke or she's delivering a heavy dose of side-eye. Keith and Mammie would have gotten along quite well.

The very last photo was of Miss Margaret Tolley and Miss Dill Dismukes. "Lifelong friends," the screen read. "Thick as thieves." The photo of the two women in their Sunday best, caught mid-chortle at some hilarious story, showed the friendship between the Nearest descendant and the Jack descendant better than words ever could.

JEFFREY'S NARRATION OF Nearest Green's story played on millions of TVs across the country. "What happens when everything we know about something changes?" the ad asked.

One month later, the extended short-film version premiered in New York City at the Tribeca Film Festival. Chuck Baker drove up from Lynchburg with his dad, Chuck Baker Sr. Neither of them had been to the city before, and they navigated their pickup through Midtown.

Aunt Tee came, too. As she tells it, I "sent for her." She remembers me just calling her up one day and saying, "Ms. Tee, you're getting on a plane and you're coming to New York." Many Green family members from St. Louis, Nashville, Houston, and Dallas were in that audience.

Clay Risen came over from Brooklyn to join us. We held the showing at the Tribeca Film Center, hosting a reception in the gleaming wood bar area and filling the seventy-two-seat screening room. We covered the brick walls with photos of Nearest's descendants and had five cases of Uncle Nearest on standby for cocktails. Guests lined up outside behind a velvet rope.

Katharine Jerkens joined us after her father's illness and passing. "You're coming as a guest," I told her. "Do not touch a thing." It was the first of our events that she'd had nothing to do with planning, and she was able to simply enjoy the party. *This is happening*, she thought. *Now, this is cool. What other company has done something like this?*

Jeffrey joined us at the premiere, looking dapper in a black blazer, blue jeans, and blue-framed glasses. He shared stories about his great-grandmother, who taught his grandfather how to distill, and his grandfather's quiet bootleg whiskey sales in the 1950s. "It's said that history is written by the victors," Jeffrey said. "Well, we're victors now, and we can tell these stories and tell them right—tell them freely, properly, in a way that celebrates who we are without bias." Then he turned to Nearest and the enduring importance of the story.

"Too often, the contributions of some have been dismissed, have been forgotten," he said. "If we don't know who we are, who came before us, who built this country, then how do we have a deeper understanding of what the collective is all about?"

He raised a glass to the descendants.

"Thank you to the family of Nearest Green," he said. "We'll have a toast to his legacy, that history, and to him, and to all of you for being here."

There are so many ways to honor someone. We'd started with the tangible, like a memorial and a bottle, and the intangible, like the scholarships. Now we'd added a little Hollywood glitz and the kind of gravitas only Jeffrey Wright's voice can convey. We'll never get to know what Nearest sounded like, but I wonder every now and then if he might've sounded like Jeffrey.

Jeffrey was struck by the family members' pride and found meeting them deeply fulfilling. It was special to him to have the film out in the world and have the family there to see it. The bottle and brand are "rooted so beautifully inside this history and the community born of this history."

So many people were there for the screening that we had to do it in shifts. The Dan Call Farm looked amazing on the big screen. And I was so proud of the film, which we would go on to show as part of our Nearest Green Distillery tours. Mostly, though, I appreciated being able to take a moment to really be present for the Green family.

OK! magazine later reported that the film "left a packed auditorium in tears."

Someone took a great photo of Chuck, his dad, and Keith at the premiere. It was a "fancy" event, Chuck recalled approvingly, and his dad had never seen its like. Chuck put the picture up in the Barrel House. His dad passed away later that same year, and Chuck still points the photo out to visitors and tells them what a great night it was.

W E OPENED our visitor center to the public in September 2019—on the 5th, naturally.

As Victoria said at the time, "Everything we do here at Uncle Nearest Premium Whiskey is done with purpose and on purpose. Nothing we do is happenstance."

The months leading up to that day were filled with a lot of hard, happy work. About six weeks before we were due to open, I got a text message from the contractor who was working on the master blender's house, which would serve as our temporary visitor center. I'd been traveling but was due back in the morning.

"Don't freak out," he wrote. "When you come back tomorrow, you're going to be able to see the sky" from inside the building.

Okay, I thought.

I could see the sky, all right. The sky, the fields, the construction equipment—I could see everything. There were no walls anymore, no ceiling, and no floor. Six weeks ahead of our opening, the contractors had stripped the entire place in order to fix an issue with the ducting.

It gets hot as hell in Tennessee in September. Going without air conditioning was *not* an option.

We couldn't push the opening back. We'd announced and publicized the date. All throughout August, people would drive up say, "Y'all are opening *when?*" and start laughing. "Y'all are crazy. There's no way."

On September 3 and 4, we did the craziest construction dance you've ever seen in your life. On any given section of the facility, there were four different people doing four different jobs. You'd literally have someone coming along to lay down electrical wiring, then someone to lay down pipes, someone closing it all up, and then someone coming along immediately behind him and painting. Our local building inspector was there every day to sign off on progress.

We were able to get the building to a place where we had the front ready, and we closed off the area that would eventually become our offices. We were able to get a certificate of occupancy the day before we opened, and only for the part of the facility where our grand opening would take place.

Our opening day was down to the absolute wire. We had nothing—*nothing*—ready for guests. The work continued through the dead of night on September 4. We got everything set up, and the painting went on until daylight. Then we had to air it out. And *then*, because it was Tennessee in September, we had to spray for flies. They were still spraying when the first guests arrived.

We gave everybody hard hats and took them on a tour of what would eventually be the distillery. We'd put up big lighted banners that told guests what each patch of dirt would become. The property still houses sixty championship walking horses and their heirs, and visitors could see them roaming in the fields and learn about the history of the Tennessee walking horse. They stopped by the welcome house and tasted our whiskeys—Uncle Nearest 1856 Premium Whiskey, Uncle Nearest 1884 Premium Small Batch Whiskey, and Uncle Nearest 1820 Premium Single Barrel Whiskey—and tried their hand at labeling the bottles in our bottling house.

We didn't even have a license to sell liquor, so for the first four weekends we were open, we had to file a special event permit. We were planning for a thousand people to show up. A month from opening, we realized we already had two thousand RSVPs, and we hadn't even begun promoting it locally—that was just folks who'd be driving in from outside Shelbyville. At groundbreaking, the crowd was bigger than we could have ever imagined. It was clear this opening was of great significance to a whole lot of people.

Katharine was joining us in person from California. Things had moved swiftly, and her focus had been on logistics. She'd seen photos and heard all about Sand Creek Farms, but now the magnitude of what we were doing fully sank in.

"Holy cow," she breathed. "This is a really, really big deal."

We began with members of our Armed Forces raising three flags on our property. First the Tennessee flag, with its brilliant red background, blue circle, and white stars; then the Uncle Nearest flag, a bright white background with black lettering and those same three Tennessee stars; and, finally, the flag of the United States of America. Someone in the crowd took a photo of Keith and me with our arms wrapped around each other's waists, with me saluting as the flag was raised. The moment I saluted, I noticed everyone around me did the same. That was an extraordinarily special moment for me, and I hold that image dear.

As the sun began to set, everyone who'd come together to celebrate our launch stood together in a big crowd on the grass as Victoria took the controls of an excavator.

As Victoria scooped a chunk of grass, fireworks filled the sky as beats from "The Greatest Show" filled the air, and we all hooted and hollered.

WHEN THE NEAREST Green Distillery opened, Jack Daniel's took out an ad in the *Tennessean* congratulating us. That's the kind of class Jack himself would have applauded. As time went by, with lots of close work with Mark McCallum and Nelson Eddy, Uncle Nearest settled into actual coexistence with Jack Daniel's. They incorporated a Nearest Green exhibit in the visitor center. They produced in-house materials to educate employees—a video, a PowerPoint, a sales sheet. It's a whole Nearest Green tool kit. It embraces the view that we're two brands with a shared history, and that "Jack would be proud that today there's now a distillery honoring his friend just down the road."

They chose a prominent, historic warehouse, the oldest on the property, named Barrel House 114. In 2021, they dedicated it the George Green Barrel House. Now the warehouse is part of their tour and, in addition to storing a small selection of whiskey barrels, it serves as their tasting room.

The distillery has speculated about whether George might have been the master distiller who came after Nearest. We know he definitely worked at the distillery in a leadership capacity, but we just don't know what role he played.

They hosted dozens of Green descendants for a family reunion and distributed pretty gift boxes to everyone in attendance. Inside was a bottle of Jack Daniel's Single Barrel Select whiskey. The bottle had a distinctive shape—still square, but with elegantly rounded edges, and a tall, textured neck. Hung around the neck on a metal chain was a small medallion that read, "JD Green Family Descendants Selection."

This was a special single barrel bottling just for the Greens, never to be sold. I've been told it was very tasty.

THIS STORY HAS always been about Nearest and Jack. Even after Jack went to make whiskey on his own and Nearest retired, the two men and their families were still friendly. I like the idea that Nearest and Jack learned from each other and then were able to take different roads.

That's how I think about Jack Daniel's and Uncle Nearest these days, too—our companies have grown together. We share a history, but we are entirely separate. We've had our challenges, but at the end of the day, we've made each other better. And we share a common goal.

"The whiskey aisle keeps getting more crowded," the *New York Times* wrote in 2018. It was true, and Uncle Nearest was an active part of that crowding. But I wanted other Black entrepreneurs' whiskies alongside Uncle Nearest in every store in America. What would be the point of doing all this if we couldn't shake up the white male stranglehold on the spirits industry? Jack Daniel's asked to join us on this journey, and we could not have been more grateful. One is great. Two is better.

In 2020, Uncle Nearest and Jack Daniel's came together to launch a not-for-profit alliance, the Nearest & Jack Advancement Initiative. It has three components. The Leadership Acceleration program creates advanced industry apprenticeships for people of color already in the spirits industry who aspire to leadership roles like head distiller or production manager. The barrier to entry in the industry is low, but between that barrier to entry and success lies a very large chasm. After about eighteen months, members of the program are prepared to become visible leaders in the industry. Tracie Franklin and Bryan Copeland were our first graduates from this individually tailored program. The Business Incubation program encourages BIPOC entrepreneurs in the spirits industry and gives them knowledge and resources.

And lastly, we established the Nearest Green School of Distilling at Motlow State University. It took quite a deal of cutting red tape to get every government body and school board to agree, but the first courses will be held soon. As an associate's degree in distilling, rather than a certificate, the program is the first of its kind.

At first I worked closely with Mark McCallum on this. Following his retirement, we became friends with him and his wife, Diane, and Mark became one of my most trusted advisors. He had more than forty-five years of experience in the consumer packaged goods space and more than sixteen years in spirits, and I knew I could use someone in my corner with that level of expertise. So I asked him to join the board of Grant Sidney Inc., which owns Uncle Nearest. Mark made the leap, he said, because "I believed, as I believe today, it's one of the greatest stories that I've ever been associated with."

After that, I worked with Melvin Keebler at Jack Daniel's. Melvin and I both understand that the standard for judging the initiative's success is how well it works in a sustained manner over a long period of time.

"As a Black American, I wish things to change overnight," Melvin has said. Me too. Still, it's been incredible to watch the success of the initiative so far.

The first graduate of the business incubation program absolutely had to be Chris Montana. Along with his wife and cofounder Shanelle, Chris started Du Nord Craft Spirits in Minneapolis in 2013. He did amazing things with very little, launching his distillery with only $60,000 and producing whiskey, vodka, gin, and liqueurs. He later told me, "If anyone came to me now and said they want to start a distillery with $60,000, I'd say, 'Go spend that $60,000 on sweet potato pie. You have no chance.'" Unfortunately, the Du Nord distillery was damaged and closed due to a fire during the George Floyd protests in Minneapolis in 2020. What the fire didn't destroy, the sprinkler system took out. Chris told me he saw the distillery as his fourth child, and "no one wants to see their baby burn."

"They needed help," Katharine Jerkens recalled. "They needed the industry's help."

The incubator program helped him rebrand, repackage, and connect with distributors that increased his sales and distribution. "Without this program, we would not be in the position we are now," Chris said.

I believe the changes we're making to this industry are fundamental. I predict that in forty years, our work on diversity will have been so transformative and effective that not only will we no longer be having this conversation, we'll look back and be shocked that we once had to.

Whiskey-making is an inherently forward-looking endeavor. Anyone who creates a product and ages it for fifteen to twenty years knows there'll come a time when they've laid down a batch they won't live to see—that it's done purely for a future generation to benefit from. The Nearest & Jack Initiative is like that. As Mammie would say, "Our blessings lie ahead."

CHAPTER

46

WHEN I first hired Uncle Nearest's CFO Michael Senzaki, I told him we were going to need a lot more money. Michael hit the ground running, working on finding new investors and connecting those who trusted us in our earliest days. But we turned down those whose North Stars didn't align with ours—namely, that Uncle Nearest was building a team that looked like America, that we would market to *all* of America, and that our ownership and investors would be a beautiful representation of America.

Within two years, Uncle Nearest was available in all fifty states, the District of Columbia, and twelve countries. I was receiving nonstop calls and emails from venture capitalists, investment bankers, private equity firms, and beverage division presidents who had previously ignored us. Each represented someone who wanted to buy a minority or majority stake in Uncle Nearest.

At first, I'd respond to everyone similarly: "Thank you for your interest, but I have no desire to sell any portion of my business."

That soon became, "Thanks, but no thanks."

Then I stopped saying anything at all—responding was futile. I just ignored them.

In 2020, Uncle Nearest became the fastest-growing Black-owned spirit brand of all time. In 2023, we were the most awarded bourbon or American whiskey for the fifth year in a row. Nearest Green Distillery became the most successful Black-owned distillery globally after crossing the $100 million mark in sales.

At the end of 2022, I had a come-to-Jesus moment with our distributors. We're going to double our numbers next year, I told them. Just look at us as one of the big guys now. You should start to promote Uncle Nearest the same way you do Johnnie Walker and Jim Beam. It will save a lot of back and forth.

Around that same time, I was with some close friends. One of them worked in an executive-level position for one of the largest spirit conglomerates.

"I'm not selling, no matter the price," I told him.

"Not even for $2 billion?" he asked.

That was a specific number, but I didn't think much about it for a while.

Then Michael received a call from a friend in the investment community for the spirits industry. He shared the valuation metrics they'd assigned to Uncle Nearest. We were the brand on everyone's radar. They valued Uncle Nearest at approximately $1.5 billion.

Having watched me turn down everyone who had come before him, Michael knew the drill: "She won't accept it. I don't even need to ask," he replied.

"The most they could go up to is $2 billion dollars," the caller said.

Michael let me know about the offer. He knew what I'd say, but he felt responsible for passing it on. "That's a big number," he said. But before he could even get the whole dollar amount out, I interrupted.

"You made it clear the answer was no, regardless of the number, right?" He assured me he had.

Uncle Nearest is about more than whiskey, and I'm never going to sell it. It's worth far more than $2 billion to me.

THE NEAREST & JACK INITIATIVE was doing critical work, but there was more to do. We decided to hold an event in 2023 that would bring together people of color in the industry that would help them understand the business and get their names out there.

In April 2023, we cohosted the first-ever Spirits on the Rise summit, with hundreds of guests from BIPOC-owned spirits brands, accredited investors, and potential allies in the liquor industry. The first night was a reception at Jack Daniel's, with greetings and speeches— the best kind of networking event, gathering several hundred of all the right people together. The following day, at the Nearest Green Distillery, was one of education and connection.

Katharine Jerkens led a panel on the route to market with key industry leaders and distributors. Folks from Brown-Forman led a panel on marketing. I led several on investing and finance. We also brought in a bunch of investors and bank presidents to consult with the BIPOC founders. The idea was to give them the real deal about how to raise capital—practical guidance about what bank to go to and when so they'd understand how to position themselves well for loans and investments before they needed them.

Then we set up a brand fair where each brand could showcase themselves and meet with players in the industry—potential investors, distributors, e-commerce sellers, hotels. It was "gorgeous," Katharine recalled. The whole event "was a magical day and a half."

Uncle Nearest is the first BIPOC-owned business ever to succeed at this level in the spirits industry. We're going to help everybody else to make sure the industry never goes back to being one that shuts out women or people of color.

After the summit, the Nearest & Jack Initiative "is supercharged to do even better going forward," Mark McCallum said. "There are enough people at Brown-Forman and at Uncle Nearest who believe in it—to keep those two companies building the legacy of Nearest Green together instead of one trying to stop the other."

Keith's advice to people trying to succeed in the industry is to take big swings—unless you're doing it purely out of love and know you'll be satisfied with a little tasting room, you need to aim really high. "It's been particularly gratifying to help people," Keith said recently. "And I also like them not making the mistakes that we made."

That's especially important considering all the help we received. When Michael Berman, Keith's mentor and Uncle Nearest's first investor, learned that he was terminally ill, one of the two things that were most important to Michael was to come visit Nearest Green Distillery. It took a lot of planning and resources, along with medical equipment and nurses, a private plane large enough to carry ten people, and a deep well of strength on Michael's part to make the journey. He made it and found it deeply fulfilling to see all that he had helped to build. Weeks later, in May 2023, he passed away. Although his obituaries rightfully focused on his decades of influence in California politics, Keith and I will always hold him close in our hearts for his faith in us and all he did to help us secure Nearest Green's legacy and Uncle Nearest's future.

THE PEOPLE IN Lynchburg have been immersed in the Nearest Green story in the press, first nationally and later by more local sources. The *Lynchburg Times* covers a lot of what we do, even though they've gotten grumbles about covering a business based in Shelbyville. Their editor and publisher, Tabitha Evans Moore, is a Lynchburg native from a well-known and esteemed family lineage. Whenever the grumbles come, she reminds them this town shares her family history as well, and she has a right to share every Lynchburg story. And the story of Nearest Green is one the majority of the residents in Lynchburg are proud to tell.

Uncle Nearest is the top advertiser in the Nashville airport, because I believe in owning your backyard. Eighteen million people fly through Nashville every year. I don't want any of them to come or go without knowing that this state is home to Uncle Nearest.

Kevin Eady, Miss Dot and Claude's son, was returning from a trip with his wife through Nashville airport when he noticed his cousin Victoria's face on the wall, staring serenely over the baggage claim.

"I turned around and was like, 'Oh, there's Vicky,'" he recalled. He pointed it out to his wife. She turned around with a start.

"Oh, it *is* Vicky!" she said.

Kevin was moved to see her up there. It's "honorable and heart-touching," he said, "knowing she's my cousin, knowing we're all family. It brings a lot of pride to our family. I'm very proud of her, and she's done great things."

THERE'S AN INERTIA in Lynchburg that hearkens back to a time when the roads were mud and the vehicles were stagecoaches. Even in recent years, people from Lynchburg tended to stay in Lynchburg—they didn't even go to Shelbyville regularly, let alone Nashville. If they wanted to go on vacation, maybe they'd drive down to Florida for the beach.

Now people from Lynchburg come up to the Nearest Green Distillery. The dynamic has changed, and people feel an urge to venture out. We only began marketing locally in 2023, and that was to mark the launch of our live entertainment venue, Humble Baron—named in honor of my favorite person on earth.

We are now the seventh most visited distillery in the world and the third most visited bourbon distillery. In 2023, we welcomed well over two hundred thousand people to our home. Most of our guests spend money elsewhere in Shelbyville while they're here. After they leave the distillery, it's always, *Well, what else do we do?* This helps bring jobs and money to Shelbyville and the region. It also helps us to build Uncle Nearest in the marketplace, with our tour guides ending each tour answering a question they receive often from our guests: "Our founders and our team are committed to cementing the legacy of Nearest Green, and we do that here every day. But there is a huge way you can help us, as well. When you go to restaurants, bars, or your local retailer, look for Uncle Nearest, ask for Uncle Nearest, and if they don't have it, insist they get it and share with them why."

The Nearest Green Distillery has helped draw many businesses here from other places, and the area has shifted greatly. People of color come here to visit the distillery, they see how beautiful Tennessee is, realize it's amazing here, and decide to move here. Not everyone, of course! But enough to notice a pattern. Keith and I have many Black neighbors now—of the people who live next to us, four of them are Black people who moved here from out of state within the last three or four years. The culture in Shelbyville is shifting around and beyond Uncle Nearest.

We're building in Shelbyville outside Uncle Nearest, too. One day Keith and I were at a Mexican restaurant for dinner. The server had just set down our chips and salsa when Keith mentioned a property for sale just off the Shelbyville square that he thought would be a great burger place and microbrewery. It was the former site of a box company, and the remnants of the building had a distinctive roof that would make for a striking visual in a restaurant. The deadline for putting forward bids was coming up quickly, but he was having a hard time coming up with a name or concept for the place.

Within two minutes, I had it: Classic Hops Brewing Co. would be an old-school carhop, with classic cars displayed inside and classic music—Motown specifically—played from jukeboxes where customers could choose their favorite songs. The outdoors would have a place people could pull up and place their orders, and servers would come out to them with the food. "Classic Hops" was a play on the cars, the music, the hops in the beer, and the classic carhop of old-school, drive-in burger joints.

"How did you just come up with a full name and concept in less than two minutes?" Keith asked me. "I've been racking my brain for two weeks just trying to think of a name!" He's used to me doing this by now, but he's still amazed every time it happens.

By the time the server came to take our entree order a couple of minutes later, I'd emailed Jane asking her to file the trademark and I'd secured all the URLs related to the concept on my GoDaddy app.

The feverish pace of so much of how we went about building Uncle Nearest and our new life in Tennessee looks a lot like that day at the Mexican restaurant.

PEOPLE WHO VISIT distilleries tend to be a specific type. I love them and welcome them to the Nearest Green Distillery every day. And I want the people who don't seek them out to come too. That's why one of the signs at our entrance reads, "Welcome to the family."

There are big Jack Daniel's fans who visit as a bit of a challenge. "There's a lot of 'What's going on?' and 'Who are these people?'" as John T. Bobo says. Let's go see what they did in here, seems to be the attitude. They figure we're small, we're young, and we clearly can't be as awesome as Jack Daniel Distillery, so it'll be fun to go and pooh-pooh us. They're curious, and I think they intend to walk away saying, Jack is so much better. After they have a blast and find they love the whiskey, I sort of enjoy that it messes them up a little bit.

We get people who clearly have a racist agenda from time to time, too, and I can spot them a mile away. We're a sprawling, working monument to Black ingenuity going back to the earliest days of the nation, so—good luck with that, I guess? It makes me think of Jo Anne's mom and the little boy with the ice cream cone. A lot of times we completely break down their walls—I've watched it happen right in front of me, and it's really cool to see that.

For dealing with the nonteachable, we have my head of security Shannon Locke—although we all just call him Sharpshooter Shannon around the distillery. He made quite the impression on *Travel + Leisure* writer Kevin West, who described him as "a man built like a brick outhouse" and someone who "exuded a palpable force field of lethal protection."

There are things Shannon and Keith handle that I don't know about and don't see. Keith serves as a filter so I can continue to walk around free as a bird. I honor him often for that. When the distillery is open to the public, the sheriffs help us with security. From the moment my vehicle drives on to the distillery grounds, there's a uniformed sheriff accompanying me.

I tell Shannon, "I don't know what the hell y'all are expecting to happen. But keep them at a distance so I don't look like I'm Beyoncé walking through here." But they stay close, and they keep a close watch.

It's important that the distillery be a destination where people are safe and free to walk the grounds, learn, and think. People of every background and race reach out to me all the time and tell me how the experience transformed the way they see their history, themselves, and the future. I want them to feel loved and cherished, and to leave inspired. Creating this safe haven is our little piece of what we're able to give back to the world.

THESE DAYS, when visitors pull off US Highway 231, the Nearest Green Distillery spreads out before them: The White House, the small white building where Keith's office is, the rickhouse, Humble Baron (which holds the Guinness World Record for the world's longest bar), the Master Blender house, Barrel House II BBQ, and the visitor center where all our tours begin: in the very same spot where Tennessee walking horses were once sold.

Visitors then go with their guide. Sometimes they're a descendant of Nearest Green; every time, they're someone passionate about our whiskey and our history. Guests stop at a series of portraits by artist Raymond Bonilla of Jack Daniel, Mammie Green, Ben Green, Clay Risen, and me—a whole wall of those of us linked by September 5th. Nearby are more portraits of Nearest's descendants in their stately and well-fashioned clothes. Just as they do in their photographed portraits, they stand with their heads high, looking confident, dressed to the nines. George Green looks directly at you from the wall, his wide-brimmed hat slightly askew.

In the next room, just below our signature horseshoe, Jack Daniel's bottle jug stencil from the Dan Call property hangs from the wall. It's a reminder of where this all began: with two men making whiskey out in the backwoods of Middle Tennessee. We've got other artifacts from the original distillery, too, including the two-ton circular millstone Nearest and Jack would've used to crush grain.

Outside, tours stop by a concession stand touting made-in-Tennessee snacks like Goo Goo Clusters, Moon Pies, and Mountain Dew, then enter Philo + Frank's, our nonalcoholic speakeasy, through a hidden door.

Everyone expects the tour to start off talking about whiskey—so what better place to do the opposite? We recently had a sober friend in town from LA who wasn't going to go on the distillery tour. "Oh, go on the tour," I told him. "It's literally been created for you."

Then everyone settles in at the bar, whose stained glass windows resemble a church and may remind visitors of the Ryman Auditorium in Nashville. I can't tell you what happens in this room, since I'm hopeful you will join us! I don't want to ruin the many surprises that will happen here.

Next is everyone's favorite part: the tasting. We've grown to a place where we now have multiple tasting rooms. But the original, our Family Tasting Room, was once the circular barn where Tennessee walking horses were cooled down before being given food and water. Today, the round walls are graced with portraits of all our team members who've been with us for at least two years. We do this because when I visited a distillery in Louisville, Kentucky, I was struck by the fact that nearly every person on the wall was a white male. And when anyone on the tour would ask about the lone woman or person of color in an image, no one seemed to have any clue who that person was. I wanted our tour guides to always be able to answer that question for our guests. So, on their second anniversary, I ask each of our team members how they want to be remembered by the world. Their answers are included beneath their images and will remain on our walls in perpetuity. It gives me great joy to dream of visitors coming into that tasting room many generations down the line, when those images look incredibly outdated, and learning about the people who helped cement the legacy of Nearest Green in the exact way each team member wanted to be remembered.

During the tasting, the guide walks everyone through the charcoal mellowing process, then lays out the seven expressions we've released of Uncle Nearest so far—including our master blend, our single-barrel whiskey, and our rye. After the tasting, visitors can walk over to Barrel House BBQ II, where Chuck Baker serves up the same "grilled cheese on crack" and his famous ribs.

A COUPLE YEARS AGO, Aunt Tee brought a bottle of Uncle Nearest to share with friends in the St. Louis bar they like to call their "little hole in the wall." Word spread, and shortly after, an acquaintance asked her to give a speech about Nearest to the ladies of the National Association of Colored Women's Club.

"I'm not a speaker," she told me. "I don't get in front of people and talk."

"You'll be just fine!" I said. I told her to call me if she needed anything. "I'm here for you. I got you." She called me once a day while she worked on her speech and hammered out the historical details about Nearest and Jack. In the end, her speech was a hit.

Now she tells people, "I'm just anxious to tell the story to anybody that will listen."

Miss Neat felt that way, too. Not long before she passed away in September 2023, she said, "I was just happy to be a part of getting the story of Nearest Green out there. That's the main thing, making the public aware of the things that African Americans have contributed to society. And I had no idea. I couldn't have imagined how far it would go."

Miss Neat often told Nearest's story to young people, visiting preschools and elementary schools to teach kids about what life was like for Black people in his day. As school principal Kevin Eady can attest, the kids listen—and remember.

Dr. Geri lost her college report on Nearest and Jack in a house fire and wished she'd been able to do more with the story. "I did not have the resources or even the ideas to do anything like" the scale of what we've accomplished with Uncle Nearest, she said recently. "I think that's great."

Jack Daniel died in 1911, but we talk about him as if he's still with us. A hundred years from now, I want people to talk about Nearest the same way—in a manner that makes you forget he's no longer here. That's my task; that's our goal.

But I'm not going to be alive that long. This is just my leg of the race. I have no doubt I was chosen to tell this story. I didn't find it; it was intended for me. I'm always going to be looking out for someone else with a September 5 birthday to join me in preserving Nearest's legacy well after my time on earth is done.

★
EPILOGUE

A S I look back on all the things that have happened in this jour-ney, all the elements that have come together, I'm overwhelmed by the forces at work that are far larger than me. The trademarks. The September 5 birthdays. The Call Farm—and the gift of a small deposit and long escrow. The four acres in the heart of Lynchburg. Sherrie being our realtor and, unbeknownst to us, the perfect person to head up operations for Uncle Nearest. Brown-Forman spending so much time hoping we'd sign the coexistence agreement that their attorneys didn't try to shut us down. On and on and on!

Today, most of the Green descendants will tell you I'm family, I'm a cousin, I'm a niece, I'm a daughter, and I'm going to find myself on the family tree at some point. It's an honor to have spent so much time with the family; to have dived into Nearest's life and honored his leg-acy by building the business I believe he could've created had he lived in a different time. It's been a delight to watch more than a dozen of his descendants pursue higher education with the Nearest Green Legacy scholarship, and believing hundreds more will do the same in the years ahead.

For me, telling Nearest's story isn't just about discovery and uncovering the past. It isn't a thing you just do once, or just print on the label on the back of the bottle. Instead, it's a process: telling the truth over and over, correcting other people's misconceptions, misinterpretations, and occa-sionally outright deliberate misunderstandings, and meeting hundreds of people who have changed my mind and expanded my world every day.

After eight years of research, I understand there are many mysteries about Nearest's life that we may never solve, but that doesn't discourage me. When I think of Nearest now, I picture him as a larger-than-life man with a contagious sense of joy in an otherwise difficult life. Nearest has always been many things to many different people: a beloved Black man in the postwar South, a wise mentor and master of his craft, an entrepreneur and visionary, a husband, father, and brother, and a great-great-grandfather whose legacy has changed generations of lives. He was the best whiskey maker the world never knew, and now he's the best whiskey maker the world will always remember.

Uncle Nearest is the world's first major spirits brand to be led by a Black woman, and it's the fastest-growing independent whiskey brand in US history. Sometimes I think I'm the Black female reincarnation of Jack Daniel. I've got PR, marketing, and whiskey-company-building prowess—which I sure didn't get from my teetotaler parents!—and like Jack, I fully believe in the innate goodness of people and I don't believe in failure. I know from experience that failure isn't failure unless you give up before you succeed.

In 2024, an early prediction of Mark McCallum's came true: Harvard Business School began teaching Uncle Nearest as a case study. What a full-circle moment for a high school dropout.

When I look at the rooms that I walked into in the spirits industry in 2017 compared to the rooms I'm walking into right now, they're completely different. Before, I was the only Black person. I was the only woman unless somebody else from my team was with me. And now everywhere I go, I see us. The 70% of America that had been standing at the gates of the spirits industry for so long have now walked in and are proudly taking up space.

That's a major shift and cause for great celebration. But there's much more to do.

When the world shut down in March 2020, Keith and I watched as other distilleries around the country stopped making whiskey, vodka, and gin and instead manufactured hand sanitizer. At Uncle Nearest, we launched the Operation Brother's Keeper Initiative, which supplied three hundred thousand masks to workers on the front line.

We committed to our team members that COVID or no COVID, revenue or no revenue, people were going to get paid. There was no question about shutting down our business. We didn't lay off anyone. In fact, when other companies downsized and laid off some of the best in the business, we hired them.

We created a "Coming Out the Gate Swinging" internal campaign to ensure that we were ready the moment we were out of quarantine, and in the years since, we've continued to grow, give back, and push ourselves and the industry as a whole.

Once we started buying property in Lynchburg and Shelbyville, we never stopped. We purchased the Tolley House, transforming it into an elegantly period-furnished bed and breakfast with a fully modern kitchen and bathrooms. The welcoming, light-filled inn, with each room named after a member of the Tolley family, sits a mile from the Lynchburg town square. More recently, we bought a historic US Bank building on the square and leased the space back to the bank. The historic building that houses the *Shelbyville Times-Gazette*—the first place we visited in order to research this story—we've now purchased. There are still a lot of records that have never been put on microfilm or digitized, and it's extremely meaningful to be able to help the Bedford County Archives preserve them.

We recently purchased an entire city block in downtown Shelbyville. First, there was an old box factory with stunning all-glass sides. Adjacent to it, on the corner, is another building that's been divided into three separate retail spaces, surrounded by two acres stretching from street corner to street corner at the town square's entrance. After acquiring that building, we negotiated with our neighbor to buy his office building on an additional 1.2-acre parcel. This allowed us to own every corner leading into the main town square.

My time researching Nearest has taught me that we can't change the past. But we must build something successful to pass on to the generations coming after us. They need us to lay the cornerstone of a firm foundation for them to continue to build.

As soon as Uncle Nearest became successful, the questions started coming nonstop: *How are you not selling? How are you not selling?* I've been impressed by my fellow Black entrepreneurs who chose to sell their businesses in order to then invest in other Black-owned businesses. They're creating an ecosystem of Black founders and investors that is critical to keeping the next generation from having to start over from scratch. But I'm never going to sell Uncle Nearest. That is not even an option. I am committed to continuing to build it and creating talent pipelines for people who have the capabilities.

I believe there must be a generation of Black founders who decide to pass our businesses down. So far, even the greatest Black entrepreneurs have been unable to establish a company so lasting that it exists for their children's children's children. But the generational wealth gap is not going to go anywhere unless Black business owners begin holding on to our companies.

I know continuing to grow a business and preserving Black ownership into the next generation is a big ask. It requires faith in yourself and in the future. But at Uncle Nearest, we have established a pioneering method for founders to build a company while retaining controlling interest and securing the capital for long-term success. I've become a vocal advocate for minority founders to follow our example, bypass traditional early start-up funding sources, and work with individual investors who are enthusiastic about actively contributing to the company's growth.

Together we can forge a more equitable and just business landscape than the one we encountered in the early days of Uncle Nearest. Major investments can come from sources beyond venture capital, private equity, and wildly wealthy investors. Making your presence as a founder widely felt can replace the need to have a strong, established network to raise capital. Each of our investors takes immense pride in helping us grow the company, proving you can raise money without giving up equity or board seats by finding investors who support your vision, growth, and success on your own unique terms.

We live in a patriarchal country, in a union still striving toward perfection. But I'm driven by my ancestors' resilience and strength, and committed to pulling others up as I climb. Over the coming years, I will mark our success by the number of women and BIPOC business owners I meet in our industry. I will revel in our triumph when the spirits industry is a viable path to individual and generational wealth for women and people of color in America. What I will never do is measure our worth by the monetary figure I could make by selling.

The Green family legacy has been handed down from Nearest the distiller to Townsend the mixologist to Victoria the master blender. And like Jack Daniel long ago, I've learned so much from Nearest Green and his family. I hope Nearest, Jack, and their legacy of love, honor, and respect will become as much of an inspiration to you as they continue to be to me.

★
NOTES

THIS BOOK is the product of almost eight years of research performed by more than thirty individuals over more than three thousand hours. We have scrutinized countless census records, nonpopulation schedules, slave schedules, birth certificates, marriage certificates and other marriage records, births/deaths/marriages recorded in family Bibles, tax books, wills, newspaper obituaries, mortality schedules, grave indexes, and cemetery records. Other records have included Masonic papers, Internal Revenue Service records, Civil War enrollment and military records, personal letters, bills of sale for enslaved people, pension applications, guardianship records, circuit and county court records and minutes, land deeds, and court testimony.

Innumerable hours were spent locating records within the Library of Congress; the National Archives in College Park, Maryland and Atlanta, Georgia; George Washington's Mount Vernon; the National Park Service; the National Register of Historic Places; the Moore, Bedford, and Lincoln County Archives; the Tennessee State Archives; the Motlow State University Center for Historic Preservation; the Middle Tennessee State University Albert Gore Research Center; the *St. Louis Globe-Democrat* photograph collection at the University of Missouri St. Louis; the *St. Louis Dispatch* newspaper morgue; Standard & Poor's and Moody's industrial manuals; and the Hoosier State Chronicles at Indiana State Library.

I'm grateful for the robust local news provided by the *Moore County News*, the *Shelbyville Times-Gazette*, and the *Lynchburg Times*. The *Indianapolis*

Recorder is one of the longest-running Black papers in America, and it maintains extensive archives that were extremely helpful. Historical issues of the *Moore County Pioneer* and *The Sentinel* were immeasurably useful for forming a sense of what Nearest's world was like.

Several of my researchers drew from many podcasts while gathering material for this book—too many to count. Some of the most helpful were Jack Daniel's *Around the Barrel* series, *We Sound Crazy, To Dine For*, and *The Fred Minnick Show*, especially the "For the Love of Whiskey, Race, Progress and Diversity" episode of the latter that was held to benefit the Du Nord Riot Recovery Fund. *Chasing Whiskey*, a documentary film about Jack Daniel's that examines the brand's roots with Nearest Green, was directed by Greg Olliver and released in 2020. Debbie, Jackie, and Jerome were interviewed and filmed at the Dan Call farm and are featured in the documentary.

Chapter-by-chapter notes appear below, followed by other works consulted.

PROLOGUE

xvi   The world has only learned: See Clay Risen, "Jack Daniel's Embraces a Hidden Ingredient: Help From a Slave," the *New York Times*, June 25, 2016.

xvii   The second was journalist and historian: See Ben A. Green, *Jack Daniel's Legacy* (Rich Printing Co., 1967). A fiftieth anniversary edition was published in 2017. I contributed a forward, and several appendices were added that draw heavily from the work of Lant Wood and articles reprinted with permission.

xvii   After my dad, Frank Wilson: For more information, see Leslie Kaufman, "Frank Wilson, Motown Songwriter and Producer, Dies at 71," the *New York Times*, October 3, 2012.

xviii   My research conclusively proved: Jack's mother's listing in the mortality schedule shows she died of Typhus Fever in January 1850 after being ill for seven days. As Jack was a few months old when she died, that would put his birth in 1849. And as Ben Green wrote, "It has been handed down through the family that Jack was born "in the fall of the year," which meant September made the most sense. See Lucinda Daniel's mortality schedule, *Federal Mortality Census Schedules, 1850–1880, and Related Indexes, 1850–1880*; Archive Collection: T655; Archive Roll Number: 26; Census Year: 1850; Census Place: Subdivision 2, Lincoln, Tennessee, p. 474 (National Archives and Records Administration [NARA], Washington DC).

1

8   **I wrote two bestselling books:** My previous books are *Happy Wives Club* (Thomas Nelson, 2014) and *The Argument-Free Marriage* (Thomas Nelson, 2015).

2

10   **As Keith returned from the buffet:** See Clay Risen, "Jack Daniel's Embraces a Hidden Ingredient: Help From a Slave."

11   **The article, bylined Lynchburg:** Clay Risen, "Jack Daniel's Embraces a Hidden Ingredient: Help From a Slave."

12   **Critics as far back as W.E.B. DuBois:** Ainissa G. Ramirez, "Black Images Matter: How Cameras Helped—and Sometimes Harmed—Black People," *Scientific American*, July 8, 2020.

12   **These four, nicknamed the "shirtsleeves brothers":** Ben A. Green, *Jack Daniel's Legacy*, p. 171. See also Emmett Gowen, "Sippin' Whisky and the Shirtsleeve Brothers," *TRUE: The Man's Magazine*, November 1954 and "Rare Jack Daniel's," *Fortune* magazine, July 1951, pp. 103, 106, 131.

13   **And they tended not to know:** This charcoal mellowing is called the Lincoln County Process.

13   **In March 2016, Jack Daniel's media relations:** Emails exchanged between Lauren Haitas and Nelson Eddy of DVL Seigenthaler (now known as FINN Partners) and Clay Risen of the *New York Times*, subject line: "The man who taught Jack to make whiskey," March 2–11, 2016.

14   **The last line of the email was key:** Emails exchanged between Lauren Haitas and Nelson Eddy and Clay Risen.

14   **Nearest's sons went to work with Jack:** Emails exchanged between Lauren Haitas and Nelson Eddy and Clay Risen.

14   **Instead of running shortly after:** See Clay Risen, "Jack Daniel's Embraces a Hidden Ingredient: Help From a Slave."

15   **The day the article was published:** Clay Risen, "Jack Daniel's Embraces a Hidden Ingredient: Help From a Slave," comments section. User "Malika," location Northern Hemisphere, June 25, 2016.

15   **The next day, another user commented:** Clay Risen, "Jack Daniel's Embraces a Hidden Ingredient: Help From a Slave," comments section. User "laura174," location Toronto, June 26, 2016.

15   **"Enslavers like Jack Daniels":** Clay Risen, "Jack Daniel's Embraces a Hidden Ingredient: Help From a Slave," comments section. User "Bo," location Washington, DC, June 26, 2016.

15   **Another commented: "It is not clear":** Clay Risen, "Jack Daniel's Embraces a Hidden Ingredient: Help From a Slave," comments section. User "Michjas," location Phoenix, June 25, 2016.

15   **There was plenty of positivity in the comments:** *Matter of Fact with Soledad O'Brien*, February 3, 2018, 9:45 mark, https://www.matteroffact.tv/february-3-2018/.

3

19   **Uncle Nearest "is the best whiskey maker":** Ben A. Green, *Jack Daniel's Legacy*, p. 28.

19   **After long hours at the still:** Ben A. Green, *Jack Daniel's Legacy*, p. 31.

19   **When Jack established his own:** Ben A. Green, *Jack Daniel's Legacy*, p. 71.

19   **Then I read toward the end:** Ben A. Green, *Jack Daniel's Legacy*, p. 133.

19   **Family lore said that Jack was born:** Ben A. Green, *Jack Daniel's Legacy*, p. 133.

20   **In his will, he had to carefully:** Jack Daniel, "Will of Jack Daniel Deceased" (April 20, 1907). In Will Books, 1872–1966. Filmed by the Tennessee State Library and Archives (1967), 194–201. County Court Clerk's Office, Lynchburg, Moore County, Tennessee.

20   **He had a fine home with a large parlor:** See Lee Andrew Enoch Jr., *Memories Around Lynchburg* (McQuiddy Printing Company, 1989).

20   **"Never have I seen a man who had":** Thomas Motlow, Letter to W. R. Thompson Jr., December 27, 1962. This letter describes Jack's attributes better than any other I've read.

20   **"Never have I seen a man with a greater":** Thomas Motlow, Letter to W. R. Thompson Jr., December 27, 1962.

21   **Although he wasn't baptized until later:** See "Jack Daniel's No 7 Still Flourishes: Capt. Daniel Denies He Has Forbidden Further Use of His Name," *Nashville Banner*, April 27, 1909, (reprinted May 29, 1909), and "Card from Capt. Jack Daniel," *Nashville Banner*, April 28, 1909 (reprinted May 29, 1909).

21   **He also had a reputation for having:** Ben A. Green, *Jack Daniel's Legacy: 50th Anniversary Edition*. Grant Sidney Publishing, 2017, p. 191.

21   **At one point he promised an elderly Black man:** Ben A. Green, *Jack Daniel's Legacy: 50th Anniversary Edition*, p. 191.

21   **"He also paid the preacher":** Ben A. Green, *Jack Daniel's Legacy: 50th Anniversary Edition*, p. 191.

4

For additional context, please see Stephen V. Ash, *Middle Tennessee Society Transformed, 1860–1870* (Louisiana State University Press, 1988); Bill Carey, *Runaways, Coffles and Fancy Girls: A History of Slavery in Tennessee* (Clearbrook Press, 2018); Darlene Goring, "The History of Slave Marriage in the United States," Louisiana State University Law Center, LSU Law Digital Commons, 2006; and *The Tennessee Encyclopedia of History and Culture*.

24 **Tennessee was the birthplace:** See Rev. E. E. Hoss, D. D., *Elihu Embree, Abolitionist* (Nashville, Tennessee, University Press Company, 1897).

25 **George Poindexter, the governor of Mississippi:** Rev. E. E. Hoss, D. D., *Elihu Embree, Abolitionist.*

25 **One Bedford County resident wrote that:** Stephen V. Ash, *Middle Tennessee Society Transformed, 1860–1870.*

25 **This truth cut across race:** See Colby Sledge. "Black Slave Owner an 'Untold Part' of History," *The Tennessean*, February 22, 2007.

26 **As someone who has gone from homeless:** In May 2023, Uncle Nearest Premium Whiskey expanded its footprint to 745 acres in Bedford and Moore Counties, making it one of the largest, if not the largest, Black landowners in Tennessee.

26 **In 1858, the attorney general's issued opinion:** *Invention of a Slave*, 9 Op. Att'y Gen. 171, 171–72 (1858). See Brian L. Frye, "Invention of a Slave," *Syracuse Law Review*, February 19, 2018; and Henry E. Baker, "The Negro in the Field of Invention." *Journal of Negro History* 2, no. 1 (January, 1917).

5

32 **I'd been doing a fair amount of research:** See Ben A. Green, "Tuscaloosa From 1861 to 1880, Tuscaloosa and Her 111 Years of City Government," *The Tuscaloosa News*, September 1931; "Ben Green Resigns Post as Editor of The News," *The Tuscaloosa News*, June 1, 1952; "May the Best Come to Ben Green," *The Tuscaloosa News*, June 1, 1952; "Ben A. Green of Banner Named Editor of National Magazine," *The Nashville Banner*, March 9, 1957; "Country Music Ambassador," *The Nashville Banner*, May 9, 1957; "Mrs. Ben Green Dies; Rites Set Saturday," *The Nashville Banner*, August 12, 1960; "Editor and Author Ben A. Green Dies," *The Commercial Appeal*, December 5, 1972; "Former Newsman Ben A. Green Dies," *The Tennessean*, December 5, 1972.

33 **At that time, Jack Daniel's didn't have:** Jack Daniel's advertisement, *Lawrence Democrat*, May 17, 1895.

33 **The book was written with Jack Daniel's collaboration:** See Ben Green, A letter to Arthur S. Hancock, July 13, 1966, on Green's letterhead.

33 **A letter Green sent to Hancock:** Ben Green, A letter to Arthur S. Hancock, July 13, 1966.

6

For additional context, please see Stephen V. Ash, *Middle Tennessee Society Transformed, 1860–1870*; "History of Tennessee, 1887, Moore County," Goodspeed Publishing

Co.; Jeanne Ridgway Bigger, "Jack Daniel Distillery and Lynchburg: A Visit to Moore County, Tennessee," *Tennessee Historical Quarterly*, Spring 1972; Joseph C. Douglas, "Miners and Moonshiners: Historic Industrial Uses of Tennessee Caves," *Midcontinental Journal of Archaeology* 26, no. 2 (Fall 2001). Abe Frizzell and W. W. Gordon. "Historical Sketch of Moore County, Tenn.," *The Sentinel* (Lynchburg), July 3, 1876; Kay Baker Gaston, "Tennessee Distilleries: Their Rise, Fall, and Re-Emergence," *Border States: Journal of the Kentucky-Tennessee American Studies Association* 12 (1999); Allen C. Guelzo, *Fateful Lightning: A New History of the Civil War and Reconstruction* (Oxford University Press, 2012); Moore County Heritage Book Committee and County Heritage, Inc. *The Heritage of Moore County Tennessee 1871–2004*, Walsworth Publishing Co.; Carol Roberts, *A Dozen Tennessee Distilleries and "Old Sport"* (Independently published, 2023); James M. Safford, Chapter VIII of *Geology of Tennessee* (Printed by the state of Tennessee, 1869); and *The Tennessee Encyclopedia of History and Culture*.

35   Not many people lived in Lynchburg: Population estimate, July 1, 2022, U.S. Census Bureau QuickFacts for Lynchburg, Moore County, Tennessee.

36   Around the same time, a small Black neighborhood: See Hope Demetris, "Remembering Highview School," *The Moore County News*, February 7, 2022.

38   The assistant librarian called the library director: "History of Hickory Hill Baptist Church—Lynchburg, TN," undated.

38   Years later, I'd read a *Salon* magazine article: Yvette J. Green, "Family History, Distilled: My Ancestor Nathan 'Nearest' Green, Jack Daniel's And My Dad's Sobriety," *Salon*, January 14, 2023.

7

For additional context, please see Moore County Heritage Book Committee and County Heritage, Inc., *The Heritage of Moore County Tennessee 1871–2004*; and the National Register of Historic Places for the Lynchburg Historic District, U.S. Department of the Interior, National Park Service, July 19, 1996.

45   Celebration turned out to be the finale: See Ben A. Green, *Biography of the Tennessee Walking Horse* (The Parthenon Press, 1960) for more history and detail on Tennessee Walking Horses and Celebration.

47   After the war, George Daniel became: "History of Tennessee, 1887, Moore County."

48   In more recent years, the avid historical community: Moore County Heritage Book Committee and County Heritage, Inc., *The Heritage of Moore County Tennessee 1871–2004*.

49   She was elated when the *New York Times*: "Whiskey company reveals that slave, not preacher, gave Jack Daniel his recipe," CBC Radio, June 28, 2016.

8

For additional context, please see Moore County Heritage Book Committee and County Heritage, Inc., *The Heritage of Moore County Tennessee 1871–2004*; "Historical Sketch of Moore County, Tenn," *The Sentinel* (Lynchburg), July 3, 1876; "History of Tennessee, 1887, Moore County"; Jane Warren Waller, *Lincoln County Tennessee Pioneers* IV, no. 3 (March 1975).

50 **The whole square—all eighty-two properties—was:** National Register of Historic Places for the Lynchburg Historic District, U.S. Department of the Interior, National Park Service, July 19, 1996.

54 **Dan Call was born in 1836:** See Ben A. Green, *Jack Daniel's Legacy*; Moore County Heritage Book Committee and County Heritage, Inc., *The Heritage of Moore County Tennessee 1871–2004*; the compiled service record of Daniel H. Call, 1862–1865; Joe M. Casey, "The Man Who Taught Jack Daniel to Make Whiskey Hailed From Lois," *Moore County Review* 20, no. 1 (Spring/Summer 2009), pp. 22–23.

55 **Between Lady Love and his wife:** "Lady Love" may have been Rose Wilson, a temperance leader who was a fixture on the lecture circuit for supporters of Prohibition and railed against its role in domestic abuse. Newspaper reports from the time detail her movements as she made extensive lecture tours of Tennessee. She would visit as many as fourteen towns in two months—a rigorous speaking schedule when you take in the state of Tennessee roads at that time. "We are fighting to bury King Alcohol so deep that he will never further destroy the happiness of mankind," she told crowds so large that local leaders planned to build larger speaking halls. She was "beaming with intelligence and kindness, and devoted to the cause," reported the *Tennessean* in 1886. (See "Temperance Lectures," *Nashville Banner*, September 3, 1885, and "Remarks of Mrs. Rose Wilson," *The Tennessean*, February 24, 1886.)

9

59 *Jack Daniel's Legacy* **tells us that to reach it they had to climb:** Ben A. Green, *Jack Daniel's Legacy: 50th Anniversary Edition*, p. 27.

10

For additional context, please see: Moore County Heritage Book Committee and County Heritage, Inc., *The Heritage of Moore County Tennessee 1871–2004*; Joe M. Casey, Jewel D. Casey, O. B. Wilkinson, and Joyce Wilkinson, "Harrison's Funeral Home," *Harrison Funeral Home*, Vol. 1, Moore County Archives, Lynchburg, TN, and Joe M. Casey, Jewel D. Casey, O. B. Wilkinson, and Joyce

Wilkinson, "Harrison's Funeral Home Funeral and Burial Records with Obituaries, 1969–1990," *Harrison Funeral Home*, Vol. II, April 1992, Moore County Archives, Lynchburg TN; Cemetery Records of Lincoln County, Tennessee, and Adjoining Counties, Vol. I, A–L, Lincoln County Genealogical Society, 2012; Jo Anne Gaunt Henderson, "History of Highview Cemetery," speech, Rededication Ceremony of Highview Cemetery in Lynchburg, TN, December 2, 2017.

11

For additional context, see the Moore County Heritage Book Committee and County Heritage, Inc., *The Heritage of Moore County Tennessee 1871–2004*.

67 **I came across a newspaper clipping:** "Aunt Annie Bell Turns 90, Honored by Family," newspaper clipping, September 5, 1991.

67 **When Mammie passed away in 2001:** Moore County Heritage Book Committee and County Heritage, Inc., "George and Annie Belle Green Eady," *The Heritage of Moore County Tennessee 1871–2004*, p. 154.

67 **"She was telling the story of Jack Daniel's":** "Episode 43 - Descendants of Nathan 'Nearest' Green," *Jack Daniel's Around the Barrel* podcast, Season 4, episode 43.

67 **"I wish I had listened to more":** "Episode 43 - Descendants of Nathan 'Nearest' Green," *Jack Daniel's Around the Barrel* podcast.

68 **In 1918, Lem Motlow deeded a house:** Lem Motlow, "Lem Motlow to Sam White" (November 1918), Deeds, 1872–1966, Vol. 14, filmed by the Tennessee State Library and Archives, 337–338 and Ophelia Motlow, "Ophelia Motlow to George Eady et Ux" (January 22, 1964), Deeds, 1872–1966, Vol. 28, filmed by the Tennessee State Library and Archives, 521–22.

68 **In 1978, the last of Jack Daniel's descendants:** "Motlow Rites Tomorrow," *The Tennessean*, March 14, 1978; "Reagor Motlow buried in Lynchburg," *Johnson City Press*, March 19, 1978.

12

73 **"The Green story is an optional part of the distillery tour":** Clay Risen, "Jack Daniel's Embraces a Hidden Ingredient: Help From a Slave."

74 **I knew that alcohol had not been regulated prior:** The Internal Revenue Act of 1862, passed to support the Civil War effort, established the first income tax in the US, divided each state into districts for efficient tax collection, and introduced excise taxes on various goods, including a tax on whiskey production.

75 **Since 2013, it's been part of state law:** See Tennessee House Bill No. 1084, Public Chapter No. 341, passed April 19, 2013, signed by Governor Bill Haslam on May 13, 2013.

75   **He left home early to live with a family friend:** See *Jack Daniel's Legacy*; and Lucinda Daniel's mortality schedule, *Federal Mortality Census Schedules, 1850–1880, and Related Indexes, 1850–1880*; Archive Collection: T655; Archive Roll Number: 26; Census Year: 1850; Census Place: Subdivision 2, Lincoln, Tennessee, p. 474 (National Archives and Records Administration [NARA], Washington DC).

76   **His father Callaway owned several enslaved people:** Ben A. Green, *Jack Daniel's Legacy*, p. 11.

76   **When he hastily left for Call's Farm, he asked Felix:** Ben A. Green, *Jack Daniel's Legacy*, p. 14.

13

81   **The 1890 census, conducted a quarter-century after:** See Jenny Ashcraft, "Destruction of the 1890 Census," Newspapers.com blog, October 14, 2019, and "U.S. Census Bureau History: 1890 Census Fire, January 10, 1921," reprinted at Census.gov.

82   **In 1799 alone, Washington sold 10,942 gallons:** "Washington's Distillery," in *The Digital Encyclopedia of George Washington*, edited by Anne Fertig and Alexandra Montgomery (Mount Vernon Ladies' Association, 2012), mountvernon.org.

82   **Six enslaved men who were skilled distillers:** "Skilled Trades," George Washington's Mount Vernon, mountvernon.org.

83   **Archaeological excavations that ran from 1999 to 2006:** "Archaeology at the Distillery," George Washington's Mount Vernon, mountvernon.org.

14

85   **Miss Margaret's obituary specified:** "Mrs. Margaret Templeton Tolley," obituary, Lynchburg Funeral Home, December 1, 2015.

87   **I dug into the history of Highview Cemetery:** See Moore County Heritage Book Committee and County Heritage, Inc., *The Heritage of Moore County Tennessee 1871–2004*; and Jo Anne Gaunt Henderson, "History of Highview Cemetery."

87   **In the old days, I learned, all the men:** Rabe Stone, "Green Brothers Work of Art Known Throughout Moore County," *Moore County News*, August 16, 1973.

87   **"That's my job I chose to earn my bread":** Rabe Stone, "Green Brothers Work of Art Known Throughout Moore County."

87   **I found records for the Harrison Funeral Home:** "Harrison's Funeral Home" and "Harrison's Funeral Home Funeral and Burial Records with Obituaries, 1969–1990."

15

90   **The McGowan twins were born in 1934 and grew up:** See Sara Hope, "A Visit with The McGowan Twins," *Moore County News*, July 26, 2022, and Moore County Heritage Book Committee and County Heritage, Inc., *The Heritage of Moore County Tennessee 1871–2004*.

91   **In a 1906 deposition that was part:** Jack Daniel deposition, Hugh Ledford vs. Lem Motlow, in Chancery Court, Bedford County, December 21, 1906, bill of costs and testimony.

16

For additional context, please see *Jack Daniel's Legacy*; David A. Powell and Eric J. Wittenberg. *Tullahoma: The Forgotten Campaign That Changed the Civil War, June 23–July 4, 1863* (Savas Beatie, 2020); Ben A. Green, *Jack Daniel's Legacy*; Allen C. Guelzo, *Fateful Lightning: A New History of the Civil War and Reconstruction* (Oxford University Press, 2012); Bobby L. Lovett, "The Negro's Civil War in Tennessee, 1861–1865," *The Journal of Negro History* 61, no. 1 (January 1976), pp. 36–50; Robert Tracy McKenzie, "Freedmen and the Soil in the Upper South: The Reorganization of Tennessee Agriculture, 1865–1880," *The Journal of Southern History* 59, no. 1 (February 1993), pp. 63–84.

96   **Dan Call left his farm to join the Confederate Army:** See *Jack Daniel's Legacy*; Moore County Heritage Book Committee and County Heritage, Inc., *The Heritage of Moore County Tennessee 1871–2004*, and the compiled service record of Daniel H. Call, 1862–1865.

96   **An 1887 history of the county:** "History of Tennessee, 1887, Moore County."

96   **Dan was wounded, and records indicate:** See *Jack Daniel's Legacy*; Moore County Heritage Book Committee and County Heritage, Inc., *The Heritage of Moore County Tennessee 1871–2004*, and the compiled service record of Daniel H. Call, 1862–1865.

96   **A Union officer wrote in late 1862:** Stephen V. Ash, *Middle Tennessee Society Transformed, 1860–1870*.

96   **A Confederate soldier marching through:** Stephen V. Ash, *Middle Tennessee Society Transformed, 1860–1870*.

97   **As early as October 1862, Lincoln County residents:** Stephen V. Ash, *Middle Tennessee Society Transformed, 1860–1870*.

98   **"In defiance of the most vicious symbol":** Allen C. Guelzo, *Fateful Lightning: A New History of the Civil War and Reconstruction*.

98   **In March 1875, there was a terrible hailstorm:** Moore County Heritage Book Committee and County Heritage, Inc., *The Heritage of Moore County Tennessee 1871–2004*.

98   Nearest and Harriet would've also lived through: "History of Tennessee, 1887, Moore County" and Moore County Heritage Book Committee and County Heritage, Inc., *The Heritage of Moore County Tennessee 1871–2004.*

99   What did he and Harriet make of the eight inches: *The Sentinel* (Lynchburg), March 24, 1876.

99   Did Nearest's hogs suffer: *The Sentinel* (Lynchburg), April 14, 1876.

99   How often were the "Negro balls" held: *The Sentinel* (Lynchburg), April 21, 1876.

17

For additional context, see Moore County Heritage Book Committee and County Heritage, Inc., *The Heritage of Moore County Tennessee 1871–2004*; and Susan Campbell Bartoletti, *They Called Themselves the K.K.K.* (Clarion Books, 2014).

18

For additional context, see Susan Campbell Bartoletti, *They Called Themselves the K.K.K.*

109   The ledger she wanted me to look at now: Lynchburg Lodge No. 318 F & A Masons 1868–1874, bylaws.

111   A Lincoln County white man in his mid-sixties: William Wyatt, quoted in Susan Campbell Bartoletti, *They Called Themselves the K.K.K.*

112   On the night of November 3, 1894: See "Four Were Lynched," *The Nashville Banner*, November 4, 1893, p. 1; "Quadruple Lynching," *Los Angeles Herald*, November 5, 1893, p. 1; "A Family Lynched: Three Men and One Woman Hanged in Tennessee," *The Boston Post*, November 5, 1893; "Hanged Four at a Time," *The Knoxville Journal and Tribune*, November 8, 1893; "All to One Tree: Four Negroes Hanged Near Lynchburg, Moore County," *The Tennessean*, November 5, 1893; "Laid in One Grave," *The Nashville Banner*, November 6, 1893, p. 3; "Moore County Lynching: Coroner's Jury Finds That the Members of the Mob Are Unknown, Bodies of the Victims Interred in One Grave at Lynchburg—Waggoner's Wife Leaves the Country," *The Tennessean*, November 7, 1893.

113   *The Knoxville Journal* called it: "True As Gospel," *The Knoxville Journal*, November 7, 1893.

114   Decades later, a 1946 book by radical white journalist: Robert Minor, *Lynching and Frame-Up in Tennessee* (New Century Publishers, 1946).

115   Nine years later, in August 1903, a Black man: See J. I. Finney, "Negro Given Cruel Death," *The Tennessean*, September 26, 1903, pp. 1 and 3; "Moore County People Horrified at Work of a Mob in Lynchburg," *The Nashville Banner*, September 25, 1903, p. 1; "Grand Jury Investigating," *The Nashville Banner*, September 26,

1903, p. 1; "Tullahoma Arrests," *The Tennessean*, September 28, 1903, p. 1; "Probing to the Bottom," *The Nashville Banner*, September 29, 1903, p. 6; "Dean Makes Clean Breast," *The Nashville Banner*, September 30, 1903, p. 5; "Serves Notice to the World: County Court of Moore Takes Strong Stand for Law and Order," *The Nashville Banner*, October 7, 1903, p. 12; "Small's Murderers: Twenty-Two of them Indicted by Grand Jury," *The Tennessean*, October 8, 1903, p. 1.

19

For additional context, see Moore County Heritage Book Committee and County Heritage, Inc., *The Heritage of Moore County Tennessee 1871–2004*; Pat Mitchamore, *A Tennessee Legend with a Pictorial of Old Bottles & Jugs* (Rutledge Hill Press, 1992); David Fulmer, *Barrels & Bottles & Tennessee Jugs*; Chuck Neese, *The Whiskey Jug Book* (The New Company Publishers, 2002).

118   Joel explained that the Motlows were one of the founding families: I'm grateful to Joel for sharing his family history with me: Felix W. Motlow, "The Motlow Family Including the Descendants of Revolutionary War Soldier John Motlow, Jr. (1757–1812) and Allied Families, 1954" (reformatted and revised by Mrs. Frank T. [Linda S.] Pitts, 2005).

119   Official records appear to show the bus: Moore County, TN, Board of Education meeting minutes, September 1, 1948.

120   Tom Motlow, Lem's younger brother, grew up farming: See Emmett Gowen, "Across Hell on a Spider Web," unpublished, 1969.

120   All Tom would find back in Lynchburg: Emmett Gowen, "Across Hell on a Spider Web."

121   "You can buy the best pickup General Motors makes": "Episode 14 - What's a Tennessee Squire?" *Jack Daniel's Around the Barrel* podcast, Season 2, episode 14.

121   Even Jack Daniel's official podcast later referred: "Episode 14 - What's a Tennessee Squire?" *Jack Daniel's Around the Barrel* podcast.

20

For additional context, see Moore County Heritage Book Committee and County Heritage, Inc., *The Heritage of Moore County Tennessee 1871–2004*; Pat Mitchamore, *A Tennessee Legend with a Pictorial of Old Bottles & Jugs*; David Fulmer, *Barrels & Bottles & Tennessee Jugs*; Chuck Neese, *The Whiskey Jug Book.*

124   "This is the only known Jack Daniel jug stencil": You can view the stencil in person at the Nearest Green Distillery in Shelbyville, TN, or online as part of this virtual Smithsonian exhibit: "The Man Behind Tennessee Whiskey," part of the National Museum of African American History & Culture's "Lesser-Known Stories," https://www.searchablemuseum.com/the-man-behind-tennessee-whiskey-distilling-the-truth.

125   When the IRS consolidated Tennessee's revenue districts: According to the Internal Revenue Service (IRS) Historical Study: IRS Historical Fact Book: A Chronology 1646–1992, January 6, 1997, Tennessee's eight tax districts were first established on May 19, 1866 (p. 40). On January 3, 1876, Tennessee's 7th and 8th districts were consolidated (p. 55), and on October 2, 1876, Tennessee's 3rd, 4th, and 5th districts were consolidated into the 5th district (p. 56).

125   Each showed Jack Daniel had agreed to lease: Daniel H. Call, "Daniel H. Call to Jack Daniel" (September 27, 1877), Trust Deeds, 1872–1966, Vol. 1. Filmed by the Tennessee State Library and Archives, 257. Register's Office, Lynchburg, Moore County, Tennessee.

21

For additional context, see *Jack Daniel's Legacy* and Moore County Heritage Book Committee and County Heritage, Inc., *The Heritage of Moore County Tennessee 1871–2004.*

133   Miss Helen had graduated from high school: "Helen Butler," obituary, Albertson's Mortuary, Indianapolis, IN, August 7, 2018.

134   A quick search proved her memory was right: See "Townsend Greene's New British Lounge Opens," *Indianapolis Recorder*, January 6, 1945; "Townsend Greene's Swank British Lounge Grand Opening Fri. Nite," *Indianapolis Recorder*, January 27, 1945; "The A-V-E-N-O-O," *Indianapolis Recorder*, February 17, 1945.

22

136   Until now, Jack Daniel's had bought: "Law Closes Distilleries," *The Tennessean*, January 1, 1910, p. 7.

136   "There have been times in my life": "Talk of Tennesseans," *The Tennessean*, July 1, 1909, p. 4.

136   In the meantime, the plan was to relocate: "Jack Daniel Old No 7 Is to Be Distilled in St. Louis," *The Tennessean*, September 2, 1933.

136   "We cannot move the distillery and it will remain intact": "Jack Daniel's No 7 Still Flourishes: Capt. Daniel Denies He Has Forbidden Further Use of His Name," *Nashville Banner*, April 27, 1909 (reprinted May 29, 1909).

137   In 1910, Jack Daniel's left Lynchburg: See "Talk of Tennesseans," p. 4.; Jack Daniel's advertisement, *St. Louis Post Dispatch*, October 20, 1910, p. 9; Jack Daniel's advertisement, *St. Louis Post Dispatch*, November 17, 1911, p. 13; and Jack Daniel's advertisement, *St. Louis Post Dispatch*, August 20, 1911, p. 3.

137   The new location ran ads in English- and German-language: Jack Daniel's advertisement in German, *Mississippi Blätter*, October 2, 1910, p. 8.

137   Ben Green wrote that Lem had precisely: Ben A. Green, *Jack Daniel's Legacy: 50th Anniversary Edition*, p. 231.

138 **Two days into the violence:** Carlos F. Hurd, "Post-Dispatch Man, An Eye-Witness, Describes Massacre of Negroes," *St. Louis Post-Dispatch*, July 3, 1917, p. 1.

139 **In 1924, the *St. Louis Globe-Democrat* reported:** "Negro Man Killed During Scuffle with Irate Wife," *St. Louis Globe-Democrat*, August 25, 1924, p. 4.

23

158 **For decades, positive mentions of him abounded:** See the many mentions of Townsend in the *Indianapolis Recorder*, including September 2, 1944, p. 12; "Comfort for Walker Patrons," *Indianapolis Recorder*, November 19, 1938, p. 3; "Bronzeville Nominees," *Indianapolis Recorder*, January 29, 1938; "Theatre Manager, Family Enjoy Stay at Idlewild, Mich.," *Indianapolis Recorder*, August 27, 1938; "Greens Vacationing," *Indianapolis Recorder*, September 5, 1953, p. 5; "The Avenoo," *Indianapolis Recorder*, October 13, 1956, p. 12.

158 **In July 1937, he was lauded:** "Seein' Stars of the Stage, Theater, Night Clubs thru The Recorder World-Wide Fotos," *Indianapolis Recorder*, July 10, 1937, p. 13.

158 **In October 1937, he was hailed:** "Walker Manager, Family Return from Vacation," *Indianapolis Recorder*, October 9, 1937, p. 2.

158 **And in 1945, Townsend and Corina:** See "Townsend Greene's New British Lounge Opens"; "Townsend Greene's Swank British Lounge Grand Opening Fri. Nite"; "The A-V-E-N-O-O."

158 **It was a true family operation:** "British Lounge Now Serving All Popular Mixed Drinks," *Indianapolis Recorder*, January 18, 1947, p. 13.

158 **They received their retail liquor license:** "British Lounge Now Serving All Popular Mixed Drinks."

158 **Townsend continued to run the lounge:** William (Skinny) Alexander, "Time for Talk," *Indianapolis Recorder*, February 19, 1966, p. 3.

161 **Take Miss Helen—education meant so much:** "Helen Butler," obituary, Albertson's Mortuary, Indianapolis, IN, August 7, 2018.

24

164 **After reading about a 1911 fire:** See "Third Successive Night Fire Burns A Big Distillery," *St. Louis Post Dispatch*, June 18, 1911, pp. 1 and 20; "Smoke Evil Lessens," *The St. Louis Star and Times*, March 28, 1911, p. 12; Jack Daniel's advertisement, *St. Louis Post Dispatch*, October 20, 1910, p. 9; Jack Daniel's advertisement, *St. Louis Post Dispatch*, November 17, 1911, p. 13; Jack Daniel's advertisement, *St. Louis Post Dispatch*, August 20, 1911, p. 3.

165 **Two-thirds or more of Tennessee sharecroppers were white:** See "Sharecropping," *Slavery by Another Name*, PBS, pbs.org; and Robert Tracy

McKenzie, "Freedmen and the Soil in the Upper South: The Reorganization of Tennessee Agriculture, 1865–1880," *The Journal of Southern History* 59, no. 1 (February 1993), pp. 63–84.

169 **"I had seen him set a man up in farming":** Emmett Gowen, "Across Hell on a Spider Web."

25

For additional context, see "Uncle Nearest Premium Whiskey: Fawn Weaver," *How I Built This* podcast, NPR, October 4, 2021; Zoe Haggard, "Weaver Talks Investing, Management," *Shelbyville Times-Gazette*, January 22, 2022; and "Uncle Nearest Tennessee Whiskey with Sherrie Moore," *The Spirit Guide Society* podcast, January 21, 2020. See also Vol. 5, No. 2 of *Bourbon+* magazine for an excellent, step-by-step photographic breakdown of the Lincoln County Process.

26

176 **In Tennessee in 1860, only one in four white Tennessee families:** Bill Carey, *Runaways, Coffles and Fancy Girls: A History of Slavery in Tennessee* (Clearbrook Press, 2018), pp. 153, 161.

177 **From 1827 to 1855, it was illegal to import:** Bill Carey, *Runaways, Coffles and Fancy Girls: A History of Slavery in Tennessee*, pp. 38–39. See also Edward Ball, "Retracing Slavery's Trail of Tears," *Smithsonian Magazine*, November 2015.

178 **Importantly, it was illegal for an enslaved person to sell alcohol:** Bill Carey, *Runaways, Coffles and Fancy Girls: A History of Slavery in Tennessee*, p. 33.

178 **Much like with Nearest, records for Harriet:** The spelling of Harriet's name varied wildly across her children's birth and death certificates.

178 **Another possibility is that her enslavers were:** See census records, estate sale records, and "Col. James H. Holman," *Proceedings of the Thirtieth Annual Meeting of the Bar Association of Tennessee*, held at Nashville, TN, May 24, 25, 26, 1911, p. 280.

27

For additional context, see Richard H. Hulan, "Middle Tennessee and the Dogtrot House," *Pioneer America* 7, no. 2 (July 1975), pp. 37–46; International Society for Landscape, Place & Material Culture; and Tennessee Valley Archaeological Research, Research Design for Archaeological Testing at the Dan H. Call Cabin Site in Moore County, Tennessee, January 2017.

28

For additional context: Moore County Heritage Book Committee and County Heritage, Inc., *The Heritage of Moore County Tennessee 1871–2004*; "From 1810 to 2010 Black History & Contribution In Lincoln County," pamphlet, author unknown, 2010; Lay Organization of St. Paul AME Church in Fayetteville, TN, "Lincoln County Black History Journal 1998," Vol. 1 and Lay Organization of St. Paul AME Church in Fayetteville, TN, "Lincoln County Black History Journal 1999," Vol. 2.

186 A member of the Bobo family wrote about: Moore County Heritage Book Committee and County Heritage, Inc., *The Heritage of Moore County Tennessee 1871–2004*.

186 Other people fondly recalled watching: Moore County Heritage Book Committee and County Heritage, Inc., *The Heritage of Moore County Tennessee 1871–2004*.

187 "There were enchanting Sunday afternoons": Moore County Heritage Book Committee and County Heritage, Inc., *The Heritage of Moore County Tennessee 1871–2004*.

187 "I remember 'Ham' Daniel": Moore County Heritage Book Committee and County Heritage, Inc., *The Heritage of Moore County Tennessee 1871–2004*.

188 I found a local history pamphlet: *From 1810 to 2010: Black History & Contribution in Lincoln County*.

29

For additional context, see: Moore County Heritage Book Committee and County Heritage, Inc., *The Heritage of Moore County Tennessee 1871–2004*; "From 1810 to 2010 Black History & Contribution In Lincoln County"; Lay Organization of St. Paul AME Church in Fayetteville, TN, "Lincoln County Black History Journal 1998," Vol. 1 and Lay Organization of St. Paul AME Church in Fayetteville, TN, "Lincoln County Black History Journal 1999," Vol. 2.

30

For additional context, see "Uncle Nearest Premium Whiskey: Fawn Weaver," *How I Built This* podcast, NPR, October 4, 2021; Zoe Haggard, "Weaver Talks Investing, Management"; and "Uncle Nearest Tennessee Whiskey with Sherrie Moore," *The Spirit Guide Society* podcast.

31

For additional context, see William Jankowiak and Daniel Bradburd, eds. *Drugs, Labor, and Colonial Expansion* (University of Arizona Press, 2003); Moore County Heritage Book Committee and County Heritage, Inc., *The Heritage of Moore County Tennessee 1871–2004*; Pat Mitchamore, *A Tennessee Legend with a Pictorial of Old Bottles & Jugs*; David Fulmer, *Barrels & Bottles & Tennessee Jugs*; Chuck Neese, *The Whiskey Jug Book*.

203 **"He traveled the world as something":** Dennis Hevesi, "Jimmy Bedford, Guardian of Jack Daniel's, Dies at 69," the *New York Times*, August 10, 2009.

209 **Some 12.5 million people were enslaved:** Henry Louis Gates Jr., "How Many Slaves Landed in the U.S.?" 100 Amazing Facts About the Negro, PBS.org.

32

210 **But we know, according to the National Museum:** "The Man Behind Tennessee Whiskey."

211 **In the 1770s, a South Carolina woman named:** Chris Middleton, "Tennessee Whiskey & Charcoal Filtering," Whiskey Academy historical case study, November 2014.

211 **An 1809 book published in Harrisburg:** John Wyeth, *The Practical Distiller* (1809, reprinted by Andrews McMeel, 2013), p. 103.

211 **"This method appeared at the dawn of distilling":** Chris Middleton, "Tennessee Whiskey & Charcoal Filtering."

215 **Michael's great talent was working with data:** See Melody Gutierrez, "Michael Berman, Democratic Strategist and Force in California Politics, Dies," *Los Angeles Times*, May 8, 2023.

33

218 **In Brown-Forman's own words:** Kenneth Roman. "Jack Daniel's The Illusion of Discovery," *Crushbrew*, October 12, 2016.

221 **The first document Nelson gave me:** Jeanne Ridgway Bigger, "Jack Daniel Distillery and Lynchburg: A Visit to Moore County, Tennessee," *Tennessee Historical Quarterly*, Spring 1972.

221 **The other was a letter:** Frank Bobo, Letter welcoming Vito Pappano as a Jack Daniel's Field Tester, on Jack Daniel Distillery letterhead, 1985.

221 **There was also a 2001 insert celebrating:** "Happy Birthday Mr. Jack," insert to Brown-Forman annual report, 2001.

34

228   He interviewed me for an article that would run: See Clay Risen, "When Jack Daniel's Failed to Honor a Slave, an Author Rewrote History," the *New York Times*, August 15, 2017.

229   "Stencils, nails, the sort of ephemera": Clay Risen, "When Jack Daniel's Failed to Honor a Slave, an Author Rewrote History."

229   "It's easy to assume that anyone who digs": Clay Risen, "Fawn Weaver: Using Whiskey and Business Savvy to Illuminate Black People's Place in Distilling History," *Bourbon+* magazine, vol. 5, no. 2 (Spring 2023).

229   Soon after, in a letter to Jack Daniel's employees: Mark McCallum, "Nearest Green: Jack Daniel's First Master Distiller," *Happnin's In The Holler*, June 2017.

35

For additional context, see "Uncle Nearest Premium Whiskey: Fawn Weaver," *How I Built This* podcast, and Zoe Haggard, "Weaver Talks Investing, Management."

36

240   Shortly after our launch in Nashville: Clay Risen, "When Jack Daniel's Failed to Honor a Slave, an Author Rewrote History."

37

For additional context, see "Uncle Nearest Premium Whiskey: Fawn Weaver," *How I Built This* podcast, and Zoe Haggard, "Weaver Talks Investing, Management."

38

250   Visiting the Call Farm made a big impression: See *Chasing Whiskey*, a documentary about Jack Daniel's directed by Greg Olliver, released 2020; and "Episode 43 - Descendants of Nathan 'Nearest' Green," *Jack Daniel's Around the Barrel* podcast, Season 4, episode 43.

250   "What she had been telling us": "Episode 43 - Descendants of Nathan 'Nearest' Green," *Jack Daniel's Around the Barrel* podcast.

252   While we had the honor of Miss Helen visiting: I've written about this visit with Helen Butler previously; see "Jack Daniel's Reparations: Special Note From Our Founder" at nearestgreen.org. Interestingly, it wound up being Jack Daniel's eldest descendant, not Nearest's, who was able to identify many Greens in other photographs. Mary Avon Motlow Boyd was Jack Daniel's great niece, and Judy

Boyd Terjen's mother. She was a remarkable woman who lived to age 105. See "Mary Boyd," obituary, *The Moore County News*, August 23, 2017.

39

257 **It was covered widely on the news:** See Wesley Lowery, "'White Lives Matter' Organizers Cancel Second Rally After Taunts from Counterprotestors," the *Washington Post*, October 28, 2017.

40

260 **"Many of the people buried here":** Jo Anne Gaunt Henderson, "History of Highview Cemetery."
262 **Melvin was from Selma, Alabama:** "Melvin Keebler: VP and Assistant General Manager at the Jack Daniel Distillery," Jack Daniel Distillery, jackdaniels.com/en-us/bhm/melvin.
263 **"The Green family is just as much a part of the history":** Ibid.

41

268 **"Some thought the company couldn't risk":** Clay Risen, "Fawn Weaver: Using Whiskey and Business Savvy to Illuminate Black People's Place in Distilling History."
271 **An October 8, 1862, issue of *Harper's Weekly* dubbed:** "The War in Kentucky," *Harper's Weekly*, October 18, 1862.
271 **A Union soldier quoted in the article:** "The War in Kentucky."
275 **The rural South is part of Jeffrey's DNA:** Fred Minnick, "A Taste of History: With Investment in Uncle Nearest, Actor Jeffrey Wright Joins a Whiskey Movement," *Bourbon+* magazine, vol. 1, no. 3 (Summer 2019).

42

For additional context, see "The Enslaved Man Who Taught Jack Daniel to Make Whiskey," *The Sporkful with Dan Pashman* podcast, October 5, 2020; "Victoria Eady Butler," *To Dine For* podcast, January 16, 2023; and "Fawn Weaver: Founder and CEO of Uncle Nearest," *To Dine For With Kate Sullivan*, PBS, aired January 12, 2023.

43

288 **"Now that everyone else knows his contributions":** "Episode 43 - Descendants of Nathan 'Nearest' Green," *Jack Daniel's Around the Barrel* podcast, Season 4, episode 43.

289 **When Soledad O'Brien interviewed Debbie:** *Matter of Fact with Soledad O'Brien*, February 3, 2018, https://www.matteroffact.tv/february-3-2018.

44

293 **One such time came while I was showing:** "'Uncle Nearest' Honors Slave Who Taught Jack Daniel to Make Whiskey," *CBS This Morning*, CBS News, July 12, 2019.

293 **We'd come a long, long way from the first time:** "The Lost Story of Nearest Green, the Slave Who Taught Jack Daniel How to Make Whiskey," *CBS This Morning*, CBS News, November 28, 2017.

294 **"They were solidly behind you":** "'Uncle Nearest' Honors Slave Who Taught Jack Daniel to Make Whiskey."

295 **We planned to release an Uncle Nearest commercial:** "Uncle Nearest Premium Whiskey - The Why," directed by David Poag. Released February 3, 2019. This sixty-second spot aired in twenty-four major media markets during *The Late Show with Stephen Colbert*, and interspersed Jeffrey Wright's scenes at the Call Farm with Uncle Nearest team members introducing the whiskey and Nearest's story across the country.

295 **Instead, we created a ten-minute film:** "The Story of Nearest Green," directed by David Poag. Premiered March 19, 2019, at The Tribeca Film Festival.

298 **"Thank you to the family of Nearest Green":** Kristen Martin, "Jeffrey Wright Helps to Tell the Story of Nearest Green During Tribeca Screening," *The Knockturnal*, March 22, 2019.

298 *OK!* **magazine later reported that the film:** Genevieve Uzamere, "Jeffrey Wright Shares 'The Story Of Nearest Green' At Tribeca Film," *OK! News*, April 10, 2019.

45

300 **As Victoria said at the time:** Nancy DeGennaro, "Why is Sept. 5 so Important for Uncle Nearest Premium Whiskey Brand?" Murfreesboro *Daily News Journal*, September 6, 2022.

304 **"The whiskey aisle keeps getting more crowded":** Ben Sisario, "Bob Dylan's Latest Gig: Making Whiskey," the *New York Times*, April 28, 2018.

304 **In 2020, Uncle Nearest and Jack Daniel's:** Learn more about the Nearest &

Jack Advancement Initiative and Spirits on the Rise at https://www.nearestand jack.com.

304 **Tracie Franklin and Bryan Copeland were our first graduates:** See "Uncle Nearest Whiskey," *Drinking With Historians*, Season 1, Episode 23 and "Bryan Copeland," Jack Daniel Distillery, https://www.jackdaniels.com/en-us/BHM/ Byron.

305 **"As a Black American, I wish things to change":** "Melvin Keebler: VP and Assistant General Manager at the Jack Daniel Distillery," Jack Daniel Distillery, jackdaniels.com/en-us/bhm/melvin.

305 **He later told me, "If anyone came to me now":** "Du Nord Benefit: For the Love of Whiskey, Race, Progress and Diversity," Fred Minnick livestream, June 1, 2020.

306 **Chris told me saw the distillery:** "Du Nord Benefit: For the Love of Whiskey, Race, Progress and Diversity," Fred Minnick livestream.

306 **"Without this program, we would not be":** "Jack Daniel's and Uncle Nearest Celebrate Du Nord Social Spirits as the First Graduate of the Business Incubation Program," press release, February 3, 2022.

46

For additional context, see "Uncle Nearest Premium Whiskey: Fawn Weaver," *How I Built This podcast*, and Zoe Haggard, "Weaver Talks Investing, Management."

314 **He made quite the impression on *Travel + Leisure*:** Kevin West, "Touring Tennessee To Discover USA's Cuisine, Craft Distilleries, and Music History," *Travel + Leisure*, November 3, 2022.

47

317 **Not long before she passed away:** Miss Neat passed away on September 13, 2023, as I was working on the final draft of this book. She was laid to rest in Highview Cemetery. See "Juanita Dunlap," obituary, J. A. Welton & Son Funeral Home via Legacy.com, September 14, 2023.

318 **Jack Daniel died in 1911:** See "Capt Jack Daniel Operated On," *The Tennessean*, April 20, 1911; Jasper Newton Daniel, Tennessee Death records 1908–1958. October 9, 1911; "Jack Daniel Dies at His Home in County of Moore," *The Tennessean*, October 10, 1911.

★
OTHER WORKS CONSULTED

BOOKS

Clark, Joe. *Lynchburg*. The Tennessee Squire Association, 1971.

Encyclopedia of African American History, 1619–1895. Oxford University Press, 2006.

Fulmer, David. *Barrels & Bottles & Tennessee Jugs*.

Marsh, Helen C. & Timothy R. *Land Deed Genealogy of Lincoln County Tennessee*, Volumes 1–3. Southern Historical Press, 1996.

Miles, Tiya. *All That She Carried*. Random House, 2021.

Miller, Alan N. *Middle Tennessee's Forgotten Children: Apprentices from 1784–1902*, Clearfield, 2004.

Mitchamore, Pat. *A Tennessee Legend with a Pictorial of Old Bottles & Jugs*. Rutledge Hill Press, 1992.

Mitchamore, Pat, with recipes edited by Lynne Tolley. *Miss Mary Bobo's Boarding House Cookbook*. Harper Horizon, 1994.

Mitchamore, Pat, with recipes edited by Lynne Tolley. *Jack Daniel's Hometown Celebration Cookbook*, Volume II. Rutledge Hill Press, 1990.

Moore, John Trotwood. *The Tennessee Civil War Veterans Questionnaires, Confederate Soldiers*, Volumes 1–5. Southern Historical Press, 1985.

"Moore County," "Lincoln County," and "Franklin County," *History of Tennessee Illustrated*. Goodspeed Publishing Co., 1886.

Neese, Chuck. *The Whiskey Jug Book*. The New Company Publishers, 2002.

Tolley, Lynne, and Pat Mitchamore. *Jack Daniel's The Spirit of Tennessee Cookbook*. Rutledge Hill Press, 1988.

Stuart, Jesse. *Up The Hollow From Lynchburg*. McGraw Hill, 1975.

NEWS ARTICLES

"Lynchburg and Moore County," *The Nashville American*, March 8, 1896.

"The Sour Mash Distillers," *The Sentinel (Lynchburg)*, March 23, 1878.

Hatcher, G. E. "Pen Sketches of Two Men," *Knoxville Sentinel*, September 8 1897.

Kimberl, Maggie. "Behind the Booze: Fawn Weaver of Uncle Nearest Whiskey," *The Alcohol Professor*, October 28, 2019.

Loh, Jules. "Under the Influence: Whiskey Is the lifeblood of Lynchburg, Tenn. - the town that Jack Daniel Built," Associated Press, March 26, 1989.

Loh, Jules. "Jack Daniel's Beginning Not Likely to Be Repeated," Associated Press, March 26, 1989. In recounting Jack's origin story, Loh notes, "Call ran a store on Louse Creek and needed an apprentice for his black slave, Nearest Green, who was a superb maker of the store's most prominent product, whiskey. . . . [Jack] moved his still a few miles to a lovely spring outside Lynchburg, brought with him Nearest Green's son, George, and prospered."

Walker, Hugh. "Jack Daniel's Pours History," *The Tennessean*, January 11, 1976.

OTHER WORKS. DOCUMENTS. AND PUBLICATIONS

Bureau of the Internal Revenue, Press release No. 39, August 9, 1934, detailing taxes on distilled spirits and wines.

Casey, Joe M. "Sketches of Moore County History: End of An Era," June 2002.

Douglas, Joseph C. "Miners and Moonshiners: Historic Industrial Uses of Tennessee Caves." *Midcontinental Journal of Archaeology* 26, no. 2 (Fall 2001). Cave Archaeology in the Eastern Woodlands.

Daniel, Jack. Three letters to Clara Boone, one dated September 29, 1892, and two undated.

Eddy, Nelson. Jack Daniel's Chronological History, compiled from various sources for the Jack Daniel Distillery, revised January 2004.

Eddy, Nelson. "Jack Crew Picture Question: Which person in the Jack Daniel's crew pictures is Lem Motlow?" March 10, 2009.

Hancock, Arthur S. Letter to Ben Morris of the Brown-Forman Distillers Corp., October 30, 1958, with enclosures detailing records from Moore and Lincoln Counties, memos regarding Jack Daniel's land, and a section titled "Notes on Lynchburg."

Higbee, Mark David. "W.E.B. Du Bois, F.B. Ransom, the Madam Walker Company, and Black Businesses Leadership in the 1930s." *Indiana Magazine of History*, Vol. 89, No. 2 (June 1993), p. 101-124.

List of Jack Daniel's Distillery employees with a separate list titled "Colored Folks" that includes several members of the Green family. Undated and handwritten on the back of a sheet of Jack Daniel's letterhead.

The Middle Tennessee Journal of Genealogy & History XI, no. 2 (Fall 1997).

Motlow, J. D. Original Jack Daniel's paychecks written to Edd Green (Nearest's son) and Minnie Lou Green (Nearest's granddaughter) with their signatures on the back. J. D. Motlow was Jack Daniel's nephew.

"Moore County, Tennessee Genealogies Extracted from Chancery Court Loose Records," undated.

"The Moore County Review," *The Moore County Historical & Genealogical Society* 14, no. 1 (Spring/Summer 2003), Vol. 18, no. 1 (Spring/Summer 2007) and Vol. 19, no. 1 (Spring/Summer 2008).

Motlow, J. D. Letter to Felix Motlow, March 21, 1930.

National Register of Historic Places for the Walker, Madame C.J. Building, U.S. Department of the Interior, National Park Service.

Photograph of a group of Jack Daniel's workers at Cave Spring that includes Motlow family members along with Nearest's sons Charlie and Eli and his grandson Ott, undated.

Rutledge, Louisa Daniel. Diary, Louisa Daniel Rutledge Papers, Albert Gore Research Center, Middle Tennessee State University. Transcribed by Donna Baker.

Sanborn maps of District of Tennessee whiskey distilleries, 1900, Sanborn Map Company.

Simmons, Rachel Ann (Waggoner), "The Waggoner Family," December 31, 2001.

Walton, Hanes Jr. and James E. Taylor, "Blacks and the Southern Prohibition Movement," *Phylon (1960–)* 32, no. 3 (3rd Qtr, 1971).

Wood, Lant. "Jack Daniel Remembrances," March 25, 1961.

★
CREDITS & ACKNOWLEDGMENTS

A T THE end of my first book, I wrote, "Now it's time for me to return to the real world"—to my life as a businesswoman, to my friends and family, and to more time with Keith. This time around, the world of the book *is* my real world, and I never left it. I'm so grateful for this life and this journey. And I am grateful that my real world now includes cementing the legacy of Nearest Green for every future generation.

Keith, you are my love, my life, and my rock. None of this would have been possible without you. God knew I would need a strong partner in this life to fulfill my purpose, and there is no greater partner in love, life, and business than you. This year, we will celebrate our twenty-first year of marriage, which means it can legally drink Uncle Nearest. ☺

This book is for all of Nearest Green's descendants, the living and the dead. So many elders interviewed for this book held on just long enough to share what they knew, then one by one began passing away. I am so grateful that before they departed for heaven, each of them knew this story would be told and their ancestor's legacy would be cemented. Those still with us have waited too long for this story to be told, and I am beyond honored and grateful to be able to share it.

To my agent, Jay Mandel, with William Morris Endeavor, you're the best in the business. Thank you for doing what only you can do.

To Charlie Melcher and the Melcher Media team, this book owes its existence to your invaluable support. The Friday before the scheduled cover reveal, when I found myself without a publisher, you stepped in seamlessly. By Monday morning, not only had you ensured the smooth execution of the cover reveal and launch, but you also embarked on a journey of mastery, infusing your unique touch into every aspect of this book. Your dedication and expertise have elevated it beyond my wildest dreams. Thank you for being every author's ideal collaborator. I eagerly anticipate the magic we will continue to create together in the years ahead.

Amy Snook, you are an absolute rock star. Before we even shipped the first copy of this book, it was already a bestseller, and that's because you didn't allow me to skip a beat in the transition from my prior publisher to Melcher. From the moment I introduced you to our marketing and PR teams, it was as if you had always been a part of our family. Thank you.

A heartfelt thank you to Susan Lynch and Bonnie Eldon, who made the transition to Melcher seamless, ensuring that we could deliver this transformative book to the world. Special gratitude to Lauren Nathan, whose meticulous attention ensured that every word in this book was perfect, and copy editor extraordinaire, Anna Wahrman. Thanks also to the rest of the team at Melcher Media: Madison Brown, Shannon Fanuko, and Megan Worman.

I also extend my thanks to Sarah Ried and copy editors Sherian Brown and Leigh Grossman. Your early work on this book was profoundly impactful, and I am deeply grateful for your contributions.

The book could not have been possible without the countless descendants of Nearest Green, Jack Daniel, and the town of Lynchburg who helped me uncover Nearest and Jack's story. Among them are Chuck Baker; Miss Helen; Miss Dot; Claude Eady; Beverly Ruth "Rabbit" Vance; Barbara Ann "Chick" Estill; L. B. and J. B. McGowan; Aunt Nell; Debbie Staples; Jackie Hardin; Jerome Vance; Victoria Eady Butler; Aunt Tee; Mickey Murphy; Michael Green; Mitchell Green; Melisa Greene; Dr. Geri Lovelace; Ben Coleman; Charles Coleman; Aarica Coleman; Marcus Green; Alton Green; Cardelia Green; Patricia Green; Thressia Green-McClure; Calvin Westbook; Sara Westbrook; Cyrus Greene; Donnie Green; James Calvin; Ed, Ophelia, and Edwina McGee; Kevin Eady; Jo Anne Gaunt Henderson; Duff Green; Frank Bobo; John T. Bobo; Clay Risen; Richard Waggoner; Wendy Moore; Tom Moore; Judy Boyd Terjen; Sherrie Moore; the congregation of the Berry Chapel AME Church.

My deep gratitude goes to Joel Pitts (who had the single largest Jack Daniel's and Lynchburg collection I've ever seen) and Miss Neat, who welcomed Keith and me into their homes, showed us around cemeteries and photo albums, and were invaluable in telling this story. I am deeply grateful for their knowledge, generosity, and the care they take to keep Lynchburg's stories alive.

Nelson Eddy, thank you for bridging the gap between Brown-Forman and me and being helpful with uncovering documents and sharing mindsets from JDD/B-F along the way so I could better understand. You were the Fawn Whisperer to B-F and the B-F Whisperer to me.

Mark McCallum, it was a rough road to start, but grace. Grace on your part and grace on mine. It was not easy to be on the Jack Daniel's side of things at the start of this, and I completely understand that, so thank you for remaining open as time went on, embracing that this story deserved to be told, and recognizing that this story could never harm the legacy of Jack. And thank you for your invaluable help and insight after retiring from Brown-Forman. I've met few people with a heart as open and as kind as yours.

Jeffrey Wright, thank you for narrating *The Story of Nearest Green* so brilliantly that this book could wait until 2024 to be completed and released. That film allowed the story to be told while this research continued.

Katharine Jerkens, Victoria Eady Butler, Damian Shine, Michael Senzaki, Steven Henderson—I could not have done this without you. Thank you.

Heartfelt thanks to rock stars of research Carol Roberts, Kathryn Hopkins, and Christine Pyrdom. For years now, Carol, Kat, and Christine have pulled countless records for me and others—often original documents from large, leather-bound books. Over and over again, they've descended into dark closets and stuffy basements and returned with tax records, land deeds, death certificates, and area maps. I could not have done this work without them.

So many others helped with my research. Travis Rael, Gayle Oserberg, Jeffrey Flannery, Jillian Rael, Chris Middleton, Dr. Bradley, Guy Hall, John Parkes, Maureen Hill, Nathan Jordan, Donna Baker, and Mike Northcutt were all instrumental in piecing together parts of this story.

Special gratitude to Stephani Aryeetey, Danielle Britt, Evette Martinez, and Caroline Rash, who provided instrumental assistance to the project and this book.

Every author deserves to have a bestseller campaign coach like Luvvie Ajayi Jones. Your seamless integration with our sales, marketing, and PR teams ensured that we maximized every opportunity. Working with you was an author's dream come true. Thank you for your invaluable contributions.

Everyone involved in the process of this book has been instrumental. But no one has been more pivotal in the writing of this book than Evelyn M. Duffy. I still don't know how I came across Bob Woodward's social media post saying his editor for the prior thirteen years was going out on her own. But I am so grateful I reached out to you and you responded! Thank you for working around my insanely full schedule with the patience of a saint. And thank you for bringing together the Open Boat Editing research team, who could take the time to reinterview the key people I interviewed and somehow bring order to my research records. I am grateful for you. God certainly blessed me, and the world, when he brought you and this book together.

Ally Glass-Katz brought her abundant insights and sharp editorial eye to every stage of this project. Her indefatigable commitment and contributions to the work extend far beyond what can be simply acknowledged, and her buoyant good humor carried the day across the miles and time zones.

Tyler Loveless and Ben Gambuzza contributed rigorous archival and genealogical research and a keen understanding of Middle Tennessee, the whiskey industry past and present, and countless topics in between. Their diligence, intellectual curiosity, and investigative skills were instrumental to building a bridge between past and present.

ACKNOWLEDGMENTS

The Open Boat Editing team would collectively like to thank the following people who helped us for their time and assistance: Mark Amatucci, John Baker, Craig Batchelor, Rachel Berry, Junebug Clark, Sam Corden, Cynthia Corn, Jesse Culpepper, Eileen Duffy, Madelyn Duffy, Qres Milan Ephraim, Tracie Franklin, Erin Wiggins Gillium, Pat Holl, Taneya Koonce, Minh Lee, Jed Lirette, Michelle Miller, Jason Morgan, Luke Parrish, Liz Provencher, Mollie Schaefer-Thompson, Dani Seiss, Mark Slagle, David Wolf, and Jennifer Young. Additionally, we thank Olivia Bates, Kayce Butler, Dr. Kevin Cason, Catherine Colbran, Lauren Hamric, Taylor McPeake, and Veronica Sales at the Tennessee State Archives, and Tranae Chatman and Debbie Shaw at the Tennessee State Museum, who provided patient, efficient, and kind assistance with records.

IMAGE CREDITS

Joe Clark HBSS: p.143; Nathan Morgan: p.155; Mark Tucker: p. 153; Tim Wiencik: p. 156; Additional historical photos courtesy of the Green family: Cover, p. ix, p. 141, p. 142, p. 144, p. 145, p. 146, p. 147, p. 148, p. 149, p. 150, p. 151, p. 152, p. 154

★
ABOUT THE AUTHOR

FAWN WEAVER boasts over a quarter-century of dynamic entrepreneurial endeavors. As the CEO and visionary founder of Grant Sidney, Inc., a discreetly held investment powerhouse, Weaver's active role in her investments has consistently positioned her in influential leadership roles behind the scenes. Recognized as a captivating presence on every media platform, including social media, Weaver is not only a *USA Today*, Amazon, and *New York Times* bestselling author but also a sought-after guest on an extensive array of radio and television talk shows across the US and around the globe, including Fox Business, *Good Morning America*, *CBS This Morning*, CNBC, and Fast Company. She is a regular contributor to *Inc. Magazine* and her episode of NPR's *How I Built This* is one of its most popular.

With an extraordinary track record, Weaver holds the distinction of being the first noncelebrity Black American woman to spearhead the creation and meteoric rise of a billion-dollar enterprise. Serving as the dynamic force behind Uncle Nearest, Inc., a company she cofounded with her spouse, Keith Weaver, in 2016 under the Grant Sidney umbrella, Fawn Weaver is the driving force behind Uncle Nearest Premium Whiskey's historic ascent. Notably, this remarkable spirit brand holds the title of the fastest-growing American whiskey and Bourbon in US history and is recognized as the top-selling African American–founded spirit brand ever. Earning a staggering array of over 850 awards, including prestigious accolades from *Whisky Magazine* and the San Francisco World Spirits Competition, Uncle Nearest Premium Whiskey has emerged as an industry leader, fueled by Fawn Weaver's transformative vision and leadership.

Weaver's legacy extends beyond business triumphs. Her commitment to reshaping narratives and uplifting communities shines through the Nearest Green Foundation, a 501(c)(3) nonprofit she founded. This foundation stands as a testament to Weaver's dedication to celebrating African American heritage, championing inclusivity, and fostering lasting change. Through initiatives like the Operation Brother's Keeper, which supported frontline workers during the COVID-19 pandemic, and the Nearest and Jack Advancement Initiative, a not-for-profit alliance with Jack Daniel Distillery aimed at promoting diversity in the spirits industry, Fawn Weaver continues to redefine success as a true visionary and advocate for positive transformation.

Fawn Weaver's illustrious journey is fortified by her exceptional education and board leadership. She holds an undergraduate degree from the esteemed University of Alabama, underpinning her multifaceted expertise. Fueled by her dedication to continuous growth, she has also earned certification as a Corporate Director from the renowned Harvard Business School.

In recognition of her unparalleled accomplishments, Fawn Weaver's influence extends to the highest echelons of the business world. In a momentous appointment, she joined the board of directors at Endeavor Group Holdings in March 2021, alongside the appointment of Elon Musk. Simultaneously, she undertook significant roles on Endeavor's 16B-3 and audit committees. Endeavor, a publicly traded entertainment and content powerhouse, is valued at over $11 billion and holds dominion over industry giants such as UFC, WWE, WME, and IMG. Fawn Weaver's board leadership underscores her exceptional business acumen and her unwavering commitment to shaping the future of the entertainment landscape.

Follow her online at fawn.weaver on Instagram and on LinkedIn. Learn more about Nearest Green at www.NearestGreen.com, about the Nearest & Jack Initiative at www.NearestAndJack.com, and about Uncle Nearest Premium Whiskey at www.UncleNearest.com.

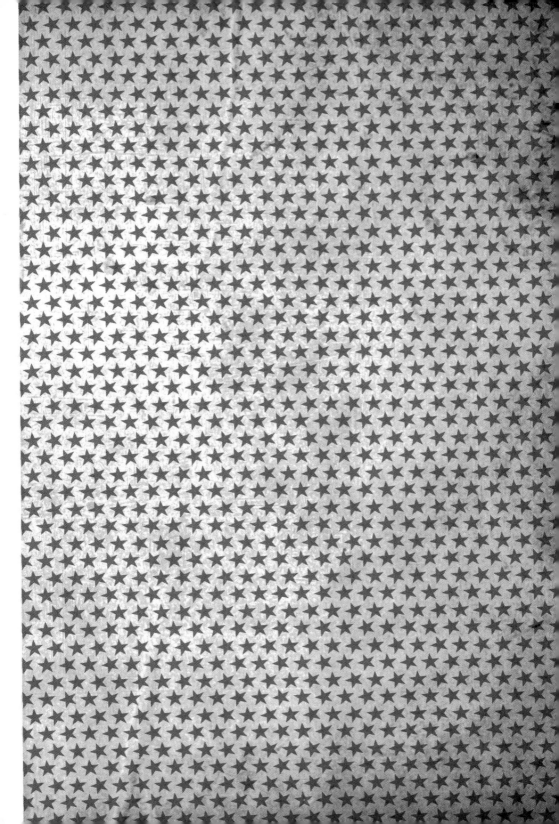